W9-ALX-141

Bikerlady

The author contemplates the journey ahead, as she lives and rides free

Photo by Bandit, www.bikernet.com

Bikerlady
Living & Riding Free!

Sasha Mullins

CITADEL PRESS
Kensington Publishing Corp.
www.kensingtonbooks.com

CITADEL PRESS books are published by

Kensington Publishing Corp.
850 Third Avenue
New York, NY 10022

Copyright © 2003 Bikerlady, Inc.

All rights reserved. No part of this book may be reproduced in any form or by any means without the prior written consent of the publisher, excepting brief quotes used in reviews.

All interviews used with permission of the subjects.

All Kensington titles, imprints, and distributed lines are available at special quantity discounts for bulk purchases for sales promotions, premiums, fund-raising, educational, or institutional use. Special book excerpts or customized printings can also be created to fit specific needs. For details, write or phone the office of the Kensington special sales manager: Kensington Publishing Corp., 850 Third Avenue, New York, NY 10022, attn: Special Sales Department, phone 1-800-221-2647.

CITADEL PRESS and the Citadel logo are Reg. U.S. Pat. and TM Off.
BIKERLADY is a trademark and service mark of Bikerlady, Inc.

Harley-Davidson Sportster, Harley-Davidson Dyna Wide Glide, Harley-Davidson Heritage Softail Classic, Harley-Davidson Dyna Low Rider, Harley-Davidson Dyna Super Glide, Harley-Davidson Heritage Springer, Harley-Davidson Road King, Harley-Davidson Road Glide, Harley-Davidson Ultra Classic Electra Glide, and Harley-Davidson Fat Boy, are registered trademarks of the Harley-Davidson Motor Company.

First printing, August 2003

10   9   8   7   6   5   4   3   2   1

Printed in the United States of America

Library of Congress Control Number: 2003101242

ISBN 0-8065-2519-3

This revvin' book is dedicated to none other than:

G O D

who gave me life, destiny, and the Holy Spirit on two wheels,

and

Ann and John Mullins

My goofy, adorable parents who ask:

"Why do you have to ride that thing?"

Because my motorcycle makes me s'mile!

©2002

experience beautiful freedom®

A torrent of thunder echoes behind you and the sound vibrates through the car floor. You glance in the side view mirror and glimpse a biker fast approaching, fresh out of a mean lean, seemingly ripping up asphalt into the wind. Right on your tail, with a "get out of the way" attitude, the biker guns the throttle, urging you to "move it!" The twisting parkway was your personal haven until the aggressive motorcyclist appeared moments ago, eager to canyon carve ahead of your sports car.

You figure, "Okay, it's cool, I'll take you on. Just try and pass me." Riding along the empty ribbons of tar lacing through mountain terrain, you slow up along the single-into-double-lane straightaway to challenge the rider in a little catch-me-if-you-can rip. You put on your best attitude face and glance left to greet the rider with a surly gaze. Your eyes meet a sensuous red-lipstick grin that flashes pearly whites. Waist-length locks silently whip the wind beneath a shiny black lid decorated with rhinestones. Curves tucked into road-worn ruby and black leathers straddle a custom V-twin of untamed cubic centimeters and performance. You manage a surprised nod and grimace as you gulp down some attitude. A gorgeous semi-gloved hand tipped with long crimson fingernails bids adieu and lips blow a kiss into the wind. She laughs and snaps the throttle open, leaving you breathless and wondering, "Just who was that bikerlady?"

. . . Catch me if you can.

Contents

Preface

What comes to your mind when you think of who a bikerlady might be? We might not be what you imagine. We are mothers, daughters, sisters, wives, grandmothers, executives, farmers, artists, entrepreneurs, waitresses, chefs, school teachers, journalists, and more—riding the open roads from all walks of life and bonding together as one giant goddess in the wind. We ride alone or in groups, bonding with each other's shared passion for the sport and learning from the easy riding freedom experienced on two wheels. Our personal journeys reveal a rainbow of reasons why we love to ride and how we decided to purchase our own motorcycles. We wear our emotions not on our sleeves, but strung as pearls around our handlebars. We uniquely characterize an inner strength and confidence by virtue of our glorious femininity and passion for motorcycling. We portray what it means to experience our beautiful freedom . . . and we gotta roarrr!

In 1910, it was taboo for a woman to wear pants, taboo for her to vote, and definitely taboo for a lady to drive a motorcycle. But society's frowns didn't stop pretty Clara Wagner from joyously hiking up her long, swirly skirt and straddling a motorcycle to compete in a 365-mile endurance run from Chicago to Indianapolis. The young woman discovered a divine independence and a unique two-wheeled form of empowerment kindred to unearthing a rare gem. The feeling was priceless, the liberty indescribable. The adventure of motorcycle riding became contagious among women, rousing the feminine spirit and beautifully freeing our individuality in a way no other experience could offer. Thus, the motorcycle contributed to the forward motion of women's social and dress reform.

"You can still be a lady and ride," declared the late Dot Robinson, former president of the first women's motorcycle club, The Motor Maids, founded in the 1940s. Born into motorcycling, she was the femme fatale who powdered her nose, smoothed her skirt, and promptly took on the American Motorcycle Association's (AMA) rule that barred women from participating in competitions. Through a petitioning effort, Dot won AMA's approval to compete and went on to win race after race, becoming an icon in women's motorcycling. Dainty and mighty Dot, a wife and mother, proudly displayed her femininity whether competing or riding cross-country. She wore pink, painted her Harleys pink, and had lipstick holders bolted to the handlebars for quick touch-ups. "I've always tried to project the best image from a motorcycle," said Dot. This impeccably dressed biker-lady owned thirty-five Harleys and rode more than one and a half million miles during her lifetime.

"Motorcycling is a way in to yourself and a way out," wrote Melissa Holbrook Pierson in her 1997 book, *The Perfect Vehicle*. "The way out of yourself that motorcycles provide is towards life." Tales from bikerladies around the world describe mysterious healings and soulfully enriching experiences gained from cruising hundreds of silent windy miles or by tearing up racetrack asphalt. Motorcycling is a journey within that not only inspires peace, but summons lost dreams to surface, encourages healing from illnesses, gives strength to overcome abusive relationships, helps us reclaim our inner beauty, and bonds us together as a sisterhood. Motorcycles entice our wild femininity to be free, to be beautiful. And oh, the fun of it!

Bessie Stringfield, an African-American, crossed the country at nineteen years old during the early 1930s, despite racial oppression. She was spunky and petite—an individualist who chipped away at social barriers by virtue of her motorcycle lifestyle. Fearless Bessie surprised everyone she met during her thousands of miles in the saddle touring around and as a motorcycle dispatcher for the army. "I was never afraid on the road because I had the Man Upstairs with me," she said. This legendary "Motorcycle Queen of Miami" owned twenty-seven motorcycles in her lifetime and became a symbol of strength and independence. The AMA recently named an award after Bessie for her extreme pioneering efforts, which have paved the way for today's women motorcyclists.

As a well-known female motorcycle journalist and spokesperson, I have been photographing and interviewing women riders for years. Their road tales and experiences are inspiring to the point of being phenomenal. Women of all ages and from various cultural backgrounds, nationalities, and lifestyles jump on their motorcycles and ride off, returning with extraordinary tales of accomplishment, self-discovery, and empowerment. These tales break down barriers and encourage community, enlightening and inspiring even the most dispirited woman. Throughout this book, I have provided profiles of sister bikerladies, in their own words. To find out more information about these ladies and others, including motorcycle resources and information, you can visit my website at www.bikerlady.com.

The experience of motorcycling is a pure and organic rapture with the wind that provides us with the freedom to discover and become the powerful women we were meant to be. "Sexy," "beautiful," and "free" define the bikerlady and the sensual feminine spirit.

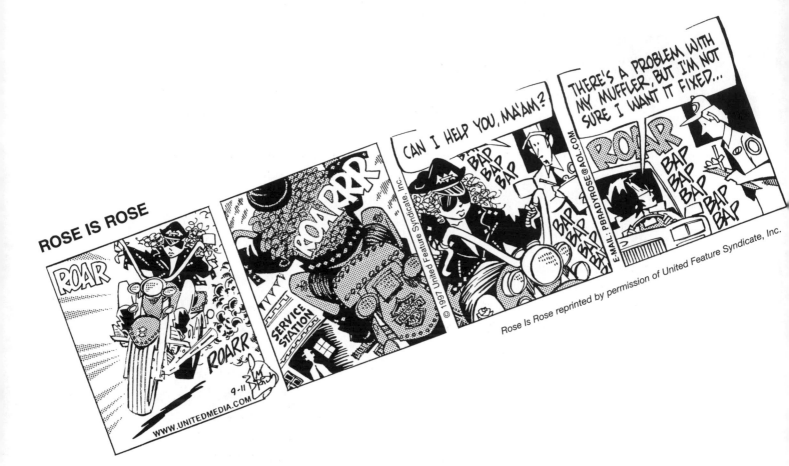

Acknowledgments

First and foremost I thank you, my wind sisters, for your beautiful voices that are testimony to the exquisite beauty of the ride. Thanks to the readers who buy this book and to my beloved motorcycle lifestyle and industry that support this book.

Huge, earth-stretching gratitude to Jim Fitzgerald, Carol Mann, and the administrators at the Carol Mann Agency . . . it's been a wild ride. I'm incredibly grateful to you for your hard work to get this project into the hands of a publisher. Jim, thank you for reaching out to me to write this book. Marly Rusoff, thank you for being the angel that whispered in his ear about my talents.

To Walter Zacharius, I am incredibly grateful for your support of my book. More earth-stretching gratitude to Bruce Bender of Citadel Press for taking the chance on my project, given the time constraints to get it to market. To Anne Ricigliano, thank you for your design artistry. Margaret Wolf and Francine Hornberger, thank you for your editorial talents. To *all* the folks at Kensington Citadel Press who worked on this book, huge hugs and gratitude. Your patience and willingness are treasured, and I am incredibly grateful. Fritz Clapp, my attorney and manager, your guidance and advice is a treasure to me. My deepest gratitude for your sincere interest in my career and for your creative input.

To Big Mike Hossack, my dear friend and the greatest drummer for the coolest rock band—the Doobie Brothers. Without you, darling, this book would never have been completed. I thank you so much for opening your home to me and putting up with my changing your office into a book- and paper-strewn writer's den. It was hard to have to give up my city-girl lifestyle, beloved NYC nest, and move across the country so I could afford to complete this project. Your love and support made my dreams become reality. Ta-da!

Thanks to my beautiful motorcycle, "Tigerlily," for bringing me here on my dream journey. Dreams do come true, and I feel like a biker Dorothy tapping her boot heels together and enjoying some smooth road for a change. Soul kisses to Annie cat, too.

Brian, Suzanne, Liam, Ryan, Sean; Laura, Garry, Sammy, Jake; Donna Marie, Big Kyle, Kyle, Jade, David; Linda, Michael, Jessica, Kimmo—siblings and nieces and nephews. I love you and your love is so yummy to me! Thanks for all photos and phone calls to remind me that I didn't fall off the earth. Elsie-doll, thank you for your prayers. Soul sistah, Kristen! Many thanks for telling Marly about me.

Skip MacLeod . . . brother of the road! Huge thanks. You've been an incredible friend and I don't know what I would have done without you during the Discovery Channel filming, Bikerlady, Inc., stuff and so forth. You definitely kept my spirits up while writing the book. Ivan Santana, the most extraordinary researcher on the planet and a gentleman, you are a gem and I am so grateful for your talent. Ann Ferrar, thank you for your incredible groundbreaking book, *Hear Me Roar: Women, Motorcycles and the Rapture of the Road*, that paved the way for more authors to write about women in motorcycling!

Bandit, your belief in me and constant encouragement when I was just a budding motojournalist made all the difference in the world. I am forever grateful to you, brother. Mark Langello, you hooked me up with the editors who took a chance on me because of your recommendation. Thank you for believing in me. Charles Salzberg, the best writing teacher in NYC, thank you for accepting this biker chick into your classroom and finding my work interesting and worthy. Biker Billy, thanks for your hot advice and fiery support.

Sonny Barger, thank you for your support. You're an inspiration! I was at your debut book-signing at Virgin Records in New York and little did I know that I'd become a published author, too, back then. We are Riders writing! How Cool! I'll see you on the road!

Rickey Santiago, you always cheer me on when the going has been really rough. Thank you for the beautiful Bikerlady logo. Bob Smith . . . meow. Maybe the creditors will stop calling me now?

Susan Kander and Warren Ashworth, the ultimate New York City land-lords, thank you for putting up with my disappearances and the new faces in my apartment while I've been chasing my dreams for the past several years. Susan Dworak, thank you, sister, for your constant encouragement. GOTH, FLAME, RaZor, thank you for keeping the K I T T E N laughing. Cris

Sommer-Simmons, you're an inspiration and a blessing to me and all women riders for cutting the journalism path of acceptance for women in this industry! Katy Wood at AMA, thanks for helping me with the history sections. Christina Shook, your artistry is exquisite and I'm honored to have your motorcycle photography in my book. Sherry Sontag—my literary sister and a brilliant author—thank you for being the first spark that launched my writing career with your precious words of encouragement.

Saving the best for last, my most heartfelt gratitude is to the ultimate biker spirit that dwells among us and within, Jesus Christ. An incredibly fine example of love, brotherhood, sisterhood, the journey, perseverance, patience, and freedom to be true to self which results in the ultimate Perfection. He encouraged my creative spirit and gifts as a writer to compose this project, and as a rider to chase my dreams and fulfill my purpose. He watches our backs forever.

Now, saddle up for a good read, friends.
This is your journey, too.

The sights, the scents, the journey—the Roarrrr of freedom!

Bikerlady

Carmella Gruttadauro
Photographer: Christina Shook © 2003

CHAPTER 1

She's Gotta Roarrr!

Seems like a dream,
Riding wild and free, an empowered diva, highway queen,
Steel horse under my reign, road is long and there ain't no end,
They told me no so I stole the asphalt, come on, Baby, catch me if you can
I'm woman, Gotta Roarrr!
My motorcycle, hot, yeah, I want more . . .

    — "Gotta Roarrr!" song lyrics by Sasha

There is a mysterious vehicle that has freed the female spirit and delivered woman into the full landscape of her femininity. It is the motorcycle. Since the early 1900s, this two-wheeled iron horsepower machine has raced women away from social, gender, and racial oppression, delivering us into an equal, respectful, and admirable position in the social and cultural fabric of life. But this has not come without challenge and sacrifice. Woman and her iron horse have had to persevere. The motorcycle has taken the pioneering chrome cowgirl upon journeys through which she has discovered the sweetest gems inside her soul, releasing the true power of her femininity. This is the inspiration for *Bikerlady: Living & Riding Free!*

For the past few years I have been observing the female motorcycle marketplace and interviewing women who ride, and I have noticed a phenomenon. The motorcycle has changed these women forever. This vehicle has ridden down the obstacles in their lives, shown them their personal meaning and truth, and freed their feminine spirit in a way in which nothing else had ever done. The motorcycle has united women from all walks in life who would never otherwise communicate with each other. It has fostered great friendships and created sisterhoods that have evolved into female motorcycle riding clubs. It has given new definition to the maternal figure-head in the family and has taught young children the power of the female spirit and that, yes, girls can be in control of their own destiny. The motorcycle has created extended families of those who ride. It has opened up riders' souls, surprising them by showing them their abilities, self-worth, and purposes in life. It has helped riders realize dreams and solve life's seemingly never-ending string of dilemmas and challenges. The motorcycle is the greatest and most soul-evoking mystery to grace a rider's life.

Even though women have forged quite a path in the lifestyle and sport of motorcy-cling, people are still quite surprised to see a female on a motorcycle. It was even more surprising prior to the 1980s when many bikes were kick-start and needed constant maintenance. But those strong women were riding since the inception of the motorcycle, heading out on the road and enjoying the uniqueness of being a female rider. As motorcycle technology has improved, more and more women have become attracted to the sport. But although female motorcyclists are the fastest growing segment of the motorcycle marketplace, the industry has been slow to respond to the needs of the female rider. No matter. Women, with their creative flair and resourcefulness, get by with riding gear that may not fit quite right,

and the ability to do light mechanical work and customize their rides to suit their needs.

Most women who ride live to ride. Riding is solitude and a blissful moment for taking care of oneself. Riding a motorcycle, one is in control of one's destiny, free in the wind. Let's face it. Women have way too much to do with all our many roles: career gal, wife, companion, mother, friend, advi-sor, leader, and so forth. When a woman rides, it's all about *her* as she roars down the highway as an easy ridin' goddess in the wind, beautiful and free.

Motorcycles turn me on. Chrome, like hard silk to the touch, mirrors the passing images on life's journey. It reflects sunlight dancing across well-hung handlebars and shimmers my silver-jeweled hands resting upon the grips, making me feel like a Queen when I ride. Between my legs is a power-house stallion of cubic inches, hot and hungry to move forward as it vibrates with a sense of adventure, awaiting my direction, as I twist the throttle and rev the engine to announce my presence to the world.

I love the way the frame gracefully cra-dles the motor and transmission within its metal uterus and each engine evolution gives birth to a new road experience. The curve of steel fenders embracing fat rubber treads inset with flame-carved rims fires my iron horse into a wild charge along free-ways, byways, highways, and good-bye waves. The octane swooshing in her belly is a perfume luring me on an escapade. A woman on a motorcycle is a modern-day Miss Liberty; her feminine spirit is the torch she holds high.

Guys love to manhandle their machines, as if wrestling them to the ground, pinning them down to show 'em who's boss. Women, on the other hand, operate motorcycles with feminine finesse. We understand the delicate balance of things and what it means to be equal, to give life to something. For men, controlling a motorcycle is all in the chest as they push that stallion around; for ladies, riding is guided by our most curvaceous places. My motorcycle and I tango along the asphalt as familiar dance partners. My hips move side to side, dipping and swaying, gliding with the machine as we lean into twisty curves and sashay down the straightaway, all to an intuitive rhythm.

Riding free. The wind is deliriously seductive. It whispers affirmations and echoes thoughts as it caresses my ears and face. It undresses layers of accumulated baggage assuring that the adventure is congruous to the purpose: freedom. The breeze strips away inhibitions piled on by everyday survival to reveal the soul of the rider—strong, with a destiny and a dream.

Motorcycle riding ripens the awareness of moment-by-moment sensualities. You are exposed to the elements, to horizons, to perspectives, to reality engaging the person into an environmental orgasm, because the rider becomes one with all of it and transforms with the changing scenery. Golden rippling prairies carpet the way to omniscient mountains that empty into barren stretches that morph into green thoroughfares that disappear into rising concrete thickets that bend into suburban order that all melt away into a body of water—the only place we cannot ride.

Motorcycles are the voice, the *roarrr* for bikerladies around the globe. And our two-wheeled freedom machines have ridden down oppressive barriers and borne us away from suffocating discrimination and suppressive situations. Throughout history, motorcycles have uniquely freed our feminine spirits, revealed our inner strengths, and empowered us, as if to exclaim on our gender's behalf: "We have roarrred onto the scene. Hey, look at me, I'm . . .

Mysterious
On my own
Tough
Original
Revived
Courageous
Youthful
Cool
Lovely
Empowered
Sexy."

Hear me roar!

The wild urge for motorcycles first surged through my tiny nine-year-old frame, then draped in a Brownie uniform complete with mini-platform shoes. It was the moment when I changed inside from geek to goddess. I was under no family influence to mount a steel horse. I hadn't been inspired by a famous person posing for the camera or a movie still showing off a rough-and-tumble actor grimacing on a bike. For me, the desire to ride a motorcycle was based on pure instinct, which became an infatuation.

One day, while waiting for my mother to pick me up after school, my blue eyes watched through bottle-thick, red-framed eyeglasses as my classmate Richard came tearing down the long, rutted playground hill on a dirt bike. Tingles raced up my spine. It wasn't an opposite sex thing. It was freedom machine allure. I was experiencing iron love at first might!

Debbie, a pretty blond Brownie peer, was also waiting for her mom. The rider swooped around the giant swing-set and roared up, skidding to a halt and sending dust swirling around us. "Who wants to ride?" asked the sweaty, panting, cutest boy in school. Debbie yelped "Me!," clearly an expression of her desire to straddle the boy instead of the machine. The invitation for adventure was irresistible, though the saliva pooling against my teeth delayed my response. Standing next to that bike caused my budding desire to become an iron Godiva, to immediately seize all manner of communication. My gold-plated scout pins rose and fell to my fluttering heartbeat.

The blue bike was a fireball of energy revvin' to go, to explore, to free wheel. The knee-knock engine sound, scent of gasoline, pipes growling like a cub, knobby, muddy tires hungry to claw terrain, and handlebars begging to be gripped by an easy little rider fascinated me. The definition of freedom and adventure was idling before me. My soul had finally found its match!

I nervously looked around, awaiting my turn. If my tough, Long Island–raised mother caught me so much as inches from the machine, she'd lay into me like a Mack truck trying to seize the hammer lane from a chopper. I closed my eyes and listened for the motorcycle engine to get louder as it continued to fade away. "Turn around! Quick! Come back for me!" I thought, jumping around.

Down the hill the two came; the arse end of the scoot bouncing left to right as dirt clouds followed them. Debbie jumped off, giggling, "Oh wow! That was so much fun. I want to go again!" All serious now, it was my turn. How I quivered with pleasure. But seconds away from freedom, there came the '72 olive-brown Duster with the tin-sounding AM radio blasting pop tunes on WABC. "Don't you dayah!" my mother yelled through the open window. The Winston cigarette between her two left fingers nodded furiously with each word. She stuck the smoldering stick between her lips, shoved the car into park, and flung open the car door. "Get in da caw, NOW!" said the lips clutching the bobbing cigarette in the corner of her mouth.

I felt the tingles escape through the bottom of my feet. Richard just shrugged and took off with Debbie again. I couldn't pick my frown up from off my toes. "I'll have my own bike someday," I thought as I slid onto the hot black vinyl seat that smelled like old baby formula and crammed in next to my squirming brothers and sisters.

After that experience, I would marginally get my fill of motorcycles watching *ChiPs* and biker flicks. For years after, the yearning for a motorcycle was my secret desire. It was the vehicle that would eventually unlock my spirit and be a companion to my enterprising soul.

So, two decades from the first time I got hot seeing a motorcycle, including several years as a drooling passenger eager to drive her own scoot, I just had to *roar* on my own! Finally, I got my first bike, a brand new Harley Davidson Sportster. There would be *no* other first bike for me. I had to have a Harley, even though my passion for motorcycles embraced all bikes. The bike was American, tough, loud, proud, and defined windy freedom, and the whole notion was sexy and beautiful to me.

A failed wedding engagement provided the down payment for the heifer among Harley hogs. That engagement ring swap for chrome was triumphant. It was time to slide forward from the back to the front seat in my life. Now I was in control of my own destiny again, and this got my inner and outer motors revvin'. The guy? Well, he had become wildly successful. I had stood by his side through all the tough times, sacrificed my career desires, the whole bit, because he was on his way to success and I knew my turn would follow. I know it was a dumb move to have so much faith in a man and relationship to sacrifice my own goals, but it was

ol' skool thinking. On top of that, I had just had surgery, which confirmed my sterility. So I had to deal with double trauma all at once: my engagement ending and learning I would never be able to have kids. I held on to the ring for a few years afterward, thinking he would change his mind, come to his senses, and return to our relationship. He didn't.

I never thought we would ever break up, so I was totally unprepared financially to live alone. Getting a roommate in New York City was just as expensive as living alone in a single-room shoebox. I eventually moved into a super small studio apartment on the Upper West Side. Being in the city, I could be distracted and not feel so lonely. I left all my furniture behind because it wouldn't fit in my three-hundred-square-foot space. And my entire income as a music industry secretary went toward making ends meet.

For years, I worked twelve- and fourteen-hour days climbing the corporate ladder in the music business, taking adult college classes here and there when I could afford it. Truly I was locked in a daily grind. No life. I kept smashing my head on the glass ceiling, and my great talents as an executive secretary were actually a disservice. My bosses had refused to promote me for fear of losing the gal who did all the work for them and made their stars shine.

My creative dreams were also put on the back burner for two reasons: lack of time and lack of desire. When my fiancé and I parted ways, and I learned the devastating fact that I could not have children, the highway lights of my journey dimmed for me and I gave up music, piano, writing, everything. I didn't have a creative inspiration in

The author cruises the streets of her beloved
New York City.
Photo: Anthony Fiorenelli

me except journal writing to help me deal with the heartache. I felt numb and just threw myself into my work-a-day routine.

Through it all, I always had my antique white gold engagement ring. It was incredibly beautiful and I sometimes took it out of its box to stare at it. Damn. Every time I looked at it, I remembered the moment he proposed and how wonderful I felt. But then one day I woke up and finally realized it was time to *get over it!* It was time to rid myself of the broken promise. It was time to move on. Get a life!

But what would I do with the money I got from selling the ring? Pay rent? Get caught up with bills? Take a college class or two? Lord knows I needed the dough. And then the idea came to me. Use the money to claim a long-lost dream.

As soon as I sat in the driver's seat of the little Suzuki school bike, I was totally committed to finally learning to ride a motorcycle. The motorcycle safety three-day intensive class was challenging but I kept focused on the prize: earning my license and getting my own bike.

Once I got my license, I started researching motorcycles. I had passengered on a few bikes and was wild for my own ride, but I couldn't afford it in my financial state. Where would I keep it? Rates for parking a motorcycle in New York City range from $150 to $250 per month. First things first, though. Sell the ring and get that down payment for a bike.

Now that I had the money to afford my dream, I started calling Harley-Davidson dealerships. I wanted an Aztec Orange

Sportster because the color reminded me of a new dawn, and that's just what this was for me. I also wanted to infuse my soul into a new bike, not a used one, because this was a huge and important step for me.

I finally found my ride. When I walked into the dealership where my bike awaited me, I felt like I was about to see my newborn child for the first time. There she was, chrome gleaming like a mirror, so spit-shiny new was she, awaiting her motorcycle mama.

It took me nearly a month to get the nerve up to ride through the insane streets of Manhattan, where I knew I would run into every single obstacle taught by the safety class in a span of three blocks. One day, I finally revved her up for her virgin ride. I took a deep breath, headed toward the country, and rode 200 miles alone. And yes, I was scared shitless. Taxis cut me off. People strolled in front of the moving bike. Rollerbladers sailed past me, sweeping in front of my motorcycle to cross the street. Chaos was my training ground. The hair stood up on my neck the entire day as I became intensely aware of everything that moved and didn't move around me. I rode defensively as if anything would take me down. My eyes searched and scanned. Once I hit the countryside I laughed out loud to myself! "I'm riding. I'm on my bike. I'm doing it!" I smiled so deeply and completely that I felt like I had turned inside out with joy.

My spirit became richer because now I had ultimate freedom in the wind, away from life's disappointments and the failed engagement that had plagued my life for much too long. I felt like a brand-new person. I felt like *me*. All my dreams began

to dance around in my heart: "Remember me? Remember me?" Motorcycles have a way of opening up your whole world, and widening a narrow perspective into a healthy spread of new opportunity and realization. It's also a great way to say *adios* to the past and roar forward in life!

My first bike is affectionately named "Tigerlily," inspired by St. Therese of Liseux, who was nicknamed "The Little Flower." Her story prompted me to think if I was a flower, what kind would I be? Immediately, the name "Tigerlily" came to mind because in life, a lady's gotta be both a tiger and a lily, especially when riding in New York City. Plus it's been said that a flower represents the gateway of communication with your guardian angels. And, gals, do I pray to my wind-whispering road angels every time I ride my Tigerlily. She gracefully overpowers taxicabs with a growl and tackles lane territory in chaotic city traffic; though she does lily wheel through the countryside and it's hard to corral her back to the urban jungle after a day's jaunt. She's the perfect diva bike for city riding, and I love to ride her cross-country, too.

"Soulo" is inscribed on my license plate. The name perfectly describes the spiritual connection I have with my Tigerlily and my preference for riding solo—though I love to ride with others, too. Having a solo seat also keeps rowdy, unpredictable folks from thumbing a ride.

Since getting my motorcycle, my entire life has changed. Tigerlily has connected me to the realization of my dreams and goals. It has been a struggle and sacrifice, indeed, and I feel every lump and bump along the journey, but I know the path that I need to be on. The wheels are always moving forward now; there are no revolutions backward. My motorcycle has become my confidante, my soul mate, and friend. The tens of thousands of miles that we have ridden together have allowed me to journey deep into my soul as a confused being and return as a clear-minded, open-hearted, refreshed spirit. I have learned so much about the world, the communities, cultures, the landscapes, and myself during my wanderlust escapades and I hunger for more experiences.

"You don't look like you ride a motorcycle!" How many female motorcycle riders have heard this statement? Okay, exactly what does a woman who rides a motorcycle look like? Well, Hollywood is responsible for those one-dimensional character sketches that usually portray a ferocious-looking chick, but that's not reality. Not at all.

Riding a motorcycle is sexy because it awakens all the senses, powerful because it requires physical, emotional, and intellectual strength to ride, and free because when someone feels free they are beautiful both inside and out.

The stories about how and why women motorcyclists were first drawn to these freedom machines describe reasons ranging from pure adventure to image identity to rebelliousness to healing to reinvention to camaraderie to curiosity and more. Women from all walks of life—from corporate to socialite to industrial, from housewives to grandmothers to teenagers—ride motorcycles. Who do you see on bikes? Wonderful, fun-loving ladies just like you and me.

Voices from the Road

The following quotes were gathered from a questionnaire posted on my website, bikerlady.com. Female bikers—from children to senior citizens and from all walks of life—give testimony to the road's magic. The question: What is your favorite aspect of riding a motorcycle?

"The solitude, a balance on the earth, the incredible sensuousness of the natural elements, the power of nature."

"Freedom—the wind hitting against you, the lean of the curves, the incredible power of the engine, the thrill of it all!"

"Riding my bike gives me power, it gives me confidence, and clears my mind. Where I came from [Saudi Arabia] women are not allowed to drive even a car. I had to leave home and come to the USA not just for the freedom of life, but the freedom to ride motorcycles because that was my biggest dream."

"I feel really sexy when I ride."

"Riding in the 'ultimate' convertible."

"The freedom of the ride. You depend on nothing but your own skill and instincts."

"On a motorcycle, you can dream forever."

"The freedom. The experiences. It's a perfect way to end and start a day."

"Not being a passenger—being able to make the decisions about where, when, and how far to ride and how fast!!"

"The feeling of independence, the attention I get, the image."

"I am a ten-year-old female dirt bike rider and I love playing in the mud with my Grandpa!"

"Riding clears my mind so things make sense again."

"I feel like I'm leaving all the baggage behind."

"When my husband and I get on our bikes it's like another world to us. We can leave our everyday B.S. behind us. We can kick back and enjoy."

"Hey, it's the power between my legs!"

"I love the wind in my face and the camaraderie in our group of riders."

"Handling a big machine gives me confidence in my life."

"Freedom, the way it restores my soul."

"The stories that are shared and the riding experiences seem endless. This year I'm looking forward to doing some long trips with people I have met over the last year."

"It's the ultimate attitude adjustment."

"The sights, smells, sound, wind in my face, the feeling of finally ignoring my mother's warning and seeking out my ultimate interest."

"Guys, guys, and, oh yeah, did I mention guys?"

"It brings out the bad girl in me and lets me express my inner attitude, and boy is it a big one!"

"The freedom and the respect I get from my fellow workers when they find out I ride my own."

"The speed, the balance, and oh, that SOUND!"

"The smells, the sights, the wind, the sound, the friends, the way it makes me feel inside."

`I love being one with my bike and the beauty of nature. Riding my bike is like being in one endless escapade that is on a constant high. Words cannot describe the feeling. I tell folks, `You just have to get out and do it !'"

"I feel at one with nature and the universe, I love the feel of the wind and feel like I am flying!"

"When I ride my motorcycle I forget about my job, kids, etc. It helps to reduce my stress."

"Riding gives me a feeling of accomplishment."

"I feel like I don't have to answer to anyone when I ride because I'm in control."

"It gives me a sense of empowerment."

"It is the only thing I do that puts me into a meditative state, yet makes me aware of everything around me!"

"The adrenaline rush and pure freedom of being outside and moving. Also the looks from guys as I blow past them on the highway are pretty good. . . ."

"My bike is my shrink. When I'm uptight, I get on my 'baby' and feel wonderful. . . ."

"Wind, freedom, challenge of learning new things all the time, tricking out my bike, seeing new places without the insulation/barrier of auto."

Risqué antique French postcard

Courtesy Jerry Hooker, www.motorcycle-memories.com

CHAPTER 2

Watch Out! Curves Ahead!

With the purr of my engine beneath me
And the warmth of the high sun above
I'll go over the distant horizon

Along the country lanes that I love.
Wild wood flowers and fruit will be growing,
Winding rivers flow down to the sea,
On my revered traveling companion,
I lay claim to a life of the free.

> —Theresa Wallach, from her biography, *The Rugged Road*[1]

The history of women in motorcycling reads like an Amazonian goddess–inspired tale, evoking powerhouse descriptions like *sexy, powerful, free, wise, adventurous, strong, beautiful, life-giving, celebratory, sensual,* and *independent*. The full history could fill a book all its own; in this chapter, I've presented a pared-down look at the very early years.

The women who pioneered the sport of motorcycling may not have realized just how important the motorcycling metaphor would become to women's freedom in life and on the road. The motorcycle has set the female spirit free in the wind; these early chrome cowgirls instigated the movement.

Before the bicycle was even introduced, women were held back under a strict social regime and gender hierarchy in which liberties were few. The cultural and social demands on everyday life for women kept our boundaries tighter than the last possible pull on the corset strings. Everything a woman did was for the family and the family's future. Rare was the woman who tended to her individual desires. However, beneath the layers of restrictive garments there were souls yearning for equality and liberty.

For the pioneer woman, life was all about the homestead—nurturing and caring for husband and children and tending to household duties, as well as hard physical labor on farms and ranches. It was extremely challenging but the pioneer woman was resourceful and prepared. She had to tear up roots and gather the family to relocate to lands uncharted, in pursuit of new opportunities. She was the devoted matriarch, but also behaved as patriarch when necessary, protecting the family against the unpredictable and harsh realities of the unknown. But still, the husband was head of the family and his wife had to stay in her place.

Rick Steber writes in his book *Women of the West*: "Eastern women were relegated to conduct themselves within strictly established social boundaries. Western women were allowed more freedom to stretch their wings and explore the realm of their existence. And in the process they tamed the Wild West."[2] Gender roles were rigidly defined with distinctive activities assigned to each. Horse and buggy was used for carting, chores, and family transport. Rarely did women have the opportunity for personal transportation. Cowgirls were forging their way on the rodeo scene doing trick riding and bucking bronco circuits. Little did they know the chrome cowgirl movement would someday kick off and women would saddle up on chrome horses.

When the bicycle was invented, it spawned a new freedom and the ability to travel solo. Society frowned upon the idea of a female entertaining herself with this new form of individual mobility. It was considered undignified. The "freedom machine" suggested that a woman might venture off on her own and away from the social boundaries that framed her as the fragile, powerless gender. Initially, most women rode velocipedes (tricycles) because it was considered more acceptable and better accommodated the restrictive garments of the era.

On standard bicycles, women had to buckle strap the hems of their street-sweeper skirts to keep them from getting caught in the wheels, and even then some of them would be sent head over handlebars by the roaming fabric. As a special bonus to women, the popularity of bicycles eventually expedited dress reform and away went the crippling fashion of corset and bustle. Women's clothing soon became more practical for bicycle riding and freedom came along with the new liberating ride. Bloomers raged onto the scene, to the joy of women cyclists and to the chagrin of enraged conservatives.

So important was the bicycle to the social life of women in the 1890s that Susan B. Anthony stated, "Let me tell you what I think of bicycling. I think it has done more for the emancipation of women than anything else in the world. I stand and rejoice every time I see a woman ride by on a wheel. It gives her a feeling of self-reliance and independence the moment she takes her seat; and away she goes, the picture of untrammeled womanhood."[3]

The freedom machine awakened women's rebellious nature, inviting it to come forth and enjoy the ride. In effect, the bicycle inadvertently expanded the territory of reform. Manufacturers quickly took note that they could double sales by marketing to women. Ads appeared in women's magazines featuring bloomer-clad female cyclists coasting downhill with their feet up; exuberance poured from the pages. Articles soon followed, discussing the physical, spiritual, and social benefits of bicycling. The bicycle was a triumphant metaphor for feminist advocates, a symbol of female empowerment, self-control, and independence.

For reform advocates like Maria E. Ward, the author of *Bicycling for Ladies* (1896), "Riding the wheel, our own powers are revealed to us. . . . You have conquered a new world, and exultingly you take possession of it. . . . you become alert, active, quick-sighted, and keenly alive as well to the rights of others as to what is due yourself. . . . To the many who wish to be actively at work in the world, the opportunity has come." She was not alone.[4]

"What years of eloquent preaching from the platform of women's suffrage have failed to accomplish, the necessities of this wheel have in a few months brought into practical use," wrote Mrs. Reginald de Koven in *Bicycling for Women* (1896). "Sighing for new worlds to conquer, I determined that I would learn the bicycle," wrote Frances Willard of the Women's Christian Temperance Union in *A Wheel Within a Wheel: How I Learned to Ride the Bicycle* (1895).[5]

Edith Mayo, a Curator of Political History, National Museum of American History, Smithsonian Institution, Washington D.C., wrote in her introduction to Frances Willard's book, *"Do Everything": The Life and Work of Frances Willard*:

In 1893 Frances Willard was fifty-three years old and not in good health but she was determined to learn to ride. She was still willing to dare and take chances and urged others to do so also. It was important to her that women take to the bicycle, and she believed her enthusiastic example would help lead women into new paths of life—ever expanding their horizons outward into the wider world. She was convinced that the thrill and exhilaration of mastering control of the bicycle would be matched by the sense of accomplishment a woman could experience in mastering control of her own personal destiny—quite a radical sentiment for that time.

David Hendrick, University of Virginia, American Studies, writes in his in-depth study on American mobility:[6]

It is precisely this sort of attitude, empowerment coupled with visions of an increasingly egalitarian future, that angered many men greatly. Simply put, the woman on wheels was a threat to the well-ingrained system of practical inferiority that men had been taking advantage of for centuries, and outraged men were quick to point to the bicycle as a threat to the social order. The cycle, it was argued, would disrupt the delicate sphere of the family unit by allowing the woman to travel beyond her previous limits without the surveillance of a knowing husband nearby. The younger woman, too, was vulnerable to a bicycle-induced lapse in morals, for it allowed her to stray farther afield with members of the opposite sex during courtship.

To further increase freedom for women, just over the horizon, a self-propelled pedal cycle was being born. In 1885, Gottlieb Daimler built the first motorcycle in Germany. Roaring into the new century, international and American manufacturers began converting pedal cycles into motorcycles and experimenting with entirely new creations. One-offs built by early custom builders in their backyards came to life. In 1901, the Hendee Manufacturing Company rolled out their version of Indian Motorcycles, and within the next two years Harley-Davidson showcased their invention.

Looking at antique photographs and artwork, it appears that European women warmed up to motorcycles earlier than Americans. Early twentieth-century French poster art is filled with scenes of women riding early model motorcycles. Historical documentation of American women on motorcycles, which often consists of not much more than handfuls of unidentified photographs and scarce media records, is elusive and hard to confirm. It's sad to think that riding the steel sculpture was so taboo. Praise that first scandalous, brave femme fatale who lifted her skirts and straddled that purring machine. She carved for us a

wonderful path to freedom and launched an arresting fashion statement, quite literally, as you'll discover later in this chapter. Hence, the bikerlady liberty was born!

The first documented woman to ride a motorcycle was Clara Wagner, the daughter of the manufacturer of Wagner motorcycles, in 1907. At 15 years old, she received her membership card #1083 from the Federation of American Motorcyclists (FAM) (predecessor to the American Motorcycle Association, AMA). In 1910, she rode her four-horsepower Wagner motorcycle, built by her father, to win a perfect score 365-mile FAM endurance run from Chicago to Indianapolis. This was a hardcore riding feat challenged by bad weather conditions, pitted and potted roads, mud soup, and a primitive motorcycle. But this 18-year-old bikerlady forged on, beautiful and strong, committed to her passion.

Discrimination quickly reared its ugly head when her famous run was declared unofficial and her trophy refused because she was a chick! But biker camaraderie among her fellow competitors was honorable, and they realized that the girl on the motorcycle was a helluva competitor and she deserved recognition. So they took up a collection among themselves and awarded her a gold pendant for her incredible accomplishment. Miss Clara Wagner went on record as the first woman in America to "unofficially" win a motorcycle competition.

Motorcycle popularity grew especially after 1910, about the same time that the automobile was gaining recognition. In 1909, the president of the Women's Motor-

De-Dion-Bouton tricycle.
Card posted June 1901 from France.
From the private collection of Jerry Hooker,
www.motorcycle-memories.com

There is an old saying, but nevertheless a very true one, that a woman can turn her hand at almost anything and in this day of advancement it is never surprising to hear of a woman accomplishing any sort of difficult feat—feats that naturally are supposed to require the strength and nerve more universally possessed by the opposite sex. It is no uncommon thing to hear of women driving automobiles, or now, even aeroplanes, and within the last year American women are beginning to ride motorcycles. . . . Once a woman has mastered the manipulation of a machine and provided she knows how to ride a bicycle she will never lose her love for the sport. . . . as in the old bicycle days when there were nearly as many women riders as men, the sport will be firmly established as the leading outdoor sport for women.

ing Club of New York, Alice Ramsey, drove to San Francisco from New York in 59 days in an open-bodied Maxwell-Briscoe automobile. Motorcycle manufacturing boomed with several new brands and styles of the two-wheeled vehicles that were economical compared to the automobile.

In the Sunday edition of *The New York Times*, January 15, 1911, is a beautiful cover feature headlined "Motor Cycling Popular Among Women." Like an art gallery display, the photographs cover the front page featuring women in their bloomers or riding skirts with children and solo on a variety of different motorcycles. The accompanying article, entitled "Motor Cycling Fad Strikes Fair Sex," written by Frank Libbey Valiant, states:

During this time, motorcyclists began to challenge themselves with longer journeys as they discovered these iron horses could go the distance. More articles appeared reporting that women were saddling up and journeying great distances on their motorcycles. That's when motorcycle riding really began to evolve as a passion that spoke to the soul. It was personal time to go freely exploring, and various riders took to the open road even though there may have been no roads in those early years. Didn't matter. The zeal to explore on this fast machine was infectious.

The Times of London, England, December 23, 1919, announced in a headline: MOTOR-CYCLING FOR WOMEN; GROWING POPULARITY;

Feminine Influence on Design. Written by an anonymous correspondent it states:

> It is true that with a fur-lined aviator's cap, a double-breasted leather jacket, and a pair of what are commonly called "trouseralls" the strenuous feminine motor-cyclist, who is as ready to face "mug-plugging" in the winter as she is the smooth clean run in summer can make herself astonishingly attractive; but the majority of women who are now taking up, or about to take up, motor-cycling wisely look on it as a means to an end rather than the end itself. So long as they are ready to "dress the part" the ordinary motor-cycle of to-day will satisfy them, and their influence on the evolution of the machine will be but trifling. If, however, they insist that the motor-cycle shall, in their interests, become something slightly different—lighter, cleaner, easier to control, more stable, quieter and so forth— their effect will be most valuable. It is probable that, among other things, it will persuade thousands of men who ought to be motorcyclists, if they only knew it to become so in fact.

In 1915, the first tube of lipstick was sold. It was also the year that twenty-one-year-old Effie Hotchkiss from Brooklyn, New York, decided "woman, go west" and indulged her love affair for motorcycles with a cross-country adventure, joined by her mother, Avis. Their round trip took over five months, logging 9,000 miles, and was widely covered by newspapers.

A new Harley for Effie and sidecar rig for Mom were purchased with inheritance money, and the women set out on the first mother-daughter transcontinental journey in history. Sidecar shopping was an ordeal because Avis was a rather Rubenesque woman who had to be "sized" for good measure. Packed inside the sidecar with Avis, who tatted (a form of crocheting) the duration of the trip, were the absolute minimal essentials for the voyage, which included a revolver, medicine kit, ax, tool-box, parts for the bike, a tent, pots, pans, and blankets. When the ladies reached San Francisco, Effie literally ran her Harley into her future husband. Accidentally, of course.

Ah, romance on the open road.

During their wild ride, Effie had to serve as mechanic, build bridges over rambling streams, and engage in numerous episodes of mud rescue and removal. Mother Avis happily tatted away but did help her daughter push the motorcycle and sidecar rig up a mountain. Details of their adventure are revealed in Effie's private journal, entitled *Wheels in My Head*, which I

Daughter Effie and mother Avis Hotchkiss
Photo Courtesy Craig A. Dove

had the pleasure of reading by virtue of her great-grandson Craig's generosity. Their trip was courageous and proved that the women were self-reliant, smart, passionate, and had loads of fortitude, and, in Effie's case, humor. Following the Hotchkiss excursion, there were other long-distance feats accomplished by daring bikerladies with a passion for forging roads on every level. These women truly astonished society and challenged the conventional mindset of the day.

Women are powerhouses. We are pillars of strength, multi-faceted, with talents as creators, nurturers, and network thinkers. The only reason we had been considered fragile is because physically we couldn't work super hard during our pregnancies. In some cultures, we were thought to be inferior because religion or society viewed us as unclean, subordinate to men, a servant to family life, and incapable, not to be trusted, and threatening overall. The motorcycle and our journeys on it have helped prove that we are capable physically, emotionally, and spiritually of doing anything we put our minds and hearts to. So there!

Back in those early days, it was perplexing for town folk or city folk to see a woman saddled on a primitive motorcycle, rolling into neighborhoods across America. In rural communities it was rare to even *see* a motorcycle, let alone a woman riding one. Inevitably, the question was asked: "Whar's the man?" We're sometimes still met with that same surprise even in the present day.

During the pre–WWI era, there were other notable women entertaining their wanderlust on two wheels and rare roads. A year after the Hotchkiss travels, two sisters, also from New York, decided to take a cross-county journey together, each on her own motorcycle. Adeline and Augusta Van Buren were determined to prove that women could be dispatchers in the military. The sisters were athletic and well cultured. Adeline, an English teacher who later went to NYU, designed their efficient travel outfits, which included breeches and leggings and leather riding caps. Their journey was sponsored in part by Hendee Manufacturing Company, who provided the two 61-cubic-inch Indian Power Plus motorcycles with tires provided by Firestone Tire Company. It was a major public relations undertaking for the two companies. Newspapers covered the event, with references to the two sponsoring companies and the sisters' masculine outfits. The ladies were a curious sight and drew spectators and reporters along their journey.

The Van Burens pioneered several record events for women during their moto-voyage. They were not only the first women to ride up the treacherous miles to Pikes Peak summit, they were the first to round-trip the mountain on motorized vehicles of any type!

The trip was mentally and physically challenging for the pair as they faced rough terrain for motorcycles. At one point, according to family relative Robert Van Buren, the women got lost in the desert with no water and absolutely no idea where they were. A kindly old gentleman seemingly appeared out of nowhere with drink and directions and sent the women on their way to California. We like to call these mysterious people that appear out of the vapor "road angels."

Both the Van Burens and the Hotchkisses proved that motorcycles are a serious form of transportation, and also showcased without a doubt that women can handle the rigors of both the road, and of life. All this even before we were allowed to vote.

The motorcycle was a trendy prop in stunt and circus shows. Following the ban on wooden board tracks on which riders would take their motorcycles on a vertical angle and compete on a half-mile or three-quarters track, the motordrome was created. Also known as "The Wall of Death" attraction, spectators look down into a drum as riders zoom along inside the 12-foot-high 30-foot-around wooden cylinder. While on the bikes, riders perform a series of tricks as they travel the treacherous wall. Machine failure sends rider and bike crashing to the bottom. Centrifugal force keeps the rider on the wall. The motordrome shows have a rich history here and overseas.

Women were popular stunt riders on their motorcycles in these shows and proved their ability and finesse, running their bikes hard and performing gracefully, making the stunts look really easy. In the 1920s, Alice Brady, known as the "Mile a Minute Girl," was a legend on the circuit, known for her high speeds inside the drum. Viola Pelaquin, another drum-riding legend and a member of the famous Pelaquin family, helped to pioneer the sport and business of Wall Riding.

Motorcycles slowly evolved into a sports enthusiast's mania. The AMA became a sanctioning body for social and competitive events, offering, in addition to organized races, the popular "gypsy tours," which were large organized group rides.

On April 22, 1912, in Melbourne, Australia, Dot Robinson, who would be known as the "first lady of motorcycling," was born into the lifestyle. Her father, James Goulding, a sidecar designer and amateur racer, carried Dot's pregnant mother to the hospital in a sidecar. The family relocated to the USA in 1918, where Goulding expanded his sidecar business and purchased a motorcycle dealership. Dot began riding at a very young age and worked as a bookkeeper at the dealership. Dot met her future husband, Earl, when he sauntered into the dealership to purchase a quart of oil. Not long after he was hired as a mechanic.

The young motor-passionate couple set the transcontinental sidecar record from Los Angeles to New York, making the trip in 89 hours and 58 minutes in 1935. Highways were nonexistent then and paved roads were not yet complete.

Dot and Earl were married and eventually bought the dealership from her father. They worked it into one of the top retailers for Harley-Davidson. The couple raised their one daughter, Betty Robinson Fauls, within their exciting motorcycle lifestyle. Dot bonded with 15-year-old Betty while on the road, taking her on an 11,000-mile cross-country trip. They became a famous mother-daughter duet, traveling countrywide and into Canada together.

Dot rode hard to win and set records in motorcycle competition. With feminine prowess and dignity, she gave her fellow competitors a run for number one. However, this petite lady rider with the immaculate appearance, fresh lipstick, and coifed hair, who rode her motorcycle like a champ, received a wire from the AMA announcing that she was barred from competing in the National Enduros because she was a woman.

With the same aggression she used in competition, Dot took on the AMA. She saddled up on her Harley like a chrome cowgirl on a mission. She rode all over the land of the free to gather signatures from fellow competitors stating that they were not opposed to a female competing. She also sent the petitions to dealerships. Thousands signed in support of Dot Robinson's ability to compete. Armed with her petitions, Dot walked into the stubborn president of the AMA's office to give him a crash course in equality. She gracefully smashed through the brick gender barrier by dumping the box of petitions on his desk. Of course, her no-nonsense attitude and quest for justice shocked him and he had no-choice but to acquiesce to this femme fatale motorcyclist.

Dot competed in grueling off-road enduros, piloting a sidecar rig and conquering a hodgepodge of near-impossible terrain. She raced in the toughest competitions such as the Flint 100 Mile Enduro, the Michigan State Championship Enduro, the Thanksgiving Day Enduro, and the granddaddy of them all, the Jack Pine Enduro, which was a two-day, 500-mile, off-road event that forced competitors to average 24 miles per hour, checking in at check points, fording rivers, and riding through sand and every other type of terrain imaginable. Dot won the Jack Pine, sidecar division, in 1940 and in 1946. She raced competitively from

Dot Robinson, the First Lady of Motorcycling
Courtesy Motor Maids

1930 until 1961. Dot rocked the world of women in motorcycling, eventually receiving AMA's Most Typical Girl Rider award in 1950. She was heralded as an example of a woman being a lady *and* riding the hell out of a motorcycle.

In 1938, Linda Dugeau, another passionate rider, launched a feverish letter-writing campaign to find other women riders. She spoke to dealers, other riders, clubs, and organizations with a goal of knitting together the growing community of female motorcycle riders. Upon contact, the women riders communicated through letters to each other. The idea to create an official organization of riders was spawned by a correspondent, Carol du Pont, who mentioned that she was a flyer with the Ninety-Nine club, a national group for women pilots. Linda approached Dot Robinson with the idea. Dot rode around the country looking for other female riders.

Between the letter writing and the meet-and-greets, fifty-one charter members launched the first women's motorcycle club in 1940. The Motor Maids received their official charter from the AMA in October 1941. Dot was appointed the first president of the club and held the position for 25 years. Linda served as secretary.

In founding the Motor Maids, Inc., Linda and Dot set out to unite women riders as a sisterhood. Dot, always polished with a fresh make-up application, stylish hairdo, and solid confidence in her femininity, paved the way for other women to saddle up on their own motorcycles. She rode cross-country when many women didn't yet drive cars. She lived life vivaciously and true to her desires to ride free, be utterly feminine, and compete against the men in tough motorcycle competition.

The Motor Maids became the symbol of women motorcyclists' ability to ride the distance, compete in the sport, and still be ladies through it all. They commanded respect by virtue of their serious passion for the sport, their continuing educational practices of motorcycle safety and activity in legislation, and their dedication to one another and the organization as a whole. Society's belief that a female who rides a motorcycle does so because she desires to be a male was completely dispelled with the presence and expanding network of the Motor Maids.

Around the same time as Dot, another woman was creating a name for herself in the motorcycle world. She was a tiny, African-American woman with a robust appetite for life, who was outgoing and possessed a serious adoration for Jesus Christ and the power of God. Her mission was to prove the hallmark of her faith: Nothing is impossible. So devout was she, she shared during interviews that before she learned to ride as a teenager, she would pray to Jesus to teach her how. She straddled her first motorcycle, an Indian Scout, during the late 1920s, and rode away into a legendary life that would inspire millions. This Harley-riding woman was Bessie Stringfield.

With her every action and a wide smile that wrapped clear around your heart, she would greet the obstacles of life head on, citing her personal mantra that "nothing is impossible with the Lord." At 19 years old, Bessie packed up her Harley-Davidson and departed on the first of many fearless cross-country excursions. Roads were in rough shape back then, when there were roads. She loved her penny trips, where she would toss a penny on a map and drive to the place where it landed. Seeing Bessie on a Harley surprised all kinds of people along her route. But she treasured traveling the outer roads, to experience the inroads that revealed her fortitude and faith.

According to Ann Ferrar's book *Hear Me Roar: Women, Motorcycles and the Rapture of the Road*,[7] Bessie would oftentimes be denied a place to sleep at night and the use of a restroom because of her heritage. But this wasn't always the case. Once, a white gas station attendant in the South was so impressed with Bessie as an African American riding a motorcycle, he gave her a free tank of gas. The sight of the tiny, spirited woman would invite far more positive experiences with those she met. Bessie could crush racial boundaries with her personality. She was humble, though, and never thought she was doing anything special.

Bessie never knew her mother, who died in childbirth, and she had been adopted by a Caucasian couple who supported her desire to ride. She fell in love with motorcycles at age 16. Bessie was an example of the power of faith, and of the strength and freedom that all women possess. She would respectfully flaunt her femininity as a show of that strength. Most of all, she asserted her equality in the face of racial adversity.

In Bessie's hometown of Miami, local police told her, according to Bessie's interview with a Miami newspaper: "Nigger women are not allowed to ride motorcycles in Miami." The police would pull her over all the time and she was constantly harassed. She couldn't even get her license to drive. Bessie got so fed up with the discrimination, she paid a visit to the police captain, "Captain Jack." He took her out to a nearby park to prove her riding abilities to him. She showed him what it means to really ride a motorcycle. From that day forward, she didn't have any more trouble from the police and she finally received her license. With that, Bessie became known as the "Motorcycle Queen of Miami" and established a great friendship with Captain Jack.

During WWII, Bessie served as a motorcycle dispatcher on secret missions. After that, she won her first attempt at Flat Track racing but didn't receive any prize money when, having let her hair down from under her helmet, it was discovered that she was a woman. She had one accident in her lifetime, when a tire blowout injured her left arm, but it never deterred her from riding a motorcycle. Bessie loved to host motorcycle parties in her backyard, too, which produced savory memories. She belonged to various clubs and organizations throughout her lifetime. An award was created in her name by the AMA for women who promote the advancement of women in motorcycling.

Friends and acquaintances, who also referred to her as "Motorcycle Bessie," loved this charming lady rider. In her 63 years of riding, she owned 27 Harleys, her favorite bike, and they were mostly new and blue, a proviso for Bessie. And, except for her poodles on occasion, the woman never rode alone because she "rode with the Man Upstairs." In 2002, she was inducted into the AMA Motorcycle Hall of Fame.

Born in 1918, motorcycle mamma Mary Shephard Cutright of Chillicothe, Ohio, became infatuated with two-wheelers at age fifteen when she won a bicycle race. As soon as she graduated high school she landed a job at a local shoe factory to stash enough money to attain her dream: her own motorcycle. Her desire came true in the form of a 1937 45-cubic-inch Harley-Davidson. She learned to ride from the local boys. She wed John Scott Cutright in 1942 and two years later her son, Johnny, was born. During her pregnancy she continued to ride her motorcycle up until the seventh month. At eight weeks, little Johnny was already riding on the motorcycle with Mom and Dad. He rode up front with Mary until he was too tall for her to see over his head. Once Johnny became a passenger behind his mother, she rode all over the country with him.

During the war years, Mary rode her 1940 61-cubic-inch Harley-Davidson back and forth to work at a Naval fireworks factory. Eventually she found out about the Motor Maids and signed up in 1949. She held several official positions within the organization. Based upon her powerful leadership skills, she was later appointed president. Mary belonged to lots of other clubs, too. She loved the camaraderie of the lifestyle. Over her lifetime she won more than 100 trophies in skill-testing competitions. Riding a Duo Glide, she participated in competitions that featured timed road runs and field meets that included pushing a barrel with the motorcycle, riding a plank, and several other detail-oriented skill tasks. In 1993, Mary was inducted into the Leadership Category of the National Motorcycle Museum and Hall of Fame.

Girls just wanna have fun.
Photo courtesy AMA and Pink Rose Publications and Marketing, www.pinkrosepub.com

Also on a mission to unite female motor-cyclists and passengers, albeit worldwide, was Louise Scherbyn. Louise competed in a variety of endurance and cross-country racing events and extensively toured the United States and Canada. She took part in the first all-woman motorcycle show in 1940 as a stunt rider. She founded the Women's International Motorcycle Association (WIMA) in 1950, which features district representation in countries throughout the world. Within the association there have been several outstanding female motor-cyclists who have established records or proved the savvy talents and accomplish-ments of women riding their motorcycles.

Theresa Elizabeth Wallach was born in 1909 and grew up in the United Kingdom. Her father, Henry Wallach, was known for charting unknown territory and exploring the far reaches of remote lands. Treasures from his journeys filled the Wallach home. According to her journals (published as *The Rugged Road*), when Theresa was a child, she found that society was terribly oppres-sive to women and vowed to rely on fate to guide her destiny. She disclosed her adven-turous dreams to see the world just as her father had done, but her parents weren't happy with her "roamantic" desires and thought that she should pursue a life as society dictated: as a dutiful homemaker. Even Theresa's friends would chide her about pursuing an alternative existence to the staid rules of the day.

Perhaps the possibility of being confined to such a mundane and droll existence fueled Theresa's passion to ride, and

Theresa began putting her dreams in for-ward motion almost immediately. She would sneak off on her brother's bicycle and teach herself to ride in secret. Having discovered the joy of two-wheeled freedom, by the time Theresa laid eyes on a motorcy-cle, she was completely smitten. Her par-ents were not happy, of course, and tried to force their rebellious daughter to conform.

Surprisingly, however, her father permit-ted Theresa to attend an engineering course at the University of London. There, she would stroll longingly past the rows of motorcycles in the back of the building. She made friends with the motorcyclists and through the graciousness of one finally learned to ride, fumbling as she struggled to hold down her skirt with one hand while trying to hand shift with the other. Soon she began to dress in trousers, much to the dis-approval of her parents, who were not aware that their daughter was learning a new sport.

Eventually Theresa purchased her own secondhand BSA motorcycle but had to keep it well hidden from her family at first. Tired of secrets, she finally revealed her passion for bikes to them. An argument ensued, her parents rehashing her "unlady-like behavior" and declaring that she would never be anyone's bride if she didn't stop riding.

Jessie Hole established the London Ladies Motorcycle Club in 1926. Theresa joined the club of serious women riders who had arranged the first ladies' race in Brooklands in 1928. She also joined the International Motorcyclists Touring Club, competing in Trials, scrambles, and racetrack, and was soon in the winner's circle with fellow women riders. She joined her first race because she had mistaken the event for a club meeting. To save face, she raised the compression ratio on her BSA and surprisingly won.

Also a member of the London Ladies Motorcycle Club was Florence "Blenk" Blenkiron, a competent racer, rider, and mechanic. Theresa and Florence became close friends, racing together and learning trick riding through their love of trials riding. As their expertise in motorcycling evolved, they began winning more trophies. At the time, Moto-ball was a popular sport that mimicked football on a motorcycle. The rider became like a contortionist while riding, and to move the machine so adeptly during this challenging game required supreme riding skill. Theresa cited that her skill at this type of riding contributed to the success of her teaching methods at the Motorcycle Riding School that she owned and operated years later.

In 1934, Florence became the first woman to break the 100-mph barrier on a motorcycle while in competition. She was described as a "Wonder Girl" and became the first woman to be awarded the British Motor Cycle Racing Club's Gold Star Award. Both Florence and Theresa immersed themselves in activities relating to motorcycles. This intense passion for riding set the stage for a much bigger journey. Florence wanted to visit relatives in South Africa, and when a friend who was to travel with her backed out, Theresa said that she would go with her and that they should go on their motorcycles. The silly suggestion turned serious

and the two embarked upon a journey of epic proportions.

Most people frowned upon their idea of a Trans-Sahara excursion to Cape Town, South Africa, and offered up dismal predictions, but nothing deterred them. Several people even supported them, seeing them off on their journey, including Lady Astor, an American who became Britain's first female member of Parliament. She told them, "I am an unrepentant feminist and convinced that whatever a man can do, women can do too." They called their Panther Redwing motorcycle and Watsonian sidecar rig "The Venture." And venture they did.

To think that these motorcyclists actually embarked upon such an incredible journey is surreal. The enormous challenges are difficult to comprehend even now. Forget roads, what these ladies traveled were actually *routes*. When you think of roads you think of something paved and chartered. The 14,000 miles they traveled included desert, jungle, and other wild terrain. According to Theresa, in a talk she gave to girls at her former school, "[Had it not been] for the kindness, hospitality, and assistance we received from everyone we met on the journey, natives and Europeans alike, we would have never got through."

The two women journeying on a motorcycle and sidecar through the African plains and jungles couldn't have been a more unusual site. "Our safe and happy arrival in Cape Town was the end of a marvelous exploit and we had the satisfaction to know it was the first north-south crossing of the African continent. We were fortunate to have seen Africa the way it was, before politicians made our journey impossible," wrote Theresa in her journal, *The Rugged Road*. She went on to serve as a motorcycle dispatch rider for the British Army during World War II.

Theresa's long-distance journeys included tens of thousands of miles traveled through the United States, Canada, Mexico, and Europe. Her solo trips were supported by several odd jobs while she was on the road. She loved the freedom of traveling through America on her Norton motorcycle because the post-war era in Europe was not conducive to experiencing travel so freely. Upon arriving in New York, Theresa met up with Louise Scherbyn, who at the time was establishing WIMA. She was invited to become an officer of the club, and served for a number of years.

Theresa went on to own a dealership in Chicago and became an incredibly accomplished mechanic. Later, she opened her own Easy Motorcycle Riding Schools and authored books on the subject. She forged an independent lifestyle from those early years when she defied society's rigid conformities for women.

Theresa Wallach is an example of will and fortitude of the human spirit, and a determination to accomplish great things in the face of adversity. She was quoted once as saying, "If you are not going to be like everyone else, you have to have the courage to go ahead alone." She was inducted into the AMA Motorcycle Hall of Fame in 2003.

These women are just a few examples of the early pioneers in the motorcycle lifestyle. The history is rich with women achieving legendary status in racing, journalism, as motorcycle rights activists, in long-distance riding, and more. The motorcycle has truly served as a kindred soul for women upon which we have been able to prove our abilities on many levels throughout these last hundred years. Right now, women are continuing to make historical contributions to the sport of motorcycling, especially in race competitions, politics, and industry.

The motorcycle brought forth the woman's inherent qualities as powerful, resourceful, and independent during a time when we were considered helpless, fragile beings who couldn't do a thing for ourselves. God works in mysterious ways. He inspired a man to create this machine, but a woman would ride that steed to a new destiny, forging a mighty path of equality for all females.

As Major H. R. Watling wrote in the foreword to Betty and Nancy Debenham's 1928 book, *Motorcycling for Women—A Book for the Lady Driver, Sidecar Passenger and Pillion Rider*, which was later reprinted in the fabulous book by Susan Hollern, *Women in Motorcycling, The Early Years*:[8]

> "Freedom" is the essence of modern womanhood, and the motorcycle is one of the gifts of the gods whereby such is attained. No longer is she dependent upon caprice of husband or brother—no longer is valid the "thou shalt not" which erstwhile debarred her from indulging in his activities—no longer does distance prevent her from full enjoyment of her multifarious interests—the motorcycle is her servant to carry her as she wills. It is her protector, the motorcycle is her iron chaperon. No

longer need she pine for lack of opportunity to indulge in outside interests. The motorcycle provides for her needs.

With the dawn of personal transportation came a horizon of unbridled opportunity. When women first disposed of the breath-defying corset, bustle, and colossal hat to straddle a bicycle, it wasn't yet realized how important two-wheeled adventure would be to women's liberation and independence. These early "freedom machine"

pioneers are to thank for expediting dress and social reform for ladies. In so doing, they passed along a freewheeling experience that brought women the joys of spiritual, physical, emotional, and intellectual liberty on their motorcycles and in life. The motorcycle nurtured the seed of equality and helped set the wheels in motion for society to accept that a woman can indeed accomplish anything she sets her mind to.

Miss "Cy" Woodman, New York to San Francisco on a Flanders 4 motorcycle, circa 1911–12
Published by Kraus Mfg. Co., New York.
From the private collection of Jerry Hooker, www.motorcycle-memories.com

Voices echoing the past

Betty Robinson Fauls, Florida
2003 Harley-Davidson Heritage Softail
Daughter of the legendary Dot Robinson

I'm going on 71 and I've ridden nothing but Harleys since I was 14 so I'm dyed in the wool. I love the mystique and the sound of a Harley; nothing sounds like it. My mother, Dot Robinson, felt the same way.

When I was fifteen, my mother and I went 11,000 miles together. It was great, of course, and all through my very early ages I used to ride in the side car at first and then behind her. We would travel all summer. We rode all through California and up Pikes Peak together, of course that was before there were really any good roads. My mother was riding a '61 Harley and I was riding a '45, and my bike just barely made it over the Peak. Bikes were kick-started back then and there was a knack to it. We worked on our bikes to a certain extent, Adjusting chains every night and oiling them. Little things like that. We had basic mechanical knowledge. We used to travel about 600 miles per day. There wasn't much suspension, but the old-time solo seats were sprung so they were very comfortable. The seats these days aren't near as good!

I used to compete in motorcycles since I was fourteen until about nineteen. I went in for cross-country endurance runs like the Jack Pine. I was the first female to compete solo in Jack Pine. Mother competed sidecar.

It was different back then compared to today. People didn't believe that we rode. We, for the most part, were always received well. Mother was always strict about appearances. We were always clean and neat and never really ran into any trouble. One time there were six of us going out to Colorado. Mother wasn't with us. We pulled into this old-time gas station and this fellow came out and insisted on filling our tanks and said, "Are you all alone?" And one of the girls said, "Oh no. We're all together." He replied, "No. I mean, where's the men?" She said, "They're working."

A lot of the girls that are taking up riding are amazed to hear about the Motor Maids being in existence since the forties. They think they're pioneers, and of course, they aren't. But it's wonderful having so many girls riding now.

Both my daughters, Denise and Dotty, ride. I will be riding with another Motor Maid from Florida to Colorado and then we'll meet up with one of my daughters and ride out together to California for the 2003 Motor Maid Convention 63rd Anniversary in Chico. I will receive my 55-year pin this year. Next year will be 57 years for me as a member of the Motor Maids. The women are unique in that we really ride. That's the reason we've existed this long. It's the riding that brings us together. It makes me humble and proud to see how far the Motor Maids have come. There isn't another group of women motorcyclists that have existed this long.

My bike never goes on a trailer. I think it's more trouble to put a bike on a trailer than it is to ride it. I go to the rallies, especially Daytona. I like going to rallies to meet friends from around the country. I like the camaraderie. I love the freedom of riding a motorcycle.

Gloria Tramontin Struck, New Jersey

Yamaha 1100 Virago; Harley-Davidson
  Daytona Special Low Rider

I've been a Motor Maid since 1946. This year it'll be 57 years. I'm 77 years young. I feel like I'm in my forties. Nobody believes my age when they see me. I've owned my first bike since 1943; it was an Indian army job. The second one was also an Indian, 1941 Bonneville Scout, and the third was a 1946 Indian Chief brand new and I wish I had it today. After that I started on Harleys.

My father had a motorcycle and bicycle shop in 1915 located in Clifton, New Jersey. I was born in a little apartment that was connected to the shop. My father passed away from a motorcycle accident in 1928 when I was just three years old. Then my mother and my brother ran the business. My brother started working in the business at 12 years old. When my mother retired in 1948, my brother started a Harley Dealership, because my mother had become an Indian dealer later on. That's when I started riding my first Harley and have owned eight since.

Believe it or not, I never wanted to learn how to ride a motorcycle, my brother made me! Then after that, he never saw me. I used to travel all around the country myself. I started going all over the place when I got my brand-new 1950 Harley. There were no interstates in those days. The highways were usually one lane coming and one going. I would go to Florida quite a bit. I'd travel around on the weekends, going to Virginia and all over.

Daytona Rally was just on Main Street back in the old days. There was a time when I didn't go for quite a while, and when I went and saw what happened to Daytona I couldn't believe it! It's expanded so much it's unbelievable. I would go to the races and they used to have the races on the beach.

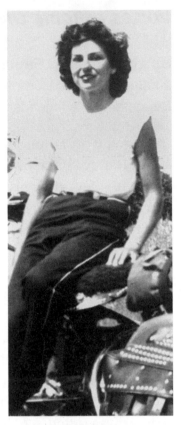

Gloria Tramontin Struck
*Photo courtesy
Gloria Tramontin Struck*

My daughter, my son, and I drive our bikes together down to Daytona from up North. Years ago, everyone just drove their motorcycles to Daytona, today they tow! I cannot imagine why. Are they motorcyclists or exhibitionists? I hate it. I get so mad. It makes me not want to go anymore.

In 1952, it was 15 degrees when I left for Daytona. I came back in slush and snow for 350 miles! When I got to Newark, New Jersey, I called my mother up because it was getting dark. I told her to come in the car to follow me home because I didn't want to get hit by a car because the driver couldn't see me. My mother came to get me and told me "You're not driving that motorcycle another inch!" So I had to park it in the service station and come back and pick it up the next day.

We didn't have the same kind of gear that they have nowadays. My mother had made me a rain suit out of some kind of plastic material and the wind just blew it apart! I wore sheepskin mitts, they helped to keep your hands warm. They were hard to wear because you couldn't hardly feel the controls and in those days you had the gear shift, so you shifted with your hand instead of your feet. The bike was a kick-start, too.

Riding around the country back then it was very unusual to see a woman riding a motorcycle. Some people would think you're a tramp and some people have different reactions. Some were excited about it and some didn't approve, saying it wasn't ladylike or whatever. But I've always been very feminine. I love my motorcycles. You can't explain how it makes you feel. And the people that I've met through motorcycling, I'm very proud to know, they are very nice people.

Pearl Hoel, South Dakota
Co-founder of the Sturgis Motorcycle Rally
1991 inductee into the National Motorcycle
  Museum and Hall of Fame

I've lived in Sturgis, South Dakota, since 1928 when Junction Avenue was just a graveled street. My husband, John Clarence (J.C.) "Pappy" Hoel, and I were in the ice business in Sturgis and when the electric refrigeration came in, of course, the ice business went out. So, we started our Indian

motorcycle shop at that time. The Jack Pine Gypsies Motorcycle club was formed in 1936. In 1938, they had their first Sturgis motorcycle rally, and we had about close to 100 men, women, and children that came to the rally. We had a big tent in our backyard over on Junction Avenue at the motorcycle shop. They slept in the tent on the bedrolls and they'd be there all evening telling their motorcycle stories. They used to come for the races more than anything. We had AMA expert races and we had some of the top riders.

The next morning they would have a trip to Mt. Rushmore. One of the women from the motorcycle club would help me and we fixed lunch for them. At four in the morning she and I would get in the truck, go downtown, and make sure we had enough food in case several more people would come into town that we didn't know about. We took our lunch and started down to Custer Park. We went ahead of the tour and got the lunch all ready. We served them and they had all they could eat for 65 cents. We would clean up everything and follow the tour into Mt. Rushmore and into Sturgis so if anybody had any trouble we'd be there to help.

From there on the rally just grew in leaps and bounds. It grew by word of mouth for several years. We fed everybody for years until it got so big we couldn't! And then the Chamber of Commerce took it over and they had a real nice program down in the park. They had a grandstand down there at that time, there was Queen of the Rally, Best-Dressed Club, and prizes for the man who rode the farthest, the Oldest rider who came the farthest, and the youngest. There weren't that many women riders back then.

I wish I had a nickel for every mile I sat behind Clarence! I rode to the fairgrounds from the shop by myself and I didn't think much of it. We were in so many places on our motorcycles. When my son, Jack, was small we had a sidecar and away we would go.

We never dreamed that Sturgis would ever get as big as it has and I was always so thrilled to think that Clarence lived to see what had happened. He had planned so much to be at the fiftieth rally anniversary, but he had passed away.

Jean Davidson, Wisconsin
College teacher, author, *Growing Up Harley-Davidson: Memoirs of a Motorcycle Dynasty, Jean Davidson's Harley-Davidson Family Album*

One of the nicest parts about writing the stories about the Harley-Davidson family is that people love to hear stories around the motorcycles, not just about the technical stuff. I love the adventure of the whole motorcycle mystique because it's a wonderful camaraderie of people.

Motorcycles came from the bicycle—that was why they were developed in the first place, because my grandfather, Walter, and his brothers wanted to get to the fishing holes faster and not have to pedal a bicycle.

Most people tell me my books bring back memories of growing up with the motorcycle. I'm out there telling the won-

derful stories of two generations, my grandfather's and my dad's. When I was growing up, I didn't want people to know who I was because every boy I went out with, as soon as he found out I was a Davidson, would say, "Hey, can your dad get me a motorcycle?" Now I feel so blessed to be born with that name.

My most memorable ride was in 1953. I was just fifteen years old and boy crazy. With just a swimming suit on and tennis shoes, I rode a motorcycle 30 miles into Milwaukee to see this boy. The only thing I was worried about is if the bike would tip over because it was so big. But I made it and I was so excited. I pulled into his driveway and I revved up the engine and his mother came out! She thought I was from the wrong side of the tracks. She sent me away!

Sarah Harley
1998 Harley-Davidson Springer Softail
Senior sales executive

When I was a little girl, my brothers would pick me up on their Harley-Davidson Super Glides with sidecars from kindergarten, first, and second grade. I would hop into the sidecar and they'd take me home. My friends grew up seeing us with motorcycles all the time. It was not a big deal. I started riding when I was a teenager. It was just a natural thing to do. You rode a bicycle and then graduated to a motorcycle. In my family anybody and everybody could ride a motorcycle. My mother Kathryn May Harley also rode and she would ride from Wisconsin to Daytona with my father for the races.

My grandfather was William S. Harley, the founder of Harley-Davidson with Arthur Davidson. His son, John E. Harley, was my father. He was vice president of Parts and Accessories. So I'm third-generation Harley. Growing up around motorcycles was very interesting. We grew up meeting different people involved in the motorcycle field, other motorcycle companies, associations, and so forth and the everyday riders. It was an inspiring atmosphere.

I remember talking about Harley Owners Group [HOG] over a kitchen table before it was even formed. We'd have dinner and we'd be talking about different things that were going on at the company. You see all that's going on today, and I've been listening to the development of these things since the late sixties, early seventies.

My most memorable time was at the 90th Harley-Davidson anniversary riding in the parade and watching people applauding and hanging out windows and waving to all of us that were riding and thinking, "This is what my grandfather started" and wishing that he were alive to see this. To think that nearly one hundred years ago my grand-

> " *To think that nearly one hundred years ago my grandfather was a founder, just really blows my mind. It's amazing.* "

father was a founder, just really blows my mind. It's amazing.

Joan Jewel, New Jersey
1994 Harley-Davidson Sportster

I started riding in 1947 and my first long ride was to Daytona Beach. My first bike was a Harley-Davidson 125. I've ridden all kinds of bikes, all kinds of brands. My favorite bike is the Triumph.

I've ridden in every state and have been back and forth to California three times. Age is not an issue. Motorcycling makes you ageless and it's a good healthy outdoor sport.

I've been in the Motor Maids for fifty-two years. I've been to at least thirty conventions. I've ridden dirt runs, road runs, and trials. I was a dealer, too. My shop was called Joan's Chain & Sprocket Sport Shop. I sold any dirt bike you could think of, but the road bike I sold was Triumphs.

I've always loved motorcycles. My husband was an American Motorcycle Association (AMA) referee and we traveled all over the country. I've met friends all over the United States and send out nearly four hundred Christmas cards a year. It's like family. Motorcyclists are one big fraternity.

Riding McClure's Pass in Colorado on route to Sturgis Motorcycle Rally, Betsy Huelskamp finds peace in the wind.

Photo: Maggie Hallahan

CHAPTER 3

The Road Is My Home

. . . many miles, I love to roam
Got the wind in my hair, got no worries and no cares . . .

  —Sasha, from the song "The Road Is My Home"

The road is her home: the woman rider is a nomad, an adventurer, a discoverer. She is curious. She is both leader and guide on the journey of life for herself, her friends, and family. She is an explorer and a pioneer, discovering layers of wisdom and talent hidden in the dull recesses of everyday life. She embodies the joy of freewheeling through moments.

Motorcycle riding piques awareness in the highest state. Rain sounds like an orchestra tumbling notes as drops strike metal, plastic, and rubber. The sky morphs a storyboard of cloudy tales. Bugs do not taste like chicken. The plethora of scents is wildly intoxicating and opens up endless chambers of self like the ultimate aromatherapy. The terrain communicates with your inner territory to address the empty barren wasteland of a personal canvas awaiting color from the brush of self-renewal.

The urban tangle becomes a mental foray into harnessing one's focus. The mountaintop becomes something not to conquer but to achieve. The wistful prairie mimics the hypnotic rolling sound of rubber humming along highway. The thick rising forest and rocky river beds reach us vertically and expand us horizontally. The lake mirrors a unique lifetime. And the asphalt ribbon never ends, leading to whatever, whenever because you are present to the beauty of each moment. These road scenarios open up dimensions of awareness. Then we realize "we," nature and humanity, are one and the ride upon which we voyage is the vehicle that delivers us into these healing, triumphant and loving epiphanies.

The motorcycle offers an intensifying voyage into joy. The rider can be complete within her celebrated femininity and discover further wonders of self on the road. "When we are weak, restless, and mentally unstable, we remain earthbound, like water. But when we become spiritualized by self-discipline and deep meditation, we soar like the wind in the omnipresence of our true soul nature." (from *Wine of the Mystic*)[9]

Sexy, powerful, and free describes the Bikerlady, the woman who rides a motorcycle whether she drives it, passengers, or races. I love the word *lady* because it describes a woman who commands respect by virtue of her feminine prowess. The feminine prowess is power. The female gender is powerful in its own right, in its own design and instinct. The female biker is in control because she is aware of her personality, her needs, her womanhood, and especially aware of all that surrounds her. Often the road that she follows to finally take hold of her destiny is filled with endless potholes, gravel, and uphill climbs, and the motorcycle rides her away from the same

old pitted, dark trail and onto her light-filled purposeful path.

The Bikerlady is a woman free to be her sensual self . . . a woman who is sexy because she allows the seduction of the road to awaken all of her senses full throttle. She lives on the edge of her own personality and grabs hold of chance opportunity. She embraces whatever the winds of change offer that will completely expose and reveal her inner radiance, even if it may tear her apart, because that will shed her old self. She rides free, exploring the open roads to get closer to and thus more familiar with her true self. She rides free to know joy and maybe to find answers. She rides free just *because*.

Let's talk about *sexy* on a motorcycle.

> *Harley-Davidson coined the phrase, "If I have to explain, you wouldn't understand."*

Sexy is all your senses fully engaged and alive, and then *awareness* kicks in; an awareness that indicates your soul stretching and laughing and floating on your quest for freedom, with hundreds of chrome, cubic-inches of power roaring between your legs. It is an awareness that unites your bodily senses, mind, and soul in an orgasmic celebration of spirit. It is sexy because we begin to love and accept ourselves, warts and all. Engaged in the passion of windy freedom on the road, we experience confidence. That is sexy. That is power.

The motorcycle. Chrome, steel, rubber. A machine. But it is more than just a two-wheeled form of transportation. Everyone who rides has her own reason to love motorcycles, but the seduction of the winding road and motorcycles cannot be explained. Harley-Davidson coined the phrase, "If I have to explain, you wouldn't understand."

Women are the fastest-growing segment of the motorcycle marketplace and currently make up 10 percent of all new motorcycle buyers. "With more U.S. women gearing up, motorcycle sales is developing a distinctly feminine form and voice," said Elisabeth Piper, Director of Corporate Affairs for the Motorcycle Industry Council. More than one-third of all Motorcycle Safety Foundation Rider Course® graduates are women. A study by the American Motorcyclist Association (AMA) showed that of its 235,000 members, 10 percent are women who have a penchant for large, touring motorcycles. Data also indicate that most women start riding in their mid-30s, and that this survey group is predominantly older, with an average age of 47.7.[19]

Riding a motorcycle takes us away from space and time into a silent abyss of oneself; the spirit is free to be and the mind can't help but release that which holds it prisoner—be it time constraints, responsibility, adversity, perceptions of others, whatever life experiences keep us from freedom and joy. Time doesn't exist. Space is boundless. Motorcycling allows us to connect with all that surrounds us because we are so vulnerable and completely exposed to our journeys. We are available to become a

character in our own road story. Whatever happens, happens and we both welcome the adventure and become it.

The motorcycle smashes down any barrier dictating what we can and cannot do. It crushes boundaries that cage our identity from free expression and breaks through glass ceilings that keep us from soaring and realizing our dreams. But why the motorcycle? Why not a car or a bicycle? The reason is that while those vehicles can also produce a free feeling, it's nothing like being on a motorcycle. A motorcycle is raw and exposed—it is a panoramic experience and perspective on life. It can gallop into a small town, a large city, or a gas station and invite camaraderie, human interest, and communication. Hey, roll down all the car windows, but you'll never escape that steel cocoon or even come close to the rush of wind and freedom you feel when galloping down the road on your steel horse.

On a motorcycle, you glide deep into uphill twists and turns. You'll never break the same sweat you would pedaling a bicycle, but the unity of flesh and steel at breakneck speed, dipping and soaring, is life transforming. You get a workout most health and fitness magazines wouldn't feature: that of the body, mind, and soul united with a chrome horse to simulate a feeling of flying. Flesh and steel become one. On this journey, one cannot go forth without the other.

Riding for hundreds of miles facing the unpredictable environmental conditions provides somewhat of a physical workout, not to mention the physical stamina needed to comb through snarled locks that have escaped the hairband. But the mind, the heart, and soul get the greatest workout. To cruise the endless ribbons of highway completely exposed to nature's mood swings, allowing every sense to open into a flora of wonder escalating into giddy out-of-the-norm experiences essential to our human nature and mapping out our journeys as a connection to our purpose are just a few

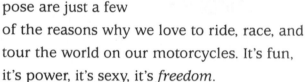

of the reasons why we love to ride, race, and tour the world on our motorcycles. It's fun, it's power, it's sexy, it's *freedom*.

Free will. Free to *be*. And what results from freedom is a banquet of gratitude that emanates from the absolute core of our souls: We are in awe of the riding experience so we thank God, the sky, the earth, the journey, our motorcycles, like an endless highway mantra. All of that gratitude brings us to a hallowed peace inside; a peace that truly is the foundation for eternal freedom.

Women from all walks of life, and I mean *all* walks of life, have told me fabulous tales about their motorcycle adventures and the revelations these freedom machines have brought into their lives that have led them on their road home to truth and joy. Yes, the men also experience much of the

same feelings we do, but women are always put in a position of facing a challenge when we engage in anything thought of as a guy thing—we've got to prove ourselves at every mile in our careers, our passions, our lives. To delve into the reasons why we are not respected as equal and capable because we are emotional creatures is another discussion. Happily, though, as we continue to celebrate our feminine qualities instead of trying to ignore our female energy, we unite as a motorcycle sisterhood, flaunting our undeniable intellect, strength, courage, and beauty. We come closer to our feminine power being accepted and respected in all facets of life as we roar forward.

Riding my motorcycle, I move as fast as I can away from the weight of the world and feel every sorrow, worry, insecurity, fear, regret, and shame rip away, like shedding an old skin. The real me is set free. Nothing remains the same, change is constant and inviting—the motorcycle is an old friend, familiar with my every move and thought. The soul of this vehicle perfectly matches human nature's desire to wander, uninhibited, with no boundaries, and just soak in the wonder. The air is plenty on the open road and it fills me with peace and fulfills every inch of me.

When I ride, oftentimes my hair stands on end, not in fear but in joyous response to my senses being completely alive. The senses are treated to a sensual communication beyond words, a knowing similar to intuition, as when you're so connected to someone that they finish your sentences. The motorcycle completes me. It finishes my sentences and answers my questions.

The road introduces us to uncommon experiences that are life transforming. When we ride, we meet people who change our lives. We enter environments that alter our perspectives. These experiences let us know that we are spirits connected with a higher power; a power that delights in our joy to know and live freedom. Marybeth Bond, author of *Gutsy Women: More Travel Tips and Wisdom for the Road*, writes: "[Travel] is about the rewards of risk-taking, living, feeling, learning, and loving; it is about having the strength to be ourselves and taking steps toward making our dreams real."[11] Truly the road becomes our home because we yearn for more adventure out there in the asphalt wilds.

Perhaps when we ate from the tree of knowledge, our punishment was that our freedom was immediately crushed. We relinquished a fantastic freedom at first bite. Before that, we celebrated our nakedness and we were playful. We loved well, ate well, and life was all about being free spirits in a gorgeous garden. Yeah, at the biker rallies, women do parade around in leather, chaps, thongs, and topless. Riding is freeing, what can I tell you? Just as I see lots of signs that say "Show Us Your Tits," I see those that retort, "Show Us Your Dicks." The women are happy to oblige, as are the men. If being modest and covering up appropriately is the sign of good soul, we're in trouble, because I've met some downright dirty folks dressed to impress in their fancy threads and I've met the greatest folks in the world dressed in minimal leather.

Riding makes you release judgment and suddenly you think, "To each her own." There are different types of riders in the motorcycle lifestyle, indeed. The culture is about freedom to be who you are, truly and sincerely that soul shining forth. I respect all riders and wish them well on their journeys. There are those who are extremely conservative, those who are extremely wealthy (known as RUBS: Rich Urban Bikers), and those who are weekend warriors who simply adopt the look with no respect for the free-spirited lifestyle. Then there are those who ride many thousands of miles around the world, completely throwing themselves into the wanderlust experience with an insatiable appetite for more road, and still more road. Of course, there are the chrome cowgirls who live and breathe the more hardcore biker lifestyle, the women riders who ride as a pastime but not as a lifestyle, and the racey ladies who love to tear up track and drag their knees in a trail of victory through wicked hairpin turns.

Riding a motorcycle creates physical and emotional health and healing for women and it may do the same for men. Bikerladies are very accepting of themselves because of the lessons learned on their journeys. They embrace body acceptance, and they come in all sizes, shapes and forms. Many wear whatever they want at the rallies. Though some may scorn them for daring to wear skimpy outfits over Rubenesque bodies, the judgment means nothing and the woman goes on about her ride and day completely thrilled with herself. A woman who is truly proud to display herself and flaunt her soul is a woman who has great self-esteem.

I love to dress in my leather skirt chaps with an itty-bitty bikini and thigh-high boots at the rallies when I'm not riding. I dress sexy for me and it's so much fun. I don't wear much, but I've got a heart the size of Texas. I love to feel that freedom of simply being me. When I'm 80 years old sifting through pictures, I want to smile sweetly at my confidence and fondly remember those days when my skin was like undisturbed silk stretched across a canvas. I don't think dressing sexy reduces my self-worth whatsoever. And the attention that I get from the male persuasion is always gentlemanly and complimentary.

The world is our playground and play we must. "Deep play," writes Diane Ackerman in her book of the same title, "unfolds in a magical space beyond the confines of everyday life, a space both physical and imaginary."[12] Riding a motorcycle is deep play time—a chance to straddle awareness and abandon. We must be wildly conscious of anything that can take us down onto the harsh pavement, but at the same time, we can get into deep play, enjoying the absence of space and time. We can be totally lost in our ride, incredibly aware of everything that surrounds us, but unaware of the chains that may bind us in real life.

And what of age? The world indeed is our playground on a motorcycle and freedom is our reality. Age becomes something entirely irrelevant to our riding experiences. We delight in a passion that has no age limitations, and joyfully piques all the treasured experiences of childhood. The wonder, the lack of time constraints, the lack of space restraints, so thoroughly lost in the passion of riding like a pioneer discovering new territory outside of us and within ourselves.

"Age is no barrier to your dreams and goals," states 50-year-old Helen Thayer, author of *Polar Dream*,[13] who skied to the North Pole. Motorcycle riding helps us focus on our dreams and goals because it clears our minds and fills us with youthful enthusiasm. Riding takes us back to childhood. We smell like the outdoors, just like when we were children, running free with our hair all wild and laughing at simply nothing at all. We didn't care if our faces were dirty then and we don't care if they're dirty from miles of road dust now. All of this—the freedom, the play, the wonder, the power of controlling our own—is the magic of riding a motorcycle.

Motorcycles attract non-riders too, like a child longing for the best toy out of the FAO Schwarz catalog. They view it from a distance; it's not theirs yet, but they connect with the toy and long to own it. Non-riders are fascinated with the mystery of the motorcycle, the art of the motorcycle. This explains the record-breaking attendance at the Guggenheim Museum for its presentation of "The Art of the Motorcycle," first shown in 1998 and still traveling, and the multi-million-dollar Harley-Davidson licensing and apparel division, supported by non-riders as well as riders.

Oh, the danger of it all. Oftentimes folks will only admire motorcycles from a distance because the machines are vulnerable to highway speeds, to dopey drivers and hapless animals. But we love that vulnerability! We love the wild road. We love exposing ourselves to the panoramic experience of life on two wheels. Life ain't a safe warm blanket! As riders, we love to open our souls to the powerful experience of riding a motorcycle and anticipating the unknown outcome of a journey. When we return from a trip, whether short or long, we have come from visiting that secret place in the wind where self meets soul; we had fun, blew out the cobwebs that entrap our minds, and arrived alive and refreshed and ready to move forward in our lives! What an experience, and it's available whenever our souls long to straddle the ride and welcome the road as our home.

The Experience: Day Trippin' with Sasha

I'm in the mood. The rising sun and blue heaven outside are inviting me to enjoy an adventure. But I have work to do. I have errands and chores that have been abandoned all week in favor of more important duties like career, family needs, and miscellaneous urgent matters screaming for my immediate attention. So much to do. I even set my alarm for a ridiculously early hour on a Saturday morning to get a jump start on the day, but where do I begin? Deep breath. Let me start by realigning my priorities. I decide to wear my leather chaps to ward off the early chill and take my rain gear just in case. I need to get the hell out of town.

With my dark Rapunzel-length hair still tousled in a bed head mess, I skip over to the parking garage a few blocks away to get my motorcycle. A silly smile rises as I mull over which route to take into the unknown. I love magical mystery–style jaunts, but planning is essential, too. The urban jungle of New York City's Upper West Side is home for me. In my neighborhood, I am affectionately known as "the motorcycle lady" or "Bikerlady."

"Hey, Bikerlady! You come to get your motorcycle? You da only one who takes your bike out all da time," the garage attendant tells me. They also always bid me good-bye with a "Be careful, darlin'" in their various accents. They get a charge out of hearing the throaty roar from the pipes

The author on the road, Mammoth Lakes, California
Photo by GOTHGIRL

announcing our dynamic duo arrival from the garage basement level. When we emerge from the elevator onto the street, passersby stop and watch in wonder, thinking, I'm sure: "A girl on a motorcycle?" I gun the throttle to let traffic know that I'm cutting in and roar away; pure elation seems to lift the machine right off the ground and I feel like I'm hydroplaning from excitement.

An unplanned, free-wheeling jaunt is outrageous fun and a tasty break from an over-scheduled lifestyle, but preparation builds confidence and fosters awareness. Preparation gives us freedom to discover and experience with reduced fear. To be

prepared is to be courageous and accepting of whatever may happen along the journey. To be prepared equals easy riding fun! Whenever I ride, there are basic essentials that I always carry just in case the wanderlust in my gypsy soul decides to extend the day trip into two days or more, and also in case the bike has her moment.

In the left saddlebag is TLC riding stuff for me: rain gear, Ziploc baggies (to keep stuff dry) containing extra panties, socks, lady moon (feminine) supplies, a first aid kit, Wetnaps, travel-size toiletries, sun block, Advil, moisturizer, a little camera, bandannas, a sweatshirt, flip-flops, cut-off shorts, and a black, silver-scripted baseball cap with "It's All Good" inscribed on the front and "Biker Chick" on the back.

In the right bag is TLC stuff for the bike: a small tool kit; extra spark plugs, fuses, and bulbs; a tire gauge and patch kit; clear eyeglasses; hundred-mile-an-hour tape (a.k.a. duct tape) and electrical tape; bungee cords; a flashlight; extra leather gloves; medical gloves; sandwich baggies (for water leaks in boots or gloves); maps; bike locks; rags; cleaner; and the bike's mini owner manual. In my waist satchel: bubble gum, a Swiss army knife, matches, antibacterial hand gel, lipstick, a mirror, earplugs, scented body oil, tissues, super glue, my wallet with ID and bike papers, vitamins, and a cell phone loaded with essential numbers.

It's both risky and risqué to ride. To be a true free spirit requires a bit of risk management, too. So the maternal instinct springs forth to offer tender loving pre-ride care. We bikers use the "T-Clock" inspection method to check the mechanical functions: Tires, Controls, Lights and electrics, Oils and fluids, Chassis and chain, Kickstand. On a Harley, it's a known fact that you've got to check for loose nuts and bolts every time you go for a ride and throughout the day. After I finish my pre-ride inspection, I run upstairs to my apartment to wash away the grease from under my perfectly manicured nails.

I finish my makeup and braid my long, brown hair into one rope laced with colorful bands. Silver Native American jewelry decorates my wrist and fingers. Then it's a last-minute check to be sure that I have all I need for today's great escape. I grab my wraparound Dior-style rhinestone sunglasses and rhinestone-studded black helmet that has three stickers on back: "New York City," "Scooter Fox," and the American flag. My two favorite leathers (a jacket and a shirt style) get layered atop each other to ward off sunrise chill. A fresh application of bright coral lipstick in the sideview mirror is my final inspection check, and now it's time to head out on the highway and discover today's escapade.

The northbound West Side Highway delivers me—bumping and shimmying all the way along its deeply worn grooves of well-traveled pavement—to the George Washington Bridge. Traffic is light and the sun has now stretched its golden rays over the skyline. The choppy waters of the Hudson River indicate the whipping winds that are playing maypole around my bike as we weave along to the exhalation of Mother Nature's breath. Suddenly it dawns on me that I should visit my sister, Lou-Lou, who lives in New Paltz, New York. I also decide that I will continue north to Woodstock, where I had once lived as a young geek and daughter to urban "greaser" parents in a small town just outside of the extreme coolness of that hippie-esque hamlet. Just over the George Washington Bridge, instead of heading southbound to the beach, I swing onto the Palisades Parkway for a gorgeous ride along the Hudson River. It's hard to imagine that a few miles north of New York City are daring cliffs that resemble the sheer drops along the Pacific coastline.

Only twenty miles from the bridge and I'm in true suburbia, sailing through the air crisply scented with bouquets of roadside flora. The canopy overhead is a lush spring green and bursts of yellow, white, orange, and red wildflowers dot the meridian and sway along to the morning breeze. As I cruise along the Palisades, I also notice lots of mowed-down fur. The dirty-gym-sock smell of fresh road kill that pierces through the otherwise perfumed atmosphere is so rancid that I breathe outward so I don't get nauseous.

A few months prior, I had hit a deer on my motorcycle but I managed to keep the bike upright. It was a dewy, pretty morning and I was on my way back to the city. I rounded a blind turn on a winding country road and there stood the animal. It dove right into my path. Oh, I handled the whole thing with sheer grace. I screamed and swerved slightly away, slamming the frightened animal back onto the side of the road. Animal parts splashed my chaps and bike. In horror, I rode to the nearest gas station to wash off, uttering "Thank you, God" and "Oh my God" all the way. Bewildered folks with their powder-dusted donut mouths, sipping coffees, watched as I hosed off my chaps and the bike. My body shook from the flight-or-fight serum that pulsed through my veins. Of course, I felt bad for hitting the poor thing, but I felt better that I wasn't the poor thing being carted away in an ambulance. Truth is, anything can try to take you down, on the road and in life. The key is to be prepared and aware.

A quick merge onto I-87 and I'm feeling so carefree that I break into singing Sheryl Crow's "Everyday Is a Winding Road." There's no room for guilt at leaving behind the "have to" chores. Those chores are always going to be there, no matter what; even if I get them all done, they'll reappear.

Time to fuel up and change the chewing gum, which has hardened into the consistency of cardboard. I pull into a full-service rest stop and over to the gas station, lean over with my cash card, punch up the numbers, and feed my hog while fishing for some fresh bubble gum. Another biker spots me and strolls over to say hi. It turns out he's on a HOG (Harley Owners Group) run with eighty other riders and I'm invited to join in. I usually allow myself to be open to the day's opportunities but I decline, explaining that I'm on my own little journey today and thanking him for the invite. We exchange business cards because I do love to keep in touch with other riders and grow my riding family outreach. I holler good-bye to the HOG members and ride away.

At the next exit I cut off onto Route 32, a winding road through the Hudson Valley farmlands that will lead me into the middle of New Paltz. As I gallop along the asphalt, I feel like an iron Godiva commanding the reins of her steel horse as my gloved hands gently operate the controls of the motor-

The author and nephew Liam on a motorcycle kiddy ride!
"Yeah, I'm teaching him to ride young."

I haven't alerted my sister that I am on my way because I like to just pop in on my family. It's more fun that way and every time I do, my nieces and nephews go wild. Familiar cars line the driveway to my sister's house. I've stumbled upon a family affair. Who knew? The back door to her ground floor apartment bursts open and four cherubic faces scream my name. My nieces and nephews run out of the house with no shoes, so happy to see their unconventional auntie. My mother's face emerges wearing that "Oh my God. Why does she have to ride that thing?"

cycle. The fringe on my chaps and jacket flutter wildly in the wind. My legs are stretched close alongside the rumbling V-Twin engine to keep warm. As I gain a mile I gain freedom, I gain my sense of true self, I gain awareness, I gain power. I leave behind the intense everyday rigors and structure necessary to keep it all together in a demanding lifestyle. Each mile can tear away at another dutiful label placed upon us—identities adopted so that we can interact accordingly in the various worlds that define our roles in life. The wind's easy elimination process is a reminder of just how lightweight the sticking power of those labels really are.

look. My sisters, Linda and Lou, and my sister-in-law, Sue, are ecstatic that I stopped by for a visit. They had a little sleepover party. I stay for coffee and let the kids sit on the bike: off and then back on, over and over again. They can't get enough of it. I think they are more amused on my motorcycle than if they were on a kiddy ride at an amusement park.

I try to leave my sister's house but of course I've got to wait while they take photos. I go through this all the time with the family and it's really sweet. My fiercely independent five-year-old niece, Jessica, is quickly trying to snap a picture with her Barbie camera upside down, and is screaming for me to "Wait, wait, I gotta get a pikcha." Everyone watches me pull away and the kids run along the lawn waving as I ride off to play in the wind.

The winding roads stimulate my creativity as a singer/songwriter. New verses to songs seem to compose themselves with every new mile. The wind and the ride are poetry in motion. Sometimes I even pull over and dial up my production team and sing the lyrics over the phone to them, and then appear in the studio to lay down the vocals to the music they have created based upon my roadside phone call compositions. That kind of creativity is God in the wind, pure and simple. I would have never known the extent of my creativity had it not been for my motorcycle.

It's just after lunchtime when I arrive in Woodstock. The town is packed with visitors and the sidewalks are lined with motorcycles of all makes and models. As soon as I park my Tigerlily, she lures people over for an "oooo" and "ahhhh" fest. She really does exemplify sexy, powerful, freedom, and feminine prowess. The town is alive with street entertainment, an outdoor art show, and a musical tribute to the 1960s.

While I stroll through town, friendly hellos are shared between fellow motorcyclists as we recognize each other as moto-passionate individuals. A large biker stuffed into crisp black leathers embossed with the Harley-Davidson logo everywhere taps me on the shoulder. "So, where you off to today, lil' lady?" he asks, watching me through thick-lensed sunglasses. Next to him is a round, bleach-blond woman with heavy fuchsia lipstick painted upon smiling lips. "Just cruisin'. And you?" I reply. "There's a pig roast over in Saugerties, next town over. It just started. These folks rent out a bunch of cabins and campsites at the KOA. You should come on over with us." And that's how bikers are—they may not even know you, but will extend an invitation to join a good time—a definition of how the world ought to be, people loving and caring toward one another no matter that they're strangers. Bikers come from all walks of life and bond together because of their love for riding and freedom. Oftentimes the connections made last a lifetime.

We make small talk about the riding day and ourselves. It turns out that George is a retired airline pilot and Margie is an environmental attorney! They met at Daytona Bike Week. I tell them I'm game for a pig roast. So I follow the giant biker and his sweet girlfriend over to the bikes. Margie's Yamaha Road Star is painted completely pink with flowers and butterflies. The inside of her windshield is taped with plastic-wrapped pictures of her grandkids, "her road angels." Her leathers are beige with red roses. She is one stylin' motorcycle mama. George rides an Ultra Touring Classic Harley-Davidson equipped with every modern convenience. They are happily retired from a previously structured existence and are now celebrating life and each other.

We head over to the roast. It's a five-dollar entry fee. The party is high octane and there's a small band playing country

GORMAN'S HARLEY-DAVIDSON SALES

Dot Robinson, the First Lady of Motorcycling
Courtesy Motor Maids

Pat Wise, first British woman racer to complete the Isle of Man TT
Photo © Pat Wise Collection

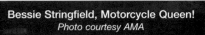

Bessie Stringfield, Motorcycle Queen!
Photo courtesy AMA

Ruth Steiner and friend, 1949
Photo courtesy Sanjoy Motorcycle Engraving

Clockwise from top left:

Woman on an Indian, circa 1912–13
From the private collection of Jerry Hooker, www.motorcycle-memories.com

Miss "Cy" Woodman, New York to San Francisco on a Flanders 4 motorcycle, circa 1911–12
Published by Kraus Mfg. Co., New York.
From the private collection of Jerry Hooker, www.motorcycle-memories.com

Clara Wagner, published by Blanchard Press, New York, 1911.
Photo only copyright by A. Loeffler, Tompkinsville, New York.
From the private collection of Jerry Hooker, www.motorcycle-memories.com

**"'Let's Go!' Easter Walters, movie star of the Pathé Film Co.," circa 1919–23,
on a Harley horizontal twin**
From the private collection of Jerry Hooker, www.motorcycle-memories.com

**"Bain't you afraid to ride it, Missy?" "No it's so simple." Posted, 1918, from England,
published by Hendee Manufacturing Co.**
From the private collection of Jerry Hooker, www.motorcycle-memories.com

CLARA WAGNER WITH HER MOTORCYCLE AT COENTIES SLIP, NEW YORK, USING THE ECLIPSE COASTER BRAKE.

MICHIGAN
HERS 2
CYCLE MAR

"Let's Go!" Easter Walters, Movie Star of the Pathe Film Co.

Clockwise from top left:

Gloria Tramontin Struck on her 1950 Harley-Davidson motorcycle
Photo courtesy Gloria Tramontin Struck

Daughter Effie and mother Avis Hotchkiss
Photo courtesy Craig A. Dov

**The lovely Viola Pelaquin, trick rider,
in the motor drome with the Pelaquin Family, 1928**
Photo by Stu Lewis, courtesy Sam Morgan

Linda Dugeau, cofounder of the Motor Maids
Courtesy the Motor Maids

Sturgis motorcycle rally

Sasha with Sonny Barger
at Sturgis

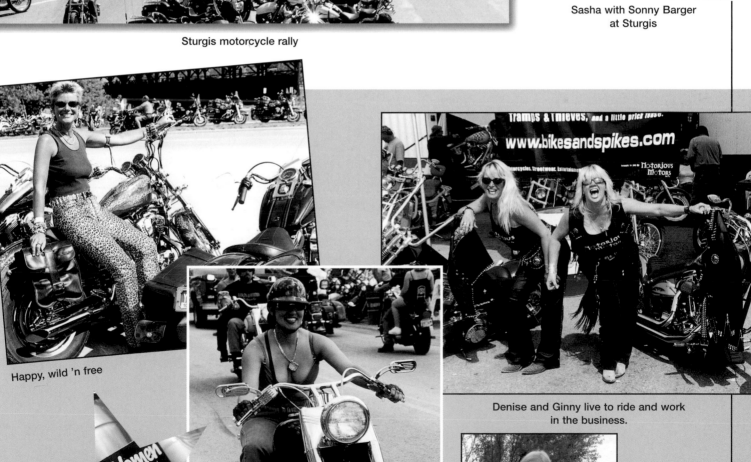

Happy, wild 'n free

Real Women ride Motorcycles

Sassy rider and her big,
beautiful Harley cruiser

Denise and Ginny live to ride and work
in the business.

Long-distance rider
Voni Glaves
*Photo courtesy
Voni Glaves*

www.bikesandspikes.com

DeAnna Goodrich

Below left: Erica B. Smith, WIMA and WIST
Photo by John F. X. Walsh, © 2002

Below right: Michele Dell, owner of Hogs & Heifers Saloon, New York City, before a pig roast party at her bar

DeAnna Goodrich

CruelGirl, of the Vixens motorcycle club says,
"Panheads rule!"
Photo courtesy CRUELGIRL

Below: Donna Raymond
in New York City
Photo by Danielle Raymond

Bottom left: She packed
everything, but gladly left the
kitchen sink.

Bottom right: Dixie Deb says,
"Ride because you love it.
Ride because you live for it."
Photo courtesy www.dixiedeb.com

Left: Lisa Bell
Photo courtesy Lisa Bell

Below: Dawn Glencer
© Doug Barber, www.dougbarber.com

Bottom: RaZor of the Devil Dolls
motorcycle club
Photo by Eddie Howell

Motorcycle Parking
on Sidewalk is
PROHIBITED
Vehicles will be towed
at owner's expense

& western tunes. It's great. Children are dangling from swing sets or playing tag among the leather-clad and tattooed bikers. Two little girls are sitting on a motorcycle sidecar rig pretending they're riding. About a hundred bikes are parked all over the woods. The host is a short fellow dressed in a ragged denim vest covered with ride pins and patches. His nickname is Peanuts, and he wears a giant grin. I find out through an amusing whisper that the Peanuts nickname was bestowed as testimony to the opposite-than-the-nickname-suggests size of the chutzpah package tucked inside his Levi's.

Peanuts and George carve the roasted pig in front of a cheering, hungry crowd. It's a potluck picnic featuring homemade road recipes from several committee bikers that spearhead the party. I hang around for three hours and in that short time, meet some really uproarious folks through George and Margie. These two road romantics know most of the people there and warmly introduce me as if I'm an immediate family member. We exchange telephone numbers. Again my riding family expands. They invite me to George's granddaughter's birthday party next month. "It'll be a biker baby birthday bash," Margie giggles.

Since I want to cruise the back roads toward New York City and get home by nightfall, I say my good-byes and head home. I love the serenity at dusk. It offers a gentle reflection of the day and serves up excitement for evening festivities. The evening ride is smooth and peaceful as I glide along the highway now. I feel deliciously relaxed as the night air rushes against my face. I'm just sweetly drifting in the wind. The road is so romantic that I almost wish I were riding alongside a fabulous chrome cowboy.

The evening also invites a bug fest and my windshield is getting pelted with all flavors. Although it feels exhilarating to ride without a shield, dead insects are better collected on it than on my face. Many of my friends hate running with a shield, and it's funny to see what they look like when we stop. Their faces are dotted with bug parts. Of course, I'm usually the one offering up the Wetnaps so they can clean the insect graveyards off their skin. I've put the bandanna that's tied around my neck over my lips so I don't get insect goo inside my

> " *The evening ride is smooth and peaceful as I glide along the highway now. I feel deliciously relaxed as the night air rushes against my face. I'm just sweetly drifting in the wind. The road is so romantic that I almost wish I were riding alongside a fabulous chrome cowboy.* "

mouth. Now I look like some outlaw chick on the run from bugs.

I'm ready for a night out on the town so I think about heading over to Hogs & Heifers Uptown, where my buddies gather with their motorcycles to enjoy some fun honky-tonk music. The tollbooths leading onto the bridge are really quiet now. During the week, the traffic is thick like an endless conveyor belt filled with matchbox cars ready for packaging. I'm sure that's what many of the drivers feel like, too. With my trusty Betty Boop Biker change purse in hand, I dig out the fare and drop the money into the gloved hand of a veteran attendant. "Oooooweeeeeeee!" she yells when she notices me. Her gospel yelp pierces through my earplugs, so I remove one to hear what she's saying to me. Her belly and enormous breasts jiggle with laughter. "You go girl, mmm, mmm, mmm, you a little thang, too." She leans out the window and studies me on the bike. "I can't believe you can drive that thang all by yourself." She puts her hand on one hip. "You scared?" she screeches.

"Nope," I reply with a giant smile.

"Oh yeah? How come you ain't scared?"

"Because I love riding my motorcycle. It's the great escape, it's freedom and it's lots of fun," I say.

"Damn. Well, maybe I ought to get me one 'cause Lawd knows I need to escape this crap and get me some freedom and fun in my life, too, know what I'm sayin?" She winks and the high shrieking laughter punctuates her every breath. "Well, you look good, girl. Oh my God. Well, I just can't believe . . . Now you jest be careful now, heah?"

I nod with a smile, stick the earplug back in, and roar off.

In the side mirror I see that she is still hanging out the window watching me. I wonder what she would have thought if I had entered the tollbooth pack wild with my other wind sisters? Bet she would have just abandoned the gig, jumped on the back of one of the bikes, and joined us. The energy that motorcycles radiate is contagious and seductive, even if the person doesn't ride, because it reflects essential human nature: freedom, power, adventure, destiny.

I ride over the George Washington Bridge and witness the energy of Manhattan in her skyline lights. Today, I leaped off the path of everyday rigors and rode away on the path of least resistance. Cobwebs are cleared away, I can think clearly now and continue moving forward in my life. In one day and two hundred fifty miles, the ride brought me both peace and an adventure. I met a new riding family, experienced the motorcycle magic through the eyes of babes, took control of my personal priorities, and let myself get spellbound with freedom and empowerment united as one with my motorcycle and the rapture of the wind. Now, back to life, back to reality.

DeAnna Goodrich, Minnesota
2001 Harley-Davidson Road King, "Blackie"
U.S. Postal Service

I'm pretty comfortable in my own skin. I
live my life with nothing to prove, be it
material or social status. I'm not a leader,
nor by any means am I a follower. I wear
my heart on my sleeve but am still strong
and confident enough to take a stand for
what I believe in. I live my life so that when
I look in the mirror, I see someone I like and
can live with. I advise women to go confi-
dently in the direction of their dreams and
to live the lives they've always wanted to live.

I've been associated with motorcycles
for the past eleven years. My coworkers
aren't as surprised that I ride as the general
public is. In Minnesota it can get a little cool
so you have to dress pretty heavily most of
the time to keep warm. So when you stop
somewhere and start taking your gear off
the expressions on people's faces are priceless. They see a 5'2" 125-pound person get
off a Road King and then they realize "It's a
girl." Riding has taught me that I can stand
up for who I am with confidence.

Erica B. Smith, New York
1992 Ducati 750SS
U.S. vice president, Women's International
Motorcycle Association (WIMA); leader for
Women in Sport Touring (WIST) e-mail
discussion group.

*M*otorcycles completely changed my
life. When I took that first ride on a
motorcycle it was shortly after an ill-fated
marriage. I was living by myself in the
middle of the country and I had to learn
how to do all my own motorcycle maintenance and restoration, and learn about
motors and how to work on them.

I met and fell in love with my second
husband at a rally. With two kids now, we
take turns riding. So riding together is something we really miss. To dance down the
road with the one that you love is one of the
neatest things in the world. If my children
are interested in riding later on, it'll be a
great excuse to get dirt bikes for ourselves.

I ride a Ducati. They have a lot of appeal
because they're lightweight, sexy, Italian
motorcycles. Once you hear the sound it's
hard to walk the other way. And I love track
days. The racetrack is a safe environment to
practice your skills and it's so much fun—
an amazing experience. You can push yourself and your bike toward your limits. The
skills you learn on the track are an asset to
street-riding skills.

Another female rider once said to me,
"Motorcycling changes women; it makes
them stronger." Riding has really helped

me find myself again and become a strong person.

Jackie Kalkhoff, Iowa
2002 Harley Davidson Low Rider
Nurse

It gives me a great deal of satisfaction to know that I can handle such a big powerful vibrating machine and ride down the road with my friends feeling so totally empowered and free. No matter how tiny I am, I can handle the big bikes just like the guys.

I'm a mother and wife and I love my kids and my work. My three children think that it's awesome that I ride, and my 18-year-old is saving for his first Harley. I love heading out on my motorcycle and forgetting all about housework, job, and responsibilities, and just being free for a couple of hours. I love the power and feeling of being out there on the road. Riding has made me much more adventurous.

Maggie Ruffo, California
2002 Suzuki SV650
Business manager

There were signs along the way, but I didn't know that someday I would become a motorcyclist. I give credit, or the blame, to my mother for providing the first sign. In 1969, when I was 11 years old, my mother took my younger brother and me to see the movie *Easy Rider*. Fast forward and it's now been five years since my first ride

in the Motorcycle Safety Foundation class. What does motorcycling do for me? It frees me by taking me out of myself. I feel powerful on my bike, after a long time of feeling powerless in my life. It gives me self-confidence and happiness.

The highlight of my riding career so far was my trip to Mono Lake and the Eastern Sierra mountains of California. We rode through Tuolumne Meadows in Yosemite on a beautiful fall day, our bikes loaded with camping gear. As we approached Tioga Pass, I was suddenly overwhelmed and awestruck by the sights around me that I could not only see, but feel and taste. Tears came to my eyes as I realized I was totally happy. That was a freeing moment. As it says on the back of my helmet: *Don't postpone joy!*

Donna Raymond, New York City
1996 Honda Magna 750, "Lucky Lady"
Recording studio manager

Motorcycles first caught my interest when I was eighteen years old. My future brother-in-law and future husband were both riders. I loved the bikes—the smells of the bikes, the sounds of the bikes, the boys, the camaraderie, the engines, and the speed.

I love the freedom motorcycle riding gives me. I love the ease of transportation, the strength of the machine beneath me. I love the "coolness" of the ride. I get thumbs-up, "Yeah, you go girl," a thoughtful nod and a wink, a good-for-you kind of look. The most important things that I learned about riding are that I can learn something new every day, to not take anything for granted, and to stay aware—to not let your guard down. Be respectful of the machine and its capabilities and it will treat you right.

Ciddie Mentzer, Florida
1994 Harley-Davidson Heritage Softail, "Louise"
Real estate investments

Whenever I am on my Harley-Davidson, "Louise," I am at one with her, free to feel the wind in my hair, to get rid of life's stresses. It becomes all about me and the freedom of the road. I feel empowered, like I am in control.

I belong to Leather and Lace Women's Motorcycle Club. I joined Leather and Lace because I like the causes that they support, but mostly because it is a sisterhood of women like me, women who understood the feeling of power when riding their own bikes. Riding has allowed me to meet my "sisters" in Leather and Lace, and that has been a life-changing experience.

If you're interested in riding just get out there and try it. It really is empowering, a feeling that you will never forget or want to give up!

Michelle Aiello, New Jersey
2002 Custom Harley-Davidson 1200 Sportster, "Isabella"; 2002 Harley-Davidson Heritage Softail "Saddie"
Attorney

I was married for 14 years and never in a million years did I ever think about riding—never mind owning—a motorcycle. When I got divorced, I wanted to live again. I was dating a guy who rode, so that's how it all started. I spent so much time on my bike that my boyfriend and I broke up because, well, I rode better then he did.

In one season of riding, I'd been to nine different states on my bike, logging about 12,000 miles. If I could ride my motorcycle 365 days out of the year, I would. My motorcycle changed my life. I love the feeling that riding gives me. I come alive when I'm on my bike. My confidence has gotten so much stronger since I've been riding. Everyday worries just disappear. It's also made me a better driver in my car! I'm more aware of my surroundings.

My life has completely changed over the past three years. Now I ride two motorcycles as well as snowboard, roller blade, play basketball, play the sax, read, golf, and do charity functions for bikers. Riding a motorcycle has given me such a sense of pride in myself because not everyone can ride a motorcycle.

I love the looks I get from people . . . it's like they want to be you even if it's just for that brief moment when they see you. My motorcycle made me realize that I don't need anyone to make me happy, as long as I'm happy. It's given me confidence and attitude to boot! I stand taller and when I talk to people about motorcycling or they find out that I ride, I tell them, "You bet I ride a hog (Harley) and *I love it!*"

Donna Kendall, Massachusetts
Harley-Davidson 883 Custom Sportster
Marketing and advertising assistant

*I*n July 2001, I was at a sales meeting for the company I work for. We had a motivation speaker come in and talk to us about "How to Double Your Sales." One of the tools was to write a list of goals—measurable goals, personal and professional, something that would make us stretch, to visualize the end result.

At the end of the meeting, I was totally motivated. I focused on my personal goals. I had wanted to learn how to ride a motorcycle for about twenty years. I always loved riding on the back of friends' Harleys—always loved the sound of the loud pipes roaring by. This was more important to me. I figured if I am happy in my personal life, it will reflect on my professional life.

The next day, I got on the Harley-Davidson website and printed out a picture of the motorcycle I really wanted. It was a purple 883 Sportster Hugger. I hung the picture in my office, so when I sat at my desk, I could see it.

My first step toward achieving this goal was to take a motorcycle safety class, and I started looking into it. In the meantime, and

as luck would have it, my husband's friend was selling his bike so I became the owner of my first motorcycle. I had never, ever driven a motorcycle before. Imagine how frustrated I was that I had this beautiful machine sitting in my garage and I had *no* idea how to ride it! I started out going back and forth across my driveway. Then I got braver and drove up and down my street (only about 150 yards long) in first gear! The second day, I wiped out, almost breaking my foot. After about a week (my foot took almost 4 months to heal completely), I got right back on. I've been riding ever since.

Betty "Jo" Whitehead, Tennessee
2000 Suzuki Intruder VS800, "Boop"
Accountant

I met a wonderful man a year after my husband died. He had ridden motorcycles his whole life. I became a passenger for a couple of years with him and then he asked me one day if I'd be interested in taking the MSF course. Once I got my license, the feeling I had when I was riding that bike solo with the wind blowing in my face was incredible.

Fresh breeze surrounding me and the scenery rushing by are things I know I can never experience sitting in a car or truck. The freedom of the road comes to life when you ride a motorcycle. There is always something new to see, new roads to ride down, and it's always fun to have someone else to share those new rides with. A women's group appeals to me because it gives us something else to do together besides share recipes! I want to promote a positive image of ladies who ride. I want to show that we can be feminine even while riding motorcycles.

Everyone at my job was surprised when they found out I ride because I "don't look like the typical biker chick" and I'm a bit reserved while at work. My son thinks it's wonderful that I ride. As a matter of fact, my son started riding about the same time I did and we ride together when he has time. He shares my passion and supports me wholeheartedly.

Riding has opened up a whole new world for me. It has taught me that I can do anything I set my mind to and that nothing is too difficult to do if you go about it with a positive attitude. It has given me the courage to know that I can do anything I want to do.

Jennifer Pfeifer, Illinois
2001 Harley-Davidson Softail Nightrain
Owner, Merle Norman Cosmetics franchise

My godfather had always ridden motorcycles. He took me on a ride around the block when I was very young and I wanted a motorcycle since that day! I took the motorcycle safety course in 1987 but wasn't able to get my license until 1999 when I finally bought a motorcycle! My one and only dream came true and it was even better than I imagined it would be!

People who think they know me are shocked when I tell them I ride a motorcy-

cle. I love the power of the machine and being in control of it. The feeling of the wind and the feeling of freedom are the best. I've been married for over 12 years and we do not have kids. I've just been too busy having too much fun with my motorcycle and my business. I can't imagine giving any of that up!

Riding a motorcycle has given me more confidence in myself just in general. I feel strong, free, and so happy. I wasn't sure I could ride a motorcycle at all but I have always been interested in it. I pinch myself every time I throw my leg over my Harley-Davidson Softail and ride away. Is it for real? Yes!

My motorcycle has fulfilled my life. It has given me more joy and wild passion for life than I thought was possible. No matter what gets me down, my motorcycle picks me up. There are so many unhappy people out there. I feel sorry for them. They need something like this in their lives. The world would be a better place.

Cheryl Rodgers, Michigan
1999 Honda CBR600 F4; 2002 Honda XR200
Graphic artist/desktop publisher

When I got my first bike, I was *hooked*! My husband and I have something to do together that we both love. We go to bike shops together, talk bikes a lot, watch motorcycle races on TV, and even lie in bed and read bike magazines!

Last year my husband bought me a brand-new dirt bike for my birthday. Everyone says you can sharpen your skills riding in the dirt, so I've been getting into riding in the dirt as well as on the street. A couple of months later he bought a dirt bike for himself as well. We love playing "cat and mouse" on our dirt bikes around the farm. Since I'm new to dirt bikes, my husband, who has ridden them since he was ten and is obviously faster, plays the "mouse." He flies around the trails we've made and I try to keep up. It's great riding experience!

I thought I couldn't ride a bike because of all that shifting and braking and stuff. I've never driven a stick shift car, let alone a motorcycle! But I soon found out that I could do it and have enjoyed every second of it. A lot of people told me not to buy a brand-new bike because I'd drop it. I was determined not to and haven't yet!

My advice to any woman who wants to learn to ride is first take the MSF course. You learn so much and will feel much more confident. Purchase and wear the proper gear. I cringe every time I see a rider without a jacket. And never drink and ride—they just aren't made for each other!

Marian Colborn, Michigan
1998 Harley-Davidson Dyna Super Glide,
  "Jack the Ripper"
Retired and a lover of life!

I belong to the Freemont Michigan Chapter of Ladies of Harley (L.O.H.), Rolling Thunder, and I started my own chapter of Woman on Wheels called the Drifters. We have 21 members. I started my own chapter

to meet other women to ride with. I rode alone for many years. I joined Rolling Thunder because the organization does good things for the vets that fought for this country.

I learned how to ride motorcycles in Chicago at age sixteen with the Blue Island Angels. Oh, neat characters there for sure. I have been married for 34 years and we have four boys. I took our boys for rides when they were young. None of them ended up liking the freedom of horses or motorcycles, but I know they are proud to say, "My mom rides a Harley."

Being retired allows me to ride free and live free more so. Since I was a kid, I've lived by no rules and no time clocks. If you have your health, tons of friends, and a clear mind, well, you've got it all. As for the whiney people, I say they need to grow up and *get* over it. Some people are not happy unless they can whine and moan about their lot in life. They need to pull themselves up by their bootstraps, be the man or woman that God intends for them to be. A motorcycle helps you to be yourself, have a good time, meet great folks, and *get over it!*

What I learned from riding is something I've always known: I'm not one to conform to anything much. I always do what I want, when I want, and I always have. I love the open road, the feeling of being in control of all that I do in life. I live and never look back, because life is short. I have always believed if women could just run this world, everything would work lots better, so we've got to hang in there and keep trying.

Jeannette Zell, Virginia
1996 Honda VFR 700 F2, "Big Red"
Technical writer

My mom is my favorite influence. She raised two daughters well after my dad left her. She was very strong and determined in her life. She was able to get through the bad times and come out on top. I greatly admire her.

I'm a bit of a fiery redhead. Riding has taught me that I can do anything I set out to do. I don't have to listen to people who tell me that I shouldn't or can't because I'm female. There aren't many females riding (compared to the amount of men) so every time another woman starts riding, I'm very supportive.

Probably my most memorable ride was on the back of my dad's bike, I hate to admit! I flew out to Colorado and then rode on the back of his bike to Sturgis, South Dakota, for the annual motorcycle rally. Seeing the countryside on the motorcycle was the most amazing experience I've ever had. One evening I saw shooting stars and a thunderstorm. We were far enough away from the storm that it didn't affect us, but I could see where it started up in the clouds and where the lightning bolts were hitting the ground below. It was a truly awesome experience.

I always wanted to ride a motorcycle since I was a little girl. I actually had dreams of being a BMX bicycle rider and broke my front tooth doing a stupid stunt down a huge hill on a little bike when I was

nine. Motorcycle riding gives me an immense feeling of accomplishment and self-confidence, of finally doing something I'd always dreamed of doing. I think I'm seen as a bit stronger and more independent than the average woman because I ride.

Shelly Hukkanen, California
2001 Suzuki Bandit 1200S, NAUTGRL
    (short for naughty girl)
Firefighter/EMT

When I am riding, I have time to think about my life, and I find this the most mind-cleansing exercise ever. If the weather is permitting and I'm feeling stressed, I hop on my bike and ride off. By the time I return home, I am so calm I can fall asleep. Riding is my life, my passion, and my love!

My favorite heroine is Tiffany Weirbach a.k.a. "Sportbike Girl." I met Tiffany through the Internet a few years ago and found out later that she had stage III melanoma that was in remission (or so we thought). Tiffany was rather young, early twenties, I believe, when she died. She had the most amazing attitude about life and I really envied her. She went for something and usually got it. She gave me the courage, you might say, to improve my riding and to make things happen in my life.

I've been a firefighter/EMT since 1988, a critical care crew member since 1998, and a member of a countywide EMS team, which evaluates the emergency services provided in the county. I'm an avid sport bike enthusiast. I love attending races from local club racing to the World Super Bike competition.

I really dislike the typical "sport bike vs. Harley" conversations, as there are no winners. If you look up the word *motorcycle* in the dictionary it says this: motorcycle (mō-tər-sī-kəl) n. "A two-wheeled motor vehicle resembling a heavy bicycle, sometimes having two saddles and a sidecar with a third wheel." I don't see anyplace where it says a motorcycle is a Harley or a sportbike. We are *all* part of a brotherhood and sisterhood: a family of people who enjoy the same thing only in different packages. I ride a *motorcycle*, and I live to ride!

Diddy "Doo Wah Diddy" Alston, North Carolina
Four Hondas: 1999 VT1100T; 1995 VT600CD; 1980 CM400T; 1974 CB125
Church secretary

I love my bikes and motorcycling in general. You can tell that a motorcycle at a church is still a novelty. My boss is amused and thinks that all pastors' secretaries need to ride a motorcycle. Of course, I think his tongue is in his cheek when he says this! There are those who have it in their heads that it is not appropriate for a motorcycle to be ridden to church on Sunday. An individual has gone so far as to mention this fact to my husband when he rode his ST1100 to church. Get off it, people. This is a two-wheeled vehicle, not the devil's spawn! At the church I attend, I receive nothing but positive comments on my VT1100T. Of

course, I get all the normal expressions of concern for my safety when I go on long trips, but they love to hear about my adventures.

Riding is like a vacation without even leaving the area in which you live. I ride to work and if I've had a really stressful day, I just hop on my scoot when I leave work and a five-minute ride home turns into a mini mind vacation of 100 miles. A bad day of riding (even in the rain) is better than a good day at work!

Motorcyclists are such generous people. You look at any motorcycle event calendar and find it full of benefits for all kinds of needy situations. Not only are these events full of people who ride, but they are full of folks who want to help put on these events. My own calendar is full of charity rides when I am not on the road to another new place.

Sandra Fries, Illinois
Yamaha TW 200, "Dutty Gyal"

I looooovvvvveeee dirt bike riding. The spill, the thrill, the agony . . . aarrrggghhhh! I really love how riding my bike takes my mind off everything else and my brain is only focused on what's ahead, the next tight turn, the hill I'm about to negotiate, the sandy track I have to gun my bike through. I belong to the Belleville Enduro Team (BETDIRT).

My husband started me out in the summer of 1999 on a Honda moped. I rode that for a week, then graduated to a Honda

70. For me, the switch from the little moped to the Honda 70 was a big climax! A couple of months later, I moved to the Yamaha TW200, which I currently ride.

Traveling is something I enjoy and I love both worlds, living in the United States and keeping a home in Jamaica, which I go back to every year. I'm just the type of person who loves the thrills but enjoys quiet moments, too. I love how riding takes my mind off everything—when it's just me and the motorcycle and the road or path ahead. Motorcycle riding teaches me that the older I get, the stronger and more beautiful I become!

Jacquie Littlejohn, New York City
2001 Ducati Monster 750, "The Dutchess";
1999 Harley-Davidson Custom Sportster,
   "WKG GRL"
Art dealer

Getting in touch with both sides of ourselves, the masculine and the feminine, is a developmental process that liberates us. When we realize that we do not have to hold back because of the conventional ideas and expectations, we are opened up to a whole range of possibilities that can enrich and expand our lives. I feel like a more accomplished woman, a stronger woman, an enormously more liberated woman, now that I ride my own bike. I have a sense of empowerment and my spirit is freer and it's so much fun!

Riding is both a solo and a group pleasure. Either way I ride, I feel an extraordinary sense of freedom and exhilaration, of exploration, a sense of self-actualization, and independence. I love to explore our glorious and diverse territories, usually with a destination in mind but not firmly tied to a particular route. I will take a left instead of a right if the landscape beckons.

Most people are usually surprised to find a woman, and of slight build at that, riding her own bike. I encounter even greater surprise because of the nature of my business, which is running an art gallery. People see this as antithetical to the prevailing idea of what kind of person a motorcyclist usually is.

Lily Johnson

Photographer: Christina Shook © 2003

CHAPTER 4

Queen of the Road

. . . she's on her own

Cruising along, riding free, feeling strong

She doesn't know what's around the next turn, but there's fuel to burn. . . .

> —Sasha, from the song "Queen of the Road"

Queen of the road: the sovereign of her destiny. Independent and manager of her life's mission. Self-sufficient and a leader governing her route.

The woman and her motorcycle—a potent combination that is both mystical and spiritual. The female motorcyclist is an iron Godiva, her feminine energy flowing, wrapping around her body and soul and uniting her as one with her steel horse. She is naked and vulnerable as she pioneers the endless roads, whether solo or with other wind sisters. She is a warrior soul as she competes in intense motorcycle race competitions and combats difficult road and weather conditions, and she is a fierce companion as a passenger on her mate's ride.

Riding a motorcycle is a delicate activity. It requires grace and balance. It requires intuition and the ability to let go. Gently squeeze the front brake while pressing on the rear brake. Ease out the clutch when switching gears. Look through the turn, lean the motorcycle, and roll open the throttle. Some guys like to wrestle with their steeds and toss 'em about to let 'em know who's in charge. Women ride iron with our hips as the guide, dipping and swaying in unison, each nurturing the other as if dancing a beautiful wind tango.

UGOGirl ready to ride Reg Kitrelle's BattleTrax rider skill course at the AMA Women & Motorcycle Conference 2002.

No more backseat driving, we're in the front now.

"Hey, I never saw a girl on a motorcycle before," shouted a man from the backseat of a New York City taxicab. I thought, "Geez, bro, where have you been?" "You look good, wow! I can't believe my eyes," he said. I wanted to have a conversation with him and investigate what he thought about this strange sight he had just beheld, but honking horns and curses hurled from impatient drivers surrounding me prevented it.

"Oh my God, look, that's a girl riding a motorcycle!" yelled this young boy on a bicycle pointing at me while I was filling up my bike in a Brooklyn gas station. He came charging over, legs pedaling hard, his friend following close behind. He skidded up and bombarded me with questions. "I should have a camera, I never seen this before. Isn't it hard for a girl to ride a motorcycle? I thought only boys ride motorcycles! Isn't that motorcycle too heavy? Wow, you must be strong. Do you lift weights, too?" He was so excited. He threw his bicycle down and studied me on the bike, and walked around it laughing and shaking his head. "I'm gonna tell my mamma and my gramma 'bout this one, man." I laughed at his sweet innocence and surprise, but damn! Here we are in the twenty-first century and this boy was totally old skool about women's abilities. "Honey, girls can do anything that boys can do and never forget that," I told him. "Yeah, right," he smirked.

Ladies, we are no longer prisoners to the backseat in life! Hell no and hallelujah. We are Queens of the road, our own road and destiny. Long ago, we slid into the front seat to command our own magnificent journey in life, setting our feminine spirit free to be and realizing our personal dreams. And still the world is amazed at our tenacity.

Too often, we put ourselves second and everyone else's needs and attention-draining situations first. This act of neglect eventually leaves us dispirited and lost, giving so much of ourselves with no reserve for our own souls. It's like standing at a gas station and watching everyone else saddle up with full tanks on their own journeys, but there's no more fuel left and there's no ride for you so you get left behind.

Our human nature as females is to nurture, provide, oversee, manage, and love. Most of us have to play the role of superwomen for the family, career, friends, and so forth. But why are we not superwomen for ourselves? It's cool and important that we nurture ourselves. Motorcycle riding helps us to connect with our needs and helps us to discover just what those needs are. There's no one else to care for except ourselves and the bike. Being alone on our journeys with just the wind in our faces gives us time to think and open up to opportunity and possibilities that drift forth from that small still place within our inner female sanctum. The wind makes us pay attention and listen to our small still voice that cries to be heard over the noisy work-a-day life routines that will not hush.

We should educate our families, spouses, and career folk about the need for "Queen-me" time. Men do it. Oh, they carve out their moments and spend time enjoying their passions and friends and developing their careers. Well, we need quality me time, too. Motorcycles provide the best me time ever invented for a female. On a motorcycle, you don't roll up to the stop light, pop on the cell phone, and say, "Oh, let me check to see if Sarah finished her homework," or "Just this one mile and I'll mop the floor." You are in forward, go motion. It's just you and the bike . . . and the "laundry" gets aired out in the wind.

Sometimes, however, we are called bitches when we demand that alone time or express ourselves. Thanks to some queen

out there that word now stands for: **B**abe **I**n **T**otal **C**ontrol of **H**erself. There are helmet stickers that reflect the new definition: "You say I'm a Bitch like it's a bad thing," "I'm not a Bitch, I am THE Bitch," and "It's MISS BITCH to you."

Motorcycles have exposed the female heart's desires in life for freedom, adventure, and the spirit of individuality. This equals evolution and revelation and revolution. Motorcycles are our dream weavers. Motorcycles help define the reborn female by fostering a reconnection with our true gender, the eternal image of the female, or Goddess, as God has created *her*: power, strength, beauty, love, leader, mother, daughter. We celebrate our femininity and our girlishness as the strength congruent to the pulsating energy of what the motorcycle represents; we are wildly female, so wildly *machisma*.

"We leak energy in any situation in which our anger or fear is controlling our ability to move forward in our lives," writes Christiane Northrup, M.D., in her book *Women's Bodies, Women's Wisdom*.[14] There are two rules of thumb for successful motorcycle riding: Don't get on the bike if you're angry and don't get on the bike if you're wrought with fear. The motorcycle will not move forward successfully and neither will the rider with those two energy-draining emotions at the helm. In fact, the act of riding a motorcycle forces the rider to "let go" of all kinds of imprisoning feelings and situations because you have to be so intensely focused and aware of your journey. Countless times I've saddled up in a jolly mood and by the end of a long journey I've been through a spectrum of emotions that bled their way through my body, mind, and soul and then were stripped away in the wind; thus, positive, healing and transformative energy has nourished the body by the end of the ride.

It takes intense concentration to successfully command the controls of a motorcycle. Moving forward is the goal. We, as queens, are the co-leaders of our destiny along with God and the Universe, with Wheels spinning, wheels churning and producing ideas in that forward "free will" and "free wheel" motion. That forward motion unites us with the present moment and we are living and knowing our dreams because we are in the forward process, on our way, achieving mile after mile, inching closer to our destiny as we discover our deepest desires, which allows us to live free.

The ride renews the spirit. It helps eliminate indecision and gives way to clear thinking. Women need to ride away from those things that will not ride away from us. We need to take time away from the daily distractions and spend quiet, reflective moments with ourselves so that when we return, we are stronger, clearer in our thinking, and able to make ready decisions.

When we travel, we are able to experience our true identity and unique gifts. The fun-loving identity we don while traveling is of the independent, resourceful pioneer in control of her destiny and on a quest to discover her inner journey. When we ride, we develop new behaviors outside of our familiar characteristics and thus a greater awareness of our potential. Riding transforms our identity, because we reach deep into that place we often do not have the opportunity to know in our everyday lives and draw upon newfound strengths and inner resources. We return to our lives from our motorcycle travels transformed and renewed.

Meeting new people charges me up. I like to open doors and welcome people into my life. People just stroll on over, check out the bike, and strike up a conversation about your journey, the ride, and how they wish that they could experience the motorcycle lifestyle. In New York City, people are the nature in the urban chaos as mountains and prairies are the nature elsewhere. The ice

breaker usually is my motorcycle. "You ride a motorcycle? You don't look like a biker!" My reply is usually "And what is a biker supposed to look like?" "I don't know, but not you!" they tell me. So that just kicks right into a high gear discussion about why I ride, where I'm going, where I'm from, and so forth. Of course, it's important to be careful about disclosing too much information about your destination to a stranger, but it's oh so fun when they realize that you're on your own. Guys especially have an awestruck look and say, "You mean you're riding a motorcycle all this way alone?" Oh yeah, honey, spit shine my boots for this Queen who *can do* all by herself. Jeez.

Getting my first bike completely changed my life. I went from working long, grueling hours in a job that just kept a roof over my head to pursuing my dreams because of this beautiful, "easy" ride. No, of course, the ride has not been easy just because I finally got my motorcycle. If anything, it's been much more difficult because I've had to face myself—the person I was meant to be, head on into the wind. Riding opens you up whether you like it or not. I had to work at stripping away my fears, other people's negative attitudes, the resentments, the nasty jealousy that I received from senior business peers that really took a toll on me, and the loss of love. When that was cleared away my dreams appeared, wanting attention like orphaned children, which, indeed, these tender dreams had become.

I had to work on myself every time I faced a motorcycle journey. The wind forces

Melissa Thomas, proud Harley girl
Photo courtesy Melissa

you to change because it forces you to smash through every internal obstacle, and the journey leads you through the hot and dusty inner desert where you feel stripped of all that you know. And you know how it strips me? Well, riding a motorcycle is so much darn fun, it makes me smile deeply to the core of my soul. The ultimate striptease. The joy of riding is so pure and powerfully simple. It strips me of the junky weightiness so I can be enlightened enough to possess what is mine in this life, and own what belongs to me in my uniqueness. Therefore, I experience a rebirth of my own inner Queenliness as God had intended me to experience my life: as a gift, pure and simple.

Motorcycling has changed our lives. We have made lifelong friends, changed career directions, become better mothers, and opened up our world to our God-given purposes, allowing opportunity to embrace us because we have become incredibly aware of all that surrounds us from riding a motorcycle. Riding produces confidence and appreciation that draws to the surface all those beautiful gifts that may have been hidden deep within. When that confidence and appreciation connects us to the fact that life is a gift and that we must live fully, the feeling of being free to be oneself bursts forth. Judgment and negativity directed at the free being becomes nothing but little stones ricocheting off the windshield of enlightenment and back at the one who scorns. Motorcycling sets the spirit free and invites positive energy. It creates a universe of respect where there may have been none. Riding free and living free is a constant celebration and reminds us that we are one of the Queen stars that we see while cruising beneath the midnight canvas high above.

The Statue of Liberty, "Liberty Enlightening the World," was our gift of independence and freedom from our French neighbors. Today, she is the mother symbol of world friendship, peace, freedom, and democracy. Since 1886, the lady has stood strong and purposeful on her pedestal in New York Harbor. Over the years, Miss Liberty has symbolized women's struggles to experience in their lives those very same values that she represents. For decades, visitors have wound their way up 192 steps to share her vision of the world. What did they see in the early part of the century? Women oppressed, an inferior gender, unable to vote, have a career, or make important choices for themselves. They saw women who were not free to simply be. But somewhere out there, during that time, was a chick that hiked up her skirt and straddled some iron.

We are each a bikerlady liberty representing an enlightenment within ourselves and toward each other as we ride free and far from the shackles of stereotypical gridlock. We are an example of the heavenly yearning to breathe free. At each gasp, negativity is evaporated and cleansed into truth by the wind as we gallop the wide-open endless roadways, living and riding free as Queens of the road!

Voices from the Road

Amber Burton Small, Indiana
1998 Honda Shadow 750 ACE, "Wild Child"
Paralegal

A little over a year ago, my best friend and I made a "Before 30" list of things we wanted to accomplish before we both turned 30. Getting our motorcycle licenses was a priority on the list. We took the requisite safety course, and got our endorsements. We've both since purchased our own motorcycles. Riding has changed my life because it's been a key factor in my ongoing metamorphosis from staid, complacent professional to a creative, evolving artist and musician.

I'm a complex woman with many interests. I work in a professional, conservative field, and I love being a wife, "nesting," and being domestic. On the other hand, I equally love adventure and traveling. I play drums in a band, I travel frequently, and I run two side businesses in interior decorating and jewelry design. I'm a nut for live music, especially the blues, and I can't get enough of either Iceland or the Caribbean. I love art and old movies, and I read voraciously. I'm a volunteer for Big Brothers and Big Sisters, and I've been matched with my little Courtney for over six months.

Riding allows me to further express my identity, to nurture my soul, to reach beyond self-imposed limits, and even to escape life at times, however briefly, when it is too stressful. It has taught me to confront my fears, overcome challenges, and exceed my own expectations.

Deborah "Dixie Deb" Cassell, Virginia
1972 Harley-Davidson Sportster Chopper, "Dixie";
1987 Evo Sportster Custom by Deb, "Black"
Owner, Computer/Internet support company

I love the people who live by, for, and through this lifestyle! A true brotherhood and sisterhood! I also enjoy the surprise when outsiders filled with awe, disdain, or fear, find a bit of themselves within this leather. I prize the solitude of riding alone.

My kids were under five when I got my chopper, so they grew up understanding my passion for motorcycles. When I show up in leathers astride Dix, they just grin and shake their heads. Though I seem wild, they and their friends know I am always there for them. They are bold, proud spirits, truly off-

spring of mine. My grandson now rides with me and he understands.

I am very positive and outgoing. I have always believed in God and his gifts of life, attitude, and responsibilities. I strive to show that religion and real life don't conflict. The saddest part of life is the lack of humility and respect; if we could walk in another's boots, fewer stones would be thrown. I have learned the most from those that have survived life and come back for more. Many are Bikers. The downside is that being an independent biker woman is a very real threat to many men. Still, I always find kindred souls. We are drawn to each other.

Riding confirmed what I already knew from about age 14: I'm basically a loner and very self-sufficient. My Harleys give me the ultimate outlet and a symbol that others know these things without having to ask. When I was 24, I met a Vietnam bro and spent the day discussing life. Before I left, he showed me a 10' chopper, "Dixie." He said I had a biker's soul and that this was my bike! I thought he was crazy as I had only just met him and didn't even know how to ride. He unexpectedly died that week but had told his mom about me and she said "come get the bike . . ." she considered it his last wish. He knew . . .

Stella LeDesma, California
2001 Harley-Davidson 883 Sportster, "MR RRITE"
Purchasing agent and water aerobics instructor

I love being the only female who rides in my large family. They are all so proud and admire me because I ride a Harley. I've always loved loud cruiser motorcycles. My boyfriend, who introduced me to the motorcycle world, rides a Harley-Davidson. I love the wind in my face, feeling free, as my alter ego emerges.

The people at my job are amazed. Nobody could imagine that the new beautiful, Harley-Davidson in the parking lot belonged to a woman. Riding has given me a lot of confidence in myself and has made me become a better car driver, too.

Marie Todd, New York

1988 Harley-Davidson FXR; 1987 Harley-
   Davidson FXR; 1979 Harley-Davidson
   K Model; 2002 Ducati 750 Monster
Director of Accounting, State University
   of New York (SUNY)

My husband, Skeeter, customizes my bikes for me. He buys wrecks and restores them. I'm always involved when he's putting the bikes together. I grew up on a farm. Getting my hands dirty is not a problem.

Motorcycle-riding is a total escape. I have a very conservative job. When I go motorcycle-riding on vacation it's a totally different world. I put on all my leathers and I'm out riding. In my work world, when people find out that I ride Harleys and take off cross-country they look at me like I have two heads, and they can't believe it and want to see pictures. I never ride my bike to work because parking one of my babies in the parking lot where I can't watch over it all day is not something I like to do. And it kinds of keeps it more of a mystery.

I go to meetings and I work with a lot of the other SUNY campuses and they all want to hear about my riding adventures. I think people have a better quality of life if they have something that they enjoy as a leisure time activity. A lot of people who are into motorcycling have that. There are times when I come home from work, especially when I've had a particularly challenging day, and all I want to do is get on my Harley and slam through the gears. Riding is a release.

Julia Blanks, Alabama

2002 Suzuki SV650S
Franchise supervisor for Domino's Pizza

I believe I can take on anything and succeed. I try to be myself no matter what. I don't compromise my opinions or what I like just because someone else doesn't agree with it.

My husband initially got a motorcycle to help cut down on gasoline costs. He had motorcycles while he was growing up so it wasn't a big deal to him. I took the MSF class and bought my first bike in 1998. My daughter loves four-wheeling and my son has a dirt bike so we are trying to get them hooked, too.

I'll never forget riding the Dragon at Deal's Gap in North Carolina. That was so fun. My husband told me stories of how some of his friends had been scared when they went through so I was a little apprehensive, but it went smooth as glass for me and I had a total blast! I rode through 318 curves in 11 miles! Woo hoo!

Riding a motorcycle has allowed me

to explore a whole other aspect of my personality—my adventurous, longing-to-be-free-from-the-bonds-of-work-home-and-kids side. It's also introduced me to some really great, cool people I might never have met otherwise. It also has given me a feeling of empowerment.

CruelGirl, Missouri

1964 Harley-Davidson Panhead, "Cruella";
1953 Harley-Davidson Panhead,
  "Yuppie Scum";
1989 Harley-Davidson FXRS, "Tarbaby";
1991 Harley-Davidson Softail, "Ms. Piggy"
Raises and rides quarter horses

I've always been a very independent woman. I live for motorcycles, and my love for nature and all living things pretty much makes up who I am. I'm a very strong-willed person, yet I have a side that most people never get to see except my closest friends. Simple things in life, like a newborn foal, can make me cry.

My father passed away and left me three thousand dollars, which became mine on my eighteenth birthday. I had been incarcerated as a teen and I was also released that year. I had read about the bikers around California while I was locked up and had an immediate desire to be a part of the biker lifestyle. I wanted a chopper. I didn't much care if other women weren't riding back then, I knew that as soon as I was released and had that cash in my hand, I was going to get me one. And that's exactly what I did. In January 1977, I bought my first chopper, a 1967 Triumph hardtail.

The best thing about riding is I love speed! I love to get out on the open road and bury the odometer. I have a 103-inch FXRS that will do close to 160 mph and I just recently put a 100-inch motor in my Softail.

CruelGirl says, "Panheads rule!"
Photo courtesy CruelGirl

The ride I'll never forget was when I was riding in a pack and a car on a multi-lane highway took down four of us at about 70 mph. No one was killed but we were all pretty seriously injured and the bikes were totaled. The guy hit and ran. They caught him a few days later, but he didn't have insurance. A local bar held a big benefit for all of us and raised enough money to help us all put our bikes together. The bands all donated their time for free. This is what sisterhood and brotherhood is all about, being there to lend a hand or parts when needed.

The most important thing I learned from riding is that I am me. I never cared that people used to frown on my tattoos or my lifestyle. Now everyone that used to frown is trying to be what I have always been: a biker!

My advice to the women buying their first bike is to buy one that you can handle. Don't run out and buy something that is too big or heavy for you that you won't be able to park or handle. This puts not only you, but others around you, at risk for serious injury. I see this all too often and it's best to learn on something that is light and easy to handle for at least a year or two and then move up to a larger bike if you want to later.

Debra Burns, California
Ron Simms Custom Build, "twysted bitch"; Ridley Nostalgia; RidleySS1
Photographer and web designer

I photograph bikes for custom bike builder Ron Simms and maintain his website. I got hooked up with Ron in 1999 after looking around for a bike and realizing that I needed one made to fit me. I am 5'3" and nearly all Harleys are just a tad bigger than I like. I wanted a big-bodied, street digger–looking bike, with forward controls that wasn't a girly looking bike. I realized that a bike would need to be either custom made or modified, so I went the custom route. I shopped around and asked a well-known local company to build one for me. After all, they had no problem building bikes for celebrities, so why not lil' ol' me? They said, "Nope, we don't build chick bikes."

So, mortified at the flat-out response they gave me and feeling totally discouraged, I called my daddy, who was a long time flat track racer during the sixties and seventies. I told him what happened and he told me to go see Simms, so I called up Ron and then went to the shop for a visit. He had me sit on a few bikes and took some measurements and next thing I knew I had a bike that fit me! There is a lot of artistry and thought that goes into a custom motorcycle that most people aren't even aware of. All the personal choices that go into each custom bike build is what makes the bike a part of you.

Debbie "Breed" Amaya, Texas
1974 Harley-Davidson Shovelhead Hardtail, "Shamu"
Customer service

I live and breathe being on two wheels. I ride because it's in my blood, my spirit, and my soul. Riding gives me the courage to be the strong and independent woman that I am. I cherish the moments I can ride with my motorcycle, "Shamu," and show other women we can all be who we want to be if we only believe and follow our dreams. I love feeling free and strong and having the power to handle such a powerful machine. Every time I ride it's memorable. Just watch me and see the smile come across my face when I kick this bad machine off and you hear the rumble.

I've been very committed for the past 16 years to the biggest toy run in Texas and I recruit women riders as Santa's Helpers every year to help me. We go to the Arlington Convention Center and help Santa distribute toys for the mentally disabled children in the hospitals in Dallas and Fort Worth. I also founded the Santa's Helpers for a local motorcycle club called the Gryphons in Ellis County.

For several years I had been going to different motorcycle benefits supporting various charities but never heard of a rally supporting the women's shelter for domestic violence. So I decided to gather up a few friends and we put our heads together and decided to call our fundraiser rally W.A.A.M (Women Against Abusive Men). We are biker women, sisters supporting sisters, and our goal is to "break the abusive cycle."

Dawn Glencer, Virginia

2001 Harley-Davidson Dyna Wide Glide,
"Baby"
Head of training for the Office of Policy
of the Secretary of Defense

When I saved up enough money and got my first Harley, I headed to the local pool hall where I met a bunch of other riders. The rest was history. I love riding in states with no friggin' helmet law and seeing guys' jaws drop when you roll in on a bike nicer than theirs. My mother is my favorite shero. She's always amazed at what I get myself into from the Marines to the CIA and now the Pentagon. My nieces and nephews love the fact that I ride. I'm the "cool aunt." And I've got a big mouth, big boobs, and a big heart.

I've also helped organize charitable benefits at my boyfriend's bar.

The proceeds have gone to everything from the Make-A-Wish Foundation to the Pentagon disaster relief fund, and to help a local teen get a kidney transplant. My latest project is the new calendar series "Deal With It," featuring local women riders from Maryland and Virginia from all walks of life, from a great grandmother to an E.R. nurse at Georgetown University Hospital.

My most memorable ride was with about 150 other riders. My boyfriend was riding behind me on his new custom with a single-swing arm. At about 70 mph, his entire back wheel came off and flew through our pack. No one was hurt, but I almost wiped out when I heard someone say he was down. I shifted from fifth to first gear and did a 180 on gravel. We got over it, though and partied on the side of the road until his brother showed up with a trailer.

If anyone is bored or disappointed with their life, getting a Harley is the first step to a major change. You know what they say:

Dawn Glencer
© Doug Barber www.dougbarber.com

"You never see a Harley parked outside a shrink's office." Take notice that women who ride look younger than everybody else. Stress blows away in the wind, sisters.

Teresa Midkiff, West Virginia
1200 Harley-Davidson Custom Sportster
Legal secretary

My father is my favorite inspiration. He owned a Harley when he got out of the service. He later married and had four children. The only bike he owned after that was a Yamaha street bike. He bought me a mini bike when I was just 12 years old. In 1996, when I first started to learn to ride again, he accompanied me to a local parking lot to practice. His legs were crippled from multiple sclerosis, but he crawled onto the motorcycle and took it for about three or four laps around the parking lot. Just seeing the joy on his face from riding was more than words could say. It was his last ride because he died the following summer.

Motorcycle-riding helped me to overcome my shyness. When you find something you love, you tend to work harder to overcome your fears. I am a very persistent person who generally doesn't take no for an answer and that is why I am where I am today.

I love the power and sexiness you feel just being a woman on your bike. Even though women have been riding for many years, it still seems to draw attention when a woman is spotted on the highway. A cell phone salesman once told me that "There is nothing sexier than a good-lookin' woman on a Harley!" This is true!

Sharon Gangell, Australia
2000 Honda VFR800, "William"
Self-employed architectural draftsperson

The sense of freedom and communing with nature is what I love most about riding. My main hobby is motorbike riding, but I also enjoy bush walking, playing on the Internet, renovating my house, and property investment. Riding has taught me to be who I really want to be. Others will like me for who I am and if they don't, they're not worth knowing.

Luisa Gervasi, Italy
2002 Suzuki GS 500, "Thessa"
Account manager

Freedom in every sense is why I love to ride! Live to ride. Ride to live. All my friends are bikers. The most important thing I learned about riding is that I *can* do it. I didn't think I could because I thought it was something only for men.

Jamie Nezbeth, Ohio
1996 Harley-Davidson Electra Glide Classic
General manager of mechanical contractor
  in Cleveland

My favorite part of riding is that after a really bad day at work, I can come home and get on the bike. It's therapy for me. It clears my head for the next day. It is a part of me as a person. It's definitely a way of life for my husband and me. I have seen so much beauty riding on the bike. I have met the most wonderful people in the world. I absolutely love it! It is a very special part of my life and I will always ride.

Riding my motorcycle taught me that I can do something if I put my heart and mind into it. I've learned that I can accept failure as well as triumphs in my life. It has made me appreciate my love of life! And I have learned that no matter what happens, I can always rely on my Harley, along with the love of my family and friends, to get me through it.

I have always loved riding, even though for many years I rode on the back. I have a lot of life experiences that I have kept in my heart about riding and I wish I could let everyone know that even if life dishes out bad things, I am a survivor. I love myself because of everything that biking has done for me. It even brought me the man I love more than life itself. He has changed my life and shown me things on that bike that I would never have seen if it weren't for him. I will always ride a Harley.

Gail Chambers on Gail's Glide
Photo by Louis Yansen

Jenny Lefferts with her babies, Leff and Kyra

Photographer: Christina Shook © 2003

CHAPTER 5

Motorcycle Mammas and Women Who Wrench

Motorcycle Mamma

Cares for family with honor

Packs her children in the saddle

Travels anywhere she wanna

She's a hard drivin' woman

Machisma super shero

Mamma to her babies or a

Mamma to her chrome

      —Sasha

Motorcycle mamma. The super shero. She bonds with her children in the wind astride her motorcycle. But the term "motorcycle mamma" has a second meaning. Although she may not have children, she's a "wench who wrenches" her bike with TLC. She babies her ride with the love and nurturing that only a "mother" can provide. In this chapter, we'll look at both types of motorcycle mammas.

The motorcycle lifestyle in general is a very loving and altruistic method of living and interacting with others. Teaching children to embrace others even if they live, act, or look differently creates a peaceable nature. The beautiful metaphors that motorcycling simmers up within the soul and consciousness of the rider can be applied to child rearing in many ways.

In life, we are mothers and fathers to ourselves. We, in association with our higher power, are responsible for our actions and interactions. We need to nurture and guide our lives in the best possible manner that will produce positive effects. Utilizing the methodology and teaching applications learned through the art of riding a motorcycle parallels life conduct on so many levels and thus we can live and ride free.

Riding a motorcycle is a very mental activity. Your brain has to absorb critical information and manage that information so that the best decisions can be made and resulting physical reactions can be performed. To operate a motorcycle, the rider must be in a constant state of awareness and in a vigilant mindset.

Let's take a look at the Motorcycle Safety Foundation's (MSF) instructions for riding

Angel and Sarah love to ride together.
Photo: Miserable George

and you'll see how riding can be compared to mothering on various levels. According to the *Motorcycle Safety Foundation's Guide to Motorcycling Excellence,*[15] gathering solid visual information is key, as is visual perception. They cite three concepts for good eye habits:

1. Concentrate (focus) on your intended path of travel and move within traffic while maintaining adequate space in all directions;

2. Aim your vision well ahead by keeping your eyes up;

3. Force your eyes to move frequently so that you will receive a wide field of information.

Just like in riding, in life we must *focus.* Too many times we are distracted by meaningless activity that drags us off our intended path, whether it's the wrong career choice, a bad relationship, or other energy-draining events that distract us from living and enjoying our purpose in life. Keeping our vision well ahead of us and our eyes upward instead of cast down opens up our world to embrace the horizons: our God-given dreams. When we look down in despair our world becomes very small and we wallow in self-pity. Looking far ahead and beyond the boundaries we or others may place upon us, we see the full scope of opportunity and potential.

Good eye habits reduce us from being drawn into target fixation. That target fixation, also known as tunnel vision, causes us to be so fixated on one thing that we smash into it or run it over. Single-mindedness versus open-mindedness.

The motorcycle will go where your eyes lead you. Fixating on the edge of the road will cause you to veer off your path. Fixation in life could come in the form of letting the little things get to you and steal your vision, causing you to crash in other areas of your life. Examples of target fixation in life are drug or alcohol addiction, a draining relationship, or simply fixating on things that just don't matter in the grand scheme of things. Keeping fixated on these things will only make the "rider" in life crash and burn.

Properly positioning yourself in your intended path of travel is crucial. You need to provide an adequate space cushion between yourself and other motorists. This means that you're constantly adjusting your position to move with the flow of traffic and to accommodate road conditions. Adjusting your position helps you find the most advantageous placement for communicating and being seen. Good positioning helps you to see situations around and ahead of you more clearly and provides you with an escape route if you need to scoot away from a dangerous situation. You don't want to collide with others by any means because we all have our own destinations in life. Even if we have the same objective, there is no other way to get there except on our own intended path of travel. That also goes for riding two up on the same bike. You'll each experience a different perspective.

Riding smart is also about being *seen*. Lots of motorcycle accidents are caused because other motorists do not see the rider. So riding is about being seen and communicating your presence to others.

And so it is in life as you communicate your presence to others, defining yourself and who you are: "Here I am! Living loud and living proud." Not all of us are extroverts, but even introverts can live loud and proud because they are being true to their hearts and themselves.

The MSF has an acronym for paying attention when riding a motorcycle. It's **SIPDE** or **SEE** which stands for:

Scan

Identify

Predict

Decide

Execute

or

See

Evaluate

Execute

Motor Maid Beverly Houser travels all over the country.

In life this translates to:

Scan or See: Scan the territory in front of you for obstacles and opportunity. Get good visual information. Look in *all* directions. Use your peripheral vision, too, to catch what's happening on the sidelines.

Identify or Evaluate: Identify obstacles and evaluate opportunities and how they will affect you.

Predict: Predict the future happenstance and options that you will have once encountering these obstacles and opportunities.

Decide: Decide what you will do in order to achieve your goal.

Execute: Make the move!

Another MSF rule when rounding the bend:

Slow to reduce approach speed to a proper entry speed prior to the turn.

Look around the bend as far as you can see to the exit point.

Lean or **Press** into the turn.

Roll steady on the throttle to stabilize the machine.

This can be translated to apply to life.

Slow as you approach the entryway to the situation forthright and pace yourself.

Look at the situation and through it as far as the eye can see.

Lean or **Press** into the twist and turns in life; press onward in the direction you intend to go; don't shy away from living.

Roll through life consistent, strong, and sure with your energy.

Never stop in a curve while in a lean. You will fall down. Think about it. You're riding through the twists and turns, going with the flow. While you're in a deep lean, some obstacle appears. If you break while in a lean, you'll lose your centrifugal force and thus your balance, and you'll drop like a rock. Straighten the bike as fast as you can and square off the handlebars as you apply the brakes to make a straight-line stop. Square off to the obstacle ahead and stop. Then deal with it.

How to deal with obstacles? Go around them. Go over them. Go through them. The MSF book suggests using evasive maneuvers. Those are swerving and surmounting. Lots of times we have to use such maneuvers in life. Strategize by not letting anything stand in the way of your forward motion. Sometimes we have had to overcome the obstacle, surmount it. Ride right over it at a 90-degree angle. How many times have we had to surmount an obstacle in life? I've used the swerving maneuver on a number of smarmy fellows looking for a date, including a potential employer who told me, "Don't worry, I won't lay ya; I've got a wife at home." Or the surmounting maneuvers for overcoming a situation that could have surely held me back where I may have just given up on everything.

Then there's handling special situations like the tire blowout. MSF states: "If a puncture should occur, keep a firm hold on the handgrips. Steer smoothly and ease off the throttle. Avoid downshifting and braking. If traffic permits, slow gradually and move off to the side of the road." This reminds me of the scenario in which someone takes the fun out of something that excites me. Here you are, all enthused, and along comes the knife that bursts your bubble. When you feel really torn up, what you need to do is keep a firm grip on your beliefs, steer smoothly and ease off a little bit, chill on the side, inflate again, and proceed full steam ahead on your course.

What to do with a broken clutch cable? Oh yes, this happens when we're operating in overdrive too much in life, or when we're in perpetual low gear or can't switch gears

Li'l Elizabeth "Ella" Steinbach with author, artist and cool biker chick Erika Lopez
Photographer: Christina Shook © 2003

properly. For switching gears with no clutch because it's burned out or the clutch cable is broken, the MSF book says to "just roll off the throttle and press hard on the shift lever. It'll be a little jerky but it works."

Indeed, I often remember having to shift gears without a "clutch support" and feeling a little jerky. Really! My high-paced New York City lifestyle has me running into over-drive and then I've got to shift gears without any clutch, just to slow down. It's no way to live and I've been learning this. How about trying to smoothly stop from high gear? According to the MSF, "Stopping smoothly is a problem—you only get one chance. Downshift one gear at a time to first and stop the engine using the engine cut-off switch." My personal engine cut-off switch

has been in the form of literally passing out for two days because I worked 72 hours in a row with no sleep. How many of us with the label "super shero" spelled out across our foreheads find ourselves in a predicament where we have taken on too much and want to slow down, but our "clutch cable" is burned out so we end up slamming through the gears?

Another special situation is having ani-mals chase us. Yeah, I've known this one in my relationship and career life, haven't you? When that uncivilized nonhuman is chasing us, MSF instructs us to "slow down until your paths are close, then accelerate away. This will throw off the animal's planned point of interception and leave it frustrated." Good show for the person trying to dog ya for your promotion. Or, how about the suave male ogre pawing at you with his tongue draping his chin, chasing you down with his eyes as if you were a prime cut of meat? I'm not one to be rude or crass so, yes, I like the way that the MSF suggests handling the "animals."

Special handling situations are required for those strong winds and gust blasts that rail you into the next lane. The MSF says, "If the wind is from the left, press on the left handgrip and the motorcycle will lean." With those strong winds of change that move through life, instead of getting bowled over like a tumbleweed across the plains, just lean into it and keep on riding with those winds.

For carrying loads, the MSF suggests considering how much the load weighs, where the load is situated, and how the load is secured. Every motorcycle has a max load capacity determined by the manufacturer. The load should be low and to the center and evenly placed side to side. Batten down the load with bungee cords and web straps. This all translates to the following life lessons:

Don't take on more than you can handle, so leave behind unnecessary baggage!

Don't carry the weight on your shoulders; keep it low and manageable.

Don't be insecure with your load and dump it for someone else to deal with.

Group riding is predicated on the buddy system and totally relies on rider responsi-

bility. You watch out for one another, communicate, and make sure that you understand what's going on. Group riding fails the moment ego enters the picture. In a group ride there is a leader who watches out for the pack and leads the group to their destination. She and sometimes a co-leader will look out for road obstacles and traffic snafus ahead. She is responsible for signaling a lane change and other movements of the pack. The person who rides sweep or shotgun or shepherd (the back or last bike position) keeps an eye on the group from behind, watching the leader's signals, helping to secure lane space for lane changes, and keeping stragglers moving forward.

Rain happens. Bad weather is inevitable. Mother Nature can do whatever she wants and if she wants to rain down and thunder on your day, she will. Rainy days can be magical. I don't mind riding in the rain most times. I love those moody days filled with their own challenges, but riding in inclement weather requires total awareness. Be prepared. Bring rain gear and wear it when the weather is bad. Save yourself from hypothermia and a really uncomfortable journey. I've ridden all day long with no rain suit on because I happened to get caught in a sun shower that didn't stop and turned into a full on rain. But it was beautiful to feel the water cooling my skin, to see it dancing as droplets on chrome, and to hear that wonderful sizzling sound the tires make on the pavement, a giant *hussssssssssshhhhhhhh*. Very soothing.

But then, of course, there are the rides where you get caught in the rain with no place to pull over and you're soaked and damn cold. Still, I'll take any rainy day on a motorcycle over a nice warm dry subway train. It's about the adventure. Life is an adventure. Sometimes life is inclement; you've just got to deal with it.

Keep your feet on the ground. Feel the earth. Maintain traction. MSF says, "Knowing where and how your motorcycle demands traction is an important part of riding with control. You already know that your potential for traction changes continuously as you ride, as does its distribution on each tire. Every riding maneuver or technique will produce a specific 'traction profile,' or set of forces that use up some of that potential." Stay grounded. The MSF book also states, "The three consumers of traction we will concern ourselves with are:

1. Side Force—includes steering forces required for tracking, balancing, and controlling your motorcycle's lean angle. The forces required to corner and overcome gravity on cross-sloping surfaces and crosswinds are also side forces. All of these forces act primarily to the side or perpendicular to the direction of forward motion.

2. Driving Force—is produced when you apply the engine's power to the rear wheel. You can use it to accelerate or just to maintain speed.

3. Braking Force—is produced when you apply the brakes, but it is also produced on the rear wheel when you 'roll off' or close the throttle. This engine-induced braking force is called 'engine breaking.' Rolling friction also contributes to braking force, acting like a small brake dragging on each wheel."

You control these factors. You control them directly with your riding skill. This is a physical example of how we bond as one with our machines. These factors are also evident in life: We are the driving force, we are the braking force, we are the steering (side) force. How these forces work in unison affects traction. For example, there's always a breaking force occurring due to rolling friction. There's also wind resistance, also referred to as aerodynamic drag. You need driving force to overcome both friction and wind resistance. With that, a dash of side force using small steering corrections is required to maintain balance and tracking while riding. "Maintaining traction permits you to maintain a reserve for reacting to the unexpected."

To be driven in life. The driving force as ambition. The side force, steering your way through your ambition. The braking force reminds me of the have-to-dos in life. They can be a real drag on your driving force. I've had to do all kinds of "have to" jobs to keep a roof over my head while I compose my projects, even while doing this book! Yep. A lot of have-tos can cause aerodynamic drag in my life. I look forward to reducing some of that drag and rolling friction have-to-do's sometime in the near future. In the meantime, I'm just alive in the moment, aware of my purpose and moving forward with that driving force within.

I am a budding motorcycle mamma. My bike is my baby. I love working on my bike. Love it, breathe it, live it. I'm still on a giant learning curve, though. I equate learning motorcycle mechanics with learning a seemingly impossible new recipe. It's about following directions and having patience. It's about listening to your intuition to know if something is wrong with your "baby." I love to cook. It comes naturally to me now. In the beginning when I would teach myself cooking, I would read recipe books and try to learn all the tricks of cooking. I find it fascinating because cooking is a wonderful art form. Working on a motorcycle is the same thing for me. It is an art form. It is a mechanical recipe to repair each component that needs attention.

Now, of course, like anything else, some of us can more easily adapt to an activity. Our intuition kicks in, and we can move beyond instruction and into our own creative application. I'm not completely technically inclined because I failed math. Let me restate that. I *miserably* failed math in junior high and high school. I just didn't have the natural ability to cozy up to the subject and "get it." Oh, it pissed me off! I even took a non-credited basic math college class from a guy that looked, sounded, and acted just like a frustrated Archie Bunker. I really wanted to show myself that I could get it. Basically, he passed me because he felt sorry for me and because I was the most courteous and well-behaved student in his class, "Listen, kid," he said, "Now, you was one of my best students, meanin' you were on time, didn't talk when I was talkin'. Ya know. I shoulda failed ya. I don't know weah you got deese dare ansahs, but you need to woik a little more at how'd ya say, formulatin'. Think about, ah, takin' the class again maybe." Ah, but I decided to ditch the math class and continue with more singing lessons, which was way more fun.

I still can't understand algebra; however, when I worked as a part-time nanny, I successfully helped a fourth grader with her math homework. She was amazed at my abilities. I felt triumphant! Sure she was only in fourth grade, but I accomplished basic math understanding on a very simple level. So what? This led me to believe that although I may not be naturally inclined to do an activity, I could surely try to overcome obstacles. That's why I know I will be able to successfully build a bike. I love the technical and mechanical aspects of motorcycles. I have an obsessive interest in learn-

Deb Powell of Powell Performance motorcycle shop in Illinois loves the art of motorcycle mechanics.
Photo by Skip MacLeod

ing everything to do with bike building and the trial and error process. And I want to give "birth" to my own "baby."

Wrenching your own bike truly is like following a noble recipe. It takes a great deal of patience, like cooking. It also takes sleuthing. First, if something's faulty on the bike, you've got to play detective and uncover the problem. Read through your manufacturer manuals and other guides to trace it. Next, determine a solution. Check the ingredients you'll need, go get the ingredients to make it work again. Then fix it. However, like cooking, mechanics involves a bunch of trial and error scenarios. You could set out to make a fabulous pumpkin pie and follow the instructions, but there are always tricks and tidbits that will make your pie even better, like chilling the dough first, or never using a non-stick pan because it shrinks the piecrust, or folding aluminum foil along the crust edges to keep them from burning. These things are not printed in that fabulous recipe. It's just what you learn through trial and error.

With a motorcycle, of course, your trial and error could end up meaning life or death depending on certain mechanical applications. Having the tools to properly work on your baby is key. I mean, it sucks not having a food processor to finely chop, dice, and slice for a recipe. A well-stocked garage makes the job inviting. However, if you're like me and live in an urban jungle where you'll get a ticket for working on your vehicle in the street, then you've got to be quite imaginative, like bumming some garage space from a friend or family member, or taking your bike for minor

repairs to some of the more lenient "hoods" and working on their streets.

I grew up with a passion for vehicles. My father (I call him Poppy) is always tinkering and repairing his cars. I grew up in a home where the men did all mechanics and repairs and we never needed to call in a specialist for anything car- or home-related. This was rather inspiring to me and fostered my sense of self-reliance. Poppy taught me how to change the spark plugs on my car; I installed a new muffler, changed my oil, and did other odds and ends. I loved helping him in the garage—the smell of grease, the sound of an engine turning over, peering under the hood into the mass mechanical haven and seeing an art form, a sculpture of driven technology.

Helping my Poppy in the garage is a treasured memory for me, and I surely did not have enough of those blessed moments. He still works on his cars a little bit, but prefers to be on the road more than in the garage these days. He still doesn't really get my love affair with motorcycles, but finds two-wheeled mobility interesting. The first time we worked together on my Harley, he was incredibly frustrated at the complexities of such a seemingly simple machine. He couldn't believe the cost of parts. Our discussion was about how the bike design should be and how easy installing saddlebag brackets should be. We ended up, per manual instructions, having to relocate the blinkers, rewire, all this stuff, just for a pair of manufacturer saddlebag brackets. It really was quite a ridiculous affair. However, having spoken with a service fellow at the dealership, I learned that the trick is to simply use Fat Boy blinkers and not relocate anything. I'm sure there were a dozen or more suggestions for easy installation of these brackets, outside of what the manufacturer kit offered. But, it was a comically frustrating endeavor to simply assemble a minor addition to the bike.

My latest endeavor is collecting all kinds of bike parts catalogs and repair books. They're quite fascinating. To me, it's like leafing through a Sears wish book as a kid. My catalog pages are dog-eared and doodled upon, with notes scratched across descriptions. There is indeed a sacred maternal relationship between rider and bike, just as so many bikers declare their beloved motorcycles are "a part of my soul." That's because so much of the rider's personality and spirit is infused into the chrome. And further, the nurturing shared and the journey the two travel together establishes a sacred bond. For many female riders, her motorcycle ownership is thought of as a mother and child union.

We, as mothers of our motorcycles, look upon our babies with adoration. The heartbeat is the engine; the pipes are the voice; the frame is its skeleton cradle; the tires represent arms reaching forward to embrace destiny and legs chasing a dream; the headlight looks ahead to the horizon; the liquids are the blood; the throttle is the energy; and the handlebars are the mechanism through which we guide our baby that has inner drive, ambition for a destination, attitude, personality, and direction.

The motorcycle is also our mother, our guide, our friend, forever teaching us to live in the moment, to be constantly aware of everything, to pay attention to details, and to love the simple things in life. The motorcycle restores our childlike wonder: playful, lighthearted, and eternally youthful at heart. The motorcycle lets us play in the road and not get yelled at. Most of all, our motorcycles teach us about the gifts within ourselves as we charge forward.

Voices from the Nest

Vicki Roberts, Wisconsin
Harley-Davidson Road King
Director, Accident Scene Management, Inc.;
   RN/EMT

Getting my bike was a life-changing event for me because it gave me time to think. I was so disappointed with life and needed to figure out what I was going to do and what life meant. The biker lifestyle itself is the camaraderie, the fact that every time you take a ride, it's an adventure and you meet people. When you're in a car, it's not like that. You don't get out of a car at a gas station and have somebody ask how you are or where are you are going? Bikers talk to each other. The bike is spiritual, too. It's a time to pray and there are no barriers between me and the sky. I feel very connected and it's my time to contemplate life and what it means. I can't imagine life without my bike.

My first bike was a 1979 Sportster that had been sitting in somebody's snowbank for about seven years. It was only $1,600, rusty, the tires needed to be replaced and the battery was dead. As a single parent at the time, that's all I could afford. I bought the bike and didn't know how to ride. The bike was top heavy with a Shovelhead motor. I had to wear high-heel boots so I could touch the ground.

I have three children and the kids thought that it was Mom just doing another one of her things. They ended up loving the motorcycles. That first winter, I tore my first bike down to the frame in my bedroom. I put it up on blocks and got all the rust off of it and cleaned it up. Once I got the tires back on it, I rolled it back into the kitchen. I had a friend come over and help me lift the engine out of it and help me with some of the bolts, other than that, I did the bike over all by myself. After I got the bike back together, I started it up in the kitchen and it caught on fire! I did something weird with the wiring when I installed the ape hanger handlebars, but we got the fire out and fixed it. I learned a lot taking my bike apart, and it was so much fun. Flash forward now and my grandkids love the motorcycles and every time they hear a bike, they think, "Oh, Grandma's coming!"

Kim Gabriele Shea, Ohio
2000 Honda Valkyrie 1520, "Dark Horse"

I love it when I snap the throttle on and my Honda Valkyrie shaft drive lifts me up—what an adrenaline rush. I love the way the motorcycle opens up communication with enthusiastic people who would not otherwise speak with you. If only we could all be that happy all the time. One time while riding, I looked over and this little girl in a car next to me gave me the thumbs up!

It simply doesn't get any better!

She melted my heart. You experience things that would never happen in a car when you ride a motorcycle.

It all started when I was a child. My step-father bought home a little, bright-yellow, mini bike chopper. I fell in love. It was so cute. When I outgrew that bike, the neighbors got a dirt bike so I rode that. Then I wanted my own motorcycle in high school. Little did I know it would be a 13-year wait before I would get my own bike again.

Three years after high school I met my husband and I rode with him a lot. We took short camping trips here and there. Then I got pregnant. We went to our last Lamaze class on the motorcycle. People in our class couldn't or didn't want to believe we rode there on a motorcycle. Our riding slowed way down for a while after our baby was born, but then we started putting her on the bike. She loved it and her dad made sure to make it as fun as possible for her. I still wanted my own bike all along but couldn't afford one. I never lost sight of what I wanted as the years rolled by. Two years after my second daughter was born, I bought my own bike.

What I love most about riding is that it wipes away your worries and concerns because you are living in the moment. It relieves my stress and makes me happy, plus it's a great way to see our beautiful country! I love the way the bike accepts you in whatever mood you happen to be. It simply doesn't get any better!

Jennifer Bromme
Photographer: Christina Shook © 2003

Jennifer Bromme, California
1994 Kawasaki ZX 7, 1977 Yamaha IT 250,
   1989 Yamaha FZR 400, 2001 Suzuki
   GSX-R 750
Motorcycle technician, Werkstatt Motorcycle
   Racing and Repair; motorcycle racer

Because I own a shop, the biggest advantage for me is that I do not have to deal with people who think women can't work on motorcycles. I do like to associate with motorcycle people; most of them are open-minded individuals. And of course I enjoy getting respect for what I'm doing from my fellow riders, my customers, and the racers on the track. When I work on a bike, I am absolutely submerged in what I'm doing, but I do that with everything. Mechanics is like meditation in a way because it's a focused process that I enjoy very much. I ride because I like the challenge, the mastery of a tool (the bike).

I built the motor for my first bike, a Yamaha XT 500, in my room while I was still living in my dad's house. I used the oven to heat up the motor to split the cases. He was pissed since the oven stank for a week from the residue oil that crusted up in it. Otherwise he was very supportive. My mom didn't like me being a mechanic, she wanted me to go to university, but ever since I fixed her car she's very proud of me.

I started doing motorcycle mechanics when I was in school. I didn't have any money to have repairs done, so I did everything myself with the help of a few friends. They were very helpful in doing things for me, but wouldn't teach me. I was told I couldn't do it because women supposedly do not have a mechanical mind. Bullshit! I enjoy everything about working on motorcycles: new technologies, using your mind in a scientific way, fast-paced summers and laid-back winters, racing, camaraderie with the other riders, challenge. Of course like all small business owners, I don't make very much money, just enough to pay the bills and go racing.

Claudia Glenn Barasch, New York City
1997 Kawasaki Vulcan Classic 1500, "Ruby"
Event planner/producer

Riding unleashes me from the rigors and normal confines of life's everyday schedules and responsibilities. Motorcycles equal travel, equals adventure, equals celebration. Riding a motorcycle enhances my life! The freedom, speed, individuality, surprise, and independence are among the many wonderful reasons why I love motorcycle riding.

My family enjoys the fact that I ride because they ride, too. My entire family plays a vital role in my life so riding with the family is a powerful experience. Riding together confirms and strengthens our bond. It provides an opportunity for my husband and me to teach important lessons to the kids using riding as a metaphor for life as well as safe riding techniques. The motorcycle riding experience with the family creates days to be together, supplies adventure, adds freshness to our daily grind, and provides lots of laughter!

Barbara O'Connell, Vermont
2000 Indian Scout; 2002 Indian Spirit
Former executive recruiter

I have two grown stepdaughters, and when they were young girls, they knew that dad and "B" were bikers. My stepdaughters' mother, who is a good friend of mine, is also a biker. I also have two teenage sons, and as young boys they would ride behind my husband and me. They now ride dirt bikes. The boys feel a real sense of pride when they say, "My mom's a biker babe." My husband and I will occasionally ride over to their school and pick them up. They feel almost like celebrities, proud that mom and dad ride these big bikes. They have a tremendous amount of respect for me as a woman and as their mother who can just go out and ride these bikes.

It's wonderful to be a part of the re-emergence of Indian Motorcycles, a classic brand. Ever since my husband, Frank, has been CEO of Indian Motorcycles, I have jumped right into it and have become like an ambassador for the Indian brand. I think it's fairly unusual for a man to go into a job as a CEO and have his wife riding her motorcycle right up front with everyone else. I'm not on the back, I'm not staying home, I'm not waving goodbye to the group. My bike is right up there with everybody else's.

I've been on many rides around the world with large groups of people. For 21 days I led the Indian Motorcycle 100th Anniversary ride across country. What a thrill to look in the mirror and see upwards of 200 headlights! The accomplishment for me, personally, as a woman having ridden nearly 5,000 miles for 21 straight days, well, I didn't want to stop. I could have ridden until I ran out of road.

There was an inner strength in me that I didn't know I possessed. From this, I have reached another level in my life that I never knew I could experience. Motorcycle-riding is a transformation, a confirmation of who I am but was perhaps afraid to tap into. I've discovered that there is more to me than I ever knew there was. Motorcycles are a very sexy thing.

Jacquelyn Cooke, Maryland
1997 Honda Magna, "Rrumblebee"
Production specialist

I learned to ride when I was 49, after a divorce that seemed like it was the end of my life but was really the true beginning. Motorcycling restored my soul.

I am a task force leader for the Columbia, Maryland, fundraising event Ride for Kids®. It puts me in touch with new faces in motorcycling almost every day. Working with Ride for Kids has fun filled and fulfilled my life. My colleagues love the fact that I ride and I collect almost $4,000 from them for Ride for Kids.

I love the independence when riding. It's when I am closest to God. I mentor a child in elementary school and am somewhat of a hit with his friends because of the bike. My own children ride with me and think I am the coolest! Motorcycles have become a family affair, a recreational activity around

which we can all have fun. My daughter, 35, rides passenger with my companion when she visits and her son, my grandson, rides passenger with me.

Lisa Martin, California
2002 Harley-Davidson Road King
Service manager, San Diego Harley-Davidson

I've always had an interest in motorcycles, mainly Harleys. My parents forbade me to ride a motorcycle, let alone work on one. I was living in New York, working on vacuum cleaners, and I thought I'd rather be working on motorcycles. I was a boiler technician in the Navy and I like wrenching. So, I went to Motorcycle Mechanics Institute (MMI). It was eye opening learning about motorcycle mechanics and exciting learning to work on the bikes. After I graduated from MMI, I went to San Diego Harley-Davidson and was hired on the spot. What makes this job especially great is working for NY Myke, the dealership owner, because we're one big family here!

Working on a motorcycle is like putting together a puzzle, and when you do it right the reward is that nothing falls off and nothing goes wrong. You test everything before you button anything up. Women pay attention to detail. We care, we get concerned about things. I'd love to hire a female mechanic or service writer.

I love riding a motorcycle, the freedom and being on the road. People look and see a female on a motorcycle and think, "wow," especially on a Harley.

Mikki Loscalzo, New York
1997 Harley-Davidson 1200 Sportster,
  "Nice Kitty"
Elementary school teacher

I teach fourth grade at the City Island School, PS 175, in New York, a wonderful school. I ride my Harley to school and the kids love it. They ask me all kinds of questions about the bike. I want them to know that women can ride. You can be an educated woman, be a lady, and ride a motorcycle. Anything a man can do a woman can do just the same.

At the end of the year, I do a special art project with the kids. I pass out an illustration of my motorcycle that's all blanked out, and they can decorate their motorcycle any way that they want. The kids love it. I also have books about motorcycles and dirt bikes in my classroom library. I'm so happy to have this passion that allows me to be free and enjoy life so much!

Val Jones, New York
1996 Yamaha Virago 750; 1996 Suzuki 200
  Dual Sport
Finance officer

I love the freedom, independence, sun on your face, wind in your hair, enjoying the countryside views from the front and not from the back of the motorcycle. You can see so much more on a motorcycle, too. If you ride, you know the feeling! It's hard to explain to someone who sees the world from a car window.

The best feeling to me is knowing that

"I did it, I bought it, I own it, and I can ride my own motorcycle." That makes me smile. I also want to pass along to my own daughter the message that "you can do it!"—whatever it is you want to do in this man's world, no matter the obstacles, no matter the doubts. As a woman, you can be intelligent, feminine, strong, independent, and confident, just *Go for it!*

I love riding dirt bikes or road bikes with my 19-year-old son, Steven. It means a lot to me because it's something just the two of us do together. After all, how many boys can say, "I ride motorcycles with my mom." My daughter, Erin, has ridden dirt bikes in the past, but is more interested in other sports right now. I've always been an active mom, participating in whatever activity they're into. But when I have time to myself I love to just get on my bike and go enjoy a solo ride.

I've learned a lot about myself through motorcycling. Riding has given me confidence, a sense of accomplishment, and a way to express myself. Riding a motorcycle is just another way for women to express themselves (like showing your true colors); showing the world you're not afraid to be a little different and still be proud to be feminine and strong at the same time.

I think it's important to recognize and respect women for their courage and to acknowledge that women who ride motorcycles can be professional at work, intelligent, feminine, strong, sexy, compassionate, caring, and loving, giving, and supportive mothers. The most important thing is balance.

Mary-Claire Burick, Maryland
2002 Sidewinder Prowler (custom bike
   I built myself)
Operations manager, Fox News Channel

Although I am a very independent woman who likes to do my own thing, I also have a pretty intense need to please others. Motorcycling is the first thing that I've gotten involved with completely outside of others' expectations. It was a big leap for me knowing that many would not approve, specifically because I was a woman. But I decided that regardless of what others thought about it, I was going to pursue this. To my amazement, everyone has supported me 100 percent. To that end, it has bolstered my self-esteem and finally given me my own "thing."

Every time I look at and ride my bike, I feel grateful for the doors that have been opened because of this new "hobby." My stepdaughter, Kristen, loves to ride and begs to ride with my husband every chance she gets. My stepson, Matt, is a bit more wary, and doesn't really like the bikes, but he does think it's pretty cool that a girl can ride!

I am notorious for biting off more than I can chew with projects. This definitely includes my recent bike build. I'd never changed the oil on a bike, but was now preparing to build my own custom from the ground up! My husband Greg and I chose a local shop, Sidewinders Motorcycle Technical Services, owned and operated by Dennis Plank. Although there were difficulties and some frustrations along the way, with the help of Greg and Dennis, it became one of my most rewarding projects.

Riding a motorcycle has absolutely changed my life! I have broadened my horizons, have had exciting new experiences, and met a wonderfully new and diverse group of people. I feel especially bonded with the women I have met through motorcycling. Each of us is so different, but yet we have this one thing that brings us together. The positive nature of the whole experience has opened my eyes and made me more receptive to new people and experiences.

Lori Eby, Michigan
1979 Harley-Davidson Superglide,
   "Sweet Bitch"
Custom Harley motorcycle painter

My husband and I own a full-service bike shop specializing in Harley-Davidsons. We also do all the custom painting ourselves. I do the artwork, and he does the bodywork/base coating and clearing. (Although I do on occasion do that, too.) Together we've been painting for almost 13 years, and running the bike shop for nine.

Motorcycles gave me the meaning of a brother/sisterhood and it gave me the power and sexiness of being in control. I love the freedom I feel being on the road and in the wind. Any problems or stress vanishes when I'm riding my scoot. Being out on the open road is a feeling you can't explain unless you're out there experiencing it. I'm very outgoing, I love life and all it throws at me. I'm happily married to a great guy who's my best friend. What was a hobby (airbrushing) turned into a full-time business which makes me thankful for being able to do what I love.

Stephanie Feld, New York
1990 Harley-Davidson FXR Police Special,
    1997 Buell S3
Motorcycle journalist, and columnist
    for *American Iron* magazine

Well, I don't really love anything about working on my bikes. If I did, I'd still own my 1957 Harley-Davidson Sportster, which required constant maintenance and repair. I work on my bikes for three reasons: 1) I want to learn as much as I can about my own machines so I can take care of them myself. I haven't found many shops whose mechanics I'd trust to change my oil, much less perform major surgery on my bike. At least if I do the work myself, I know exactly what was done; 2) I can't afford to pay a shop to fix my motorcycles; 3) I don't want to wait a month for a shop to fix my motorcycle.

If you want to learn mechanics, start simple, with oil changes and maintenance. Work up gradually from there; installing brake pads, changing clutch plates, removing and installing the wheels for tire changes. Always read the service manual *before* taking on a new project, and keep it next to you while you're working. (Tip: Place all the pages of your Service Manual into plastic sheet protectors, and store them in a ring binder.) Make sure you have the proper tools to do a job, and don't be afraid to spend the money to buy good-quality tools. Having the right tools can mean the

difference between a quick, simple repair job and a weekend-long nightmare. In the end there's nothing you can't learn to do.

Riding. There's definitely more than one thing that I love about it: I love moving directly through my environment; the way you can smell trees, flowers, dirt, rain; the way you feel the slight changes in temperature and humidity as you dip into hollows or climb hills. And I love the way that sunlight flickers through the trees in the summer, and the autumn leaves whirl up behind as you ride down a leaf-strewn road. I love the way that a good, willing motorcycle feels when you lean into a turn or roll on the throttle.

A good bike always feels like it's tugging at the bit, egging you on to unleash its power. It's not just a machine, it's an accomplice; a wicked imp urging you to act in a most socially irresponsible manner. I love the way it feels when I master a new facet of riding. Nailing a corner that's been giving me fits, or the way I felt when I first learned to countersteer; that feeling of accomplishment is something that's sorely missing from most of our lives.

Diane Marafioti, New York
1999 Kawasaki Drifter 1500cc;
1985 Harley-Davidson FLHT 1340cc,
    "Toro"
Motorcycle Safety Instructor

We are a four-generation motorcycle-riding family, "a family that rides together, stays together." I am just an average American mother and housewife who loves motorcycles, motorcyclists, motorcycle mechanics, and motorcycle wannabes who I love to teach to ride. I feel like the Mother Teresa of the motorcycling world. I feel as though each person I teach to ride is family.

I became an MSF Instructor in 1984 and soon started the American Motorcycle School. In the suburbs, most people thought it was a joke. But students came from all over NY, NJ, CT, and PA! Then my third daughter, Christine, joined me to help teach. We got too busy, so I enlisted my sister, Lee, to help. Together, we have taught people from all walks of life. The students who have enhanced our lives are too numerous to mention. But we care about them all, as we have watched them transform into new motorcyclists! One of my proudest moments as an instructor was when one of my students, Ralph Lauren of Polo, passed his motorcycle road test. He looked at me and said, "This is one of my proudest accomplishments." He went on to tell me, "I'm just a kid from the Bronx, and all my dreams came true."

Motorcycles taught me to love life, live every day sharing, and to give back the joy I receive from riding. You can only love someone if you learn to love yourself. If you give everything to everyone, there's nothing left for you. Be good to you. It's okay to fall down, but get up and finish the ride. You, too, can dream the dream and make it happen.

Michelle Meek, Kentucky
2002 Hyosung Alpha 250
Waitress

When I ride I am in total control. I'm not a control freak, but close. Riding gives me the ability to control my own freedom on the road. It's kind of like a visual statement that points out independence, strength, and (positive) aggressiveness that is achieved through control. Okay, to be less technical, *it's fun!*

My only son is almost four. He says that he likes my motorcycle and that it is okay that I ride. Right now he does not ride with me or anyone else (I think he's too little). The first time he asked if he could go for a ride I told him that when his feet reach the foot pegs he can. He likes to hop on my bike often just to see if he's grown enough! For my son to get a dirt bike he would have to show responsibility and discipline. For raising a child you need a certain amount of self-discipline and the ability to instill self-discipline. Lessons of riding a motorcycle include self-discipline because you have to be willing to learn, practice, not be discouraged, and be aware of all your surroundings. No one else can do that for you when riding a motorcycle, and this applies to life in general.

Leilehua Yuen, Hawaii
1982 Honda Nighthawk 450, "Li'l Black"
Writer, artist, mechanic

*H*aving only a bike really caused me to simplify my life. If you understand how your bike works, you'll be a better rider. Take a good riding course and apply the lessons to the rest of your life as well—especially the part about looking ahead on the road so you can see trouble and avoid it before it reaches you.

I advise women to learn to do their own maintenance and basic wrenching on their bikes and this is how I devised my "Hula and the Art of Motorcycle Maintenance" philosophy, because much of the same philosophy from dancing applies to maintenance: You break the process down into steps, understand each step, and practice. I first came to understand how riding and hula are similar when my MSF instructor, frustrated by my clumsiness, yelled, "I've seen you dance hula, now *dance* with that bike!" So I did, and suddenly the bike and I were moving as a unit, rather than as two entities at odds with each other.

Other women I meet congratulate me on my courage and strength, but I really don't think of it that way. I ride full time out of necessity, just like women have always done many things out of necessity. I'm grateful that I am able to ride a bike, because otherwise I'd not be able to go the places I need to go to do my work. I believe we each tap into the essential life force, and that it is either male or female. If we choose to perceive vitality, strength, and drive as either male or female, I think that is a function of our own prejudices.

Linda Robertson, Maine
2001 Triumph Bonneville, "Abigail"
Graphic designer

*L*ike most women I'm many people, depending on what I'm doing and who I'm with. I'm a loving partner, a proud mom, a "girly girl" out shopping and dining with my girlfriends, a wild woman riding alone on her bike snarling at tourists in cars, a tough broad who can take care of herself, and a delicate flower who sometimes needs to curl up in her partner's lap and feel taken care of. Riding taught me that I can do it alone; that I'm stronger and more self-sufficient than I had ever imagined; that I can do anything I put my mind to.

Riding a motorcycle is all about making decisions and having confidence in yourself and your own abilities. When you're out on the road you have to be confident that you can handle anything that comes around the corner, and be able to decide what you're going to do *now*. All the analyzing has to take place in a split second. For me this is actually very relaxing and revitalizing—to have this time for myself, with myself, where I am totally in control of my condition and have to live completely *now*.

Denise A. Kora, Michigan
1997 Honda Valkyrie; 1983 Honda
   1000 CB Custom
Project manager, Ford Motor Company

*W*ell, I'm a doting mother of three shih tzu dogs. The oldest, Rosie, used to ride with me, but she's getting a little too old for the biker life. Imagine a shih tzu with a bow in her ponytail, riding in the "Rosie

Pod" on my Valkyrie. It was quite the sight! (She was well protected and harnessed, of course!) The other two, Blue and Katie, are too young yet, but I suspect they will want to follow in their older sister's pawsteps someday.

I am an independent, self-supporting, driven woman; a true free spirit. I gather my energy and strength from the four natural elements (at least three are usually available when I ride): wind, earth, water (rain), and fire. There are so many aspects I love about motorcycling. I explain to non-riders that it is the closest thing to riding a magic carpet. Motorcycling has allowed me to travel and explore the lands on a new level. I appreciate life a notch or two more than I did before I rode. I know it's a bit riskier to ride a motorcycle, but it's worth the risk. It saddens me to think that some will never know what it is like to experience the joys of riding or that they are too closed-minded to try and understand that it is a major part of my life and soul.

Robin Galguera, California
1983 Kawasaki GpZ 550, "Issa" (after the
    Japanese poet)
Writer

I've spent most of my life playing it safe, being the family peacemaker, etc. Riding a motorcycle has been a powerful metaphor for my desire to live my life on my own terms, to accept risk rather than shy away from it. I love being able to feel the nuances of weather while riding a motorcycle. When I ride down into a redwood canyon, I feel all the little pockets of warm and cold air. I feel

as though I'm out in the world in an active way. I have to admit that I really dig the speed, too.

Accepting risk is part of life. I have to say, however, that since becoming a mom, I'm questioning whether or not motorcycle riding is truly a risk I want to take. My son has always seen me as a rider, so it doesn't surprise him at all. I'd rather be on a track than on the street with all of the crazy, idiotic drivers. I'm thinking of taking up dirt biking.

I was a super-shy child and feel as though I'm finally growing into myself. At age 38, I got my first tattoo, a small blue spiral on my right wrist. For me, it symbolizes a journey, both inward and out. People don't expect me—the nerdy poet with the graduate degrees—to sport a tattoo, and that's partly what it's about. It's a way of saying, "I know I'm a bundle of contradictions. Look at me, look at *all* of me."

Darlene Bish, Ohio
1980 Harley-Davidson Sturgis Dyna Glide;
1990 Harley-Davidson Electra Glide Classic
    with a sidecar;
1991 Harley-Davidson Sturgis Dyna Glide;
1977 Harley-Davidson Super Glide,
    "Miss Piggy"
Accountant

I'm a biker down to my soul and the lifestyle is very dear to me. My daughter loves motorcycle-riding. She thinks it's "cool"! That's why my husband, Bill, and I got the sidecar so she could be a part of our passion, too. She started riding at five months. Now she's learning to ride her bicycle well so that Mommy will buy her one of those little motorcycles so that she can ride her own, too. Riding pregnant, overall, it was great! In my belly she would just settle down when we were riding, like her own rocking chair, and six years later she still doesn't mind the sound of loud pipes!

I've found from an early age that I felt comfortable, capable, and alive on two wheels. I was somewhat of a tomboy and occasionally a frilly girl, never quite fitting into anyone's mold, and the motorcycle provided me with a way to be accepted for who I am. I want to teach my daughter what the motorcycle has taught me—with all its supposed danger—that life is worth living! I want her to grab the brass ring each day and enjoy each smell, each flower, each road that is offered because it is a gift from God. I have a strong religious faith and belief in God and Jesus Christ. You don't know when your time is up and I do believe in the amount of destiny that He gives you. Certain risks have given us beautiful things in life. If you are out there riding the bike, enjoying the world, cherishing the freedom, finding new friends, appreciating the day for what it is, you've got to be thankful, for you have more than most!

The gals of the Discovery Channel's *Motorcycle Women* documentary
on the road as wild wind sisters (*left to right*): Sasha, Claudia, Michelle, GOTHGIRL,
Flame, Betsy, Qian

CHAPTER 6

Wild Wind Sisters

The Goddess archetype doesn't replace God; she merely keeps him company. She expresses his feminine face. . . . Now the Goddess is returning—she is making her way up—and people without eyes to see will be completely in the dark about the journey of women all around them.

—Marianne Williamson, *Woman's Worth*[16]

Picture a pack of motorcycles roaring toward your SUV "cage." First, the sound. A muffled thunder approaches, overtaking the sound of the videotape playing to divert the kids' attention from their relentless battle over who ate the last peanut butter sandwich. Your eyes scan the rearview mirror: a line of chrome is fast approaching, one headlight, two headlights, that is not a car, no, three then four headlights and the headlights keep on coming with the rolling rumble. Then lights begin to disappear to your left to pass your cage in formation.

The kiddie video is no longer entertaining the children. "Awesome!" yells the boy. As you turn your head to check out the bikes cruising by, you realize it's all girl power. Women on the run. You can't contain your fascination and your lips curl into a smile as your soul stirs to join them. Their agenda? A good time. Freedom. Cama-raderie. Bonding as wind sisters. A few gals toss a wave your way and a thumb's up to the kiddies. You nod with a grin in reply and grip the steering wheel tight, imagining it to be handlebars. "Mom! They're all girls!" screeches your daughter, her fingers jabbing at the window and leaving a peanut butter print. Your gaze is forward as if riding shot-gun, herding the flock back into right lane formation. "Wow! I didn't know that many girls can ride motorcycles!" says the boy. "That's cuz girls can do anything they want to, right, Mom?" replies the girl who sticks her tongue out at her brother. "*Right mom?*" They are awaiting your answer. But you've left the cage and joined the pack, wild and free in your mind and easy ridin' in your heart.

Wind sisters. There's a bond between females riding the wind on two wheels in an exclusive women-only riding club or group. It is the ultimate girl-power display of strong women who share a passion for the wind's embrace, a wanderlust. Chicks on bikes chasin' the sun on the run; motorcy-cles connecting with female cycles and the circle of sisterhood, giggling like schoolgirls because the fun is contagious and hard to contain, saying oh yes *i can*, I'm in control of my destiny, watch out world, here I come. Estrogen galore. To be surrounded by women who share a passion for the open road and freedom is powerful, exciting, and comforting. Being a part of a sisterhood is tapping into clan-like human nature, know-ing that within your club there are other females that will look out for one another, and share adventure and friendship.

Women motorcyclists enjoy a lifestyle filled with a passion for two wheels and a freedom to be ourselves. We enjoy tradi-tional female activities together like cook-ing, crafts, child-rearing, gardening, shopping, socializing, and so forth, but it becomes quite a bonding experience when all of these traditions revolve around the bond of motorcycles, freedom, and adven-ture. We can commune as celebrated indi-viduals, too, and share the very essence of our independence with other free-spirited women. When a female biker is seeking to resolve an issue in her life, share, or cele-brate, she has an entire goddess network of freedom-seeking, love-for-life, empowered wind sisters. With that, you can be sure that she's going to find some very deep healing energy, strength, and support from her women rider friends. This, in turn, con-tributes to the individual's positive, forward motion in life and wild abandon.

When women get together and share adventure and freedom, magic happens. The alpha Valkyrie appears. That energy unites feminine wisdom, the life force, a rebirth, a renewal, a celebration of being a woman—balanced, too, with our masculine yang. It is a fervent watching out for one another and a deep, heartfelt caring for the others' well being, and not just on the bike, but in life, too. Sharing reaches beyond the road's bond to establish a sacred circle of camaraderie and support for one another. Cultures worldwide recognize the feminine force, a source of life and the binding element in all of Mother Nature. We are women motorcy-clists bonding together, roaring down the highways of life, beautiful and free to be ourselves away from the social and the media's distortion of who or what the perfect female should be.

How natural for us to bond in the environment of the holy Mother Nature and with such intense energy, experiencing complete freedom and quiet reflection, yet fierce camaraderie all at once. There are no inhibitions. We are women completely connected to the locations reeling past us and deeply in sync with one another as we ride and we're totally exposed to the experience as our six senses come alive like some hyper-intensive 3-D film.

Females gunning the throttle become a highway symphony of pipes roaring together as the leader watches over the pack of sister riders behind her, carefully calculating the route, lane changes, stops, and keeping an eye on hazards in the road and careless drivers. Within the pack, each woman keeps an eye on the riders surrounding her. The shepherd who sweeps the pack is in sync with the leader, watching out for her signals and guiding the pack for lane changes, communicating with the pack and the leader as needed. It is perfect harmony as the group rides tighter than a belt drive.

Most female clubs and organizations that I've ridden with ride deliciously Hard Core. Yes, both words with capital letters. I love to ride this way, at an intensely determined pace. Of course, tooling around riding is fun, too, winding along the back roads loose and free. I really dig the intensity of getting to a day's destination with excellent experiences along the way, no matter if I'm hammering down the road or wandering like an easy rider.

Communing with the environment is just as important as communing within the sisterhood. When sisterhood road experiences happen, we create our own feel-good, chick-flick, stand-up-and-cheer moments— better than in *Thelma and Louise*. Oh, the stories we experience in group riding and adventures, moments that you never forget—like when a bee flies into your jacket, or your taillight gets knocked out by a rock and only some other sister's red underwear stretched over the lens will do the trick for the time being, or running out of gas somewhere in the middle of South Dakota and flagging down a trailer housing a custom bike and siphoning gas out of it till the next stop, or sleeping in Wal-Mart lounge chairs overnight waiting for repair materials, or sleeping on your bike all night. Campfire chats, and dining on home-style meals at roadside diners, giggling about breaking the diet and celebrating the act of breaking bread together as a family. The stories are endlessly hilarious and make for wonderful family tales, which may seem quite tall to those who don't ride, but they are so very real and life transforming, too.

And that's the adventure of the road and camaraderie, of course. It's where stories happen and dreams manifest and memories are made. The road on two wheels is truly where lifelong friendships are made and sisterhood is strengthened.

"Remember slumber parties? I do! Having close friends gives girls self-esteem, offers much-needed support and provides unforgettable memories," says Carol Weston, teen expert and respected author of *For Girls Only: Wise Words, Good Advice*

(HarperCollins, 1998) and *Girltalk: All the Stuff Your Sister Never Told You* (Harper-Perennial, 1997). "Friends make life fun, and one of the best ways to encourage female bonding is to throw all-girl get-togethers." Hey, even though we're adults, we're still girls at heart. We want to have fun, make friends, and experience a common bond together.

There is also a need for establishing a community and a place of trust for women to foster friendship and relationships. Motorcycling invites sisterhood and creates a sense of trust because riding delivers the rider into the realm of self-discovery, and provides a sense of adventure and abandonment of judgment, which, in turn, promotes self-confidence and a trust for sharing experiences with one another. "One of the greatest calls we have heard, one of the greatest needs we have encountered, is the necessity of establishing community. Where women have been taught to distrust and compete with each other, we must foster Sisterhood," writes Jhenah Telyndru in *Sisterhood of Avalon*.[17]

A sisterhood, a circle of women coming together, establishes a place where the female can fully engage in the hard-won concept of a woman's worth. Joining in a motorcycle club or organization creates a venue where a woman can experience her personal power and the collective power of a sisterhood of female motorcycle riders. This collective relationship of journey-women who share a passion for the open road, completely exposed to nature astride their iron horse, establishes a synergy of lifelong sisterly friendships, with an urgency to nurture these relationships, which, in regular everyday life, would all too often otherwise get shoved to the back burner of life.

The camaraderie between motorcycle riders goes beyond the level of a perfunctory hello; it reaches to the soul because it exists between kindred spirits who share the passion for two-wheeled freedom and adventure. Motorcycle clubs and organizations are a place where people can come into their own and share the power of the road or the track. The friendships become so sacred; it is why bikers refer to their circle of friends as family, true family. And oftentimes we may consider our circle of freedom-seeking road comrades more family to us than our own flesh and blood.

The sisterhood also extends to the brotherhood of motorcycle riders. Harley Owners Group (HOG) has an extension to their club called Ladies of Harley, in which women riders from the HOG chapter ride and commune together. While my focus here is the female motorcycle clubs and organizations, many women find sisterhood and brotherhood with other riders in the coed clubs.

The goddess energy of female motorcycle riders on a ride is quite powerful. Women from all walks in life, all ages, different cultures, and different riding styles unite because of their shared passion for motorcycle riding from which their spirits are released to live free and truthful. It's almost like belonging to a spiritual group. For what other type of union would bring together women from such different backgrounds as a tightly knit sisterhood? These friendships become so deeply rooted in the concept of empowerment, freedom, independence, personal enlightenment, and plain ol' fun that wild horses couldn't drag these women apart; in fact, it's the wild iron horses that fiercely establish such bonding.

On the other hand, however, like in anything bickering does exist! "Divatude" happens just like anyplace else. But divatude stuff just has no place in a motorcycle club or organization and eventually fizzles out. The experience of riding is so incredibly sweet and transforming that bullshit just can't exist.

I'm an independent, which means I don't belong to any club, but I love the idea of being a club sister. I'm on the road so much that it's tough to dedicate my time to an organization. I enjoy being close friends with members of all the different clubs, organizations, and chapters and remain neutral, especially since I am a writer and participate in many aspects of the lifestyle and sport. But I do think belonging to a club or organization is important and has wonderful benefits. Community is essential in life. I've met lots of women who, prior to joining a club, were immersed in their own little worlds. Once they decided to join an organization, their worlds opened up, as did they, feeling much more fulfilled in life because of a newfound community of like-minded women with a passion for the road and for setting their spirits free from convention.

So, what do clubs and organizations do for fun? First of all, they have fundraisers. Bikers have the biggest hearts along with a healthy appetite for fun and are known for their altruistic spirits. Motorcycle fundraising events are sponsored worldwide and often raise the highest dollars of any group. There are tens of thousands of fundraising events initiated by the generous two-wheeled donors each year.

Most individual clubs and organizations sponsor fundraising runs that benefit a plethora of causes. Sometimes the fundraising is simply to fund more club fun in the future, strengthening membership or providing resources for the club. Women motorcycle clubs and organizations have potluck dinners, barbecues, weekend camping trips, parties, family days and events, and hold seminars on various topics of interest. The get-togethers are endless and so necessary in life. What fun to come together with a bunch of great pals that reach beyond your traditional neighbors or friend circles, to join together with other women riders from different walks of life! Talk about group dynamic and a chance for relative evolution and self-reflection. Sharing this fun pastime, which is really an ageless activity that makes the rider feel equally youthful, gives way to a bevy of laughter and good times in the most simple and unusual circumstances: Breaking down on your ride is actually okay when you're with other riders. It can make for a great road tale.

The best part about being in an organization or club is the camaraderie and the personal growth experienced from meeting and riding with women whom you may have never gotten to know otherwise. A student befriends a woman old enough to be her grandma, establishing a friendship closer than a high school bond. An attorney shares recipes with a mother hen biker who oversees the family farm and a nest of children. A feminist lesbian becomes racing buddies with a Ducatiste fashion editor. I think many women organizations and clubs and women in general would benefit from uniting with the same methods as the female motorcycle groups, which provide a beautiful space to be heard, share a passion for the idea of journey, commune on all levels, and partake in the ride of their lives.

Motors revvin'—I hear the call of the wild, or could it be Avalon? Well, let's all join in for a wild ride and explore the mist-laden roads to Avalon on our chrome. Now, that would be the most awesome motorcycle run. Gear up, biker goddesses. The sisterhood awaits us.

Following are profiles of some of the larger women's clubs and organizations. There are many more worldwide to consider. Check www.bikerlady.com for more info.

The Motor Maids, Inc.

The Oldest Motorcycling Organization for Women in North America

The Motor Maids, Inc., is a diverse group of women motorcyclists united through a passion for riding while fostering a positive image and promoting safe riding skills," states their web page. The history of the organization is rich with courageous stories of women taking to the open road, competing in motorcycle races, and establishing a sisterhood.

The idea for the first official female motorcycle club was conceived in the late 1930s by rider Linda Dugeau of Providence, Rhode Island. She thought that there must be other women motorcyclists out there interested in riding together. She underwent a search to find other wind sisters. She wrote to motorcycle dealers, other riders, and anyone she thought could connect her with other female riders. Her extensive research resulted in a list of riders that would become the 51 Charter members of the Official Motor Maids Motorcycle Club, established in 1940. The American Motorcycle Association recognized the club in 1941 by issuing it charter #509.

"The First Lady of Motorcycling," Dot Robinson of Detroit, Michigan, was appointed the first official president of the Motor Maids, a position she held for 25 years. She remained active in the organization until her death in 1999. She was inducted into the National Motorcycle Museum and Hall of Fame in 1991 and inducted into the AMA Motorcycle Hall of Fame in 1998.

The founding mission of the Motor Maids Motorcycle Club is to unite women in promoting motorcycle interests. The initial constitutional article establishing the requirements for membership has remained the Motor Maid hallmark since the first meeting: Membership shall consist of women who legally own and operate their own motorcycle or one belonging to a family member.

One of the great bylaws in the Motor Maids, Inc., constitution is Number 7: "*It shall be illegal to pull your motorcycle on a trailer to or from a Motor Maid, Inc.- sponsored event.*" These women ride hard. The National Convention is held each year in July in a different part of the country. Consistent with their mission to promote a positive image of women in motorcycling, they have a say on what a Motor Maid member can wear for formal events. The official Motor Maid, Inc., uniform consists of gray slacks, royal blue shirt, western-type white tie, white boots or white shoes with white socks, and white gloves for parades. The Motor Maids became known as the "Ladies of the White Gloves" in 1941 after they paraded at the Charity Newsies Race. Over the years, the Motor Maids have appeared in several parades.

The Motor Maids state that they "honor their past while riding towards the future. We believe it is important to *ride*, and we are proud to be a riding club. We believe that we should have *fun* in what we do. We believe in the importance of our history and in its *preservation*. We believe in our *traditions*. We believe that presenting a positive image of women motorcyclists demonstrates our *respect* for each other and for ourselves."

Women in the Wind (WITW)

Promoting a Positive Image of Women Motorcyclists Since 1979

Wanted: Women who love to chase yellow asphalt ribbons while cruising on their two-wheeled freedom machines!

Becky Brown's passion for motorcycles led her to place an ad in a local Ohio newspaper to find other women bikers. Groovy, cool, and hip, Becky was a rare sight in the 1970s as a solo female prowling highways on her own chrome. Why not find other wind sisters out there to share the fun? Ten women responded to the ad and together they became the heartbeat of what would evolve into the Women in the Wind motorcycle organization. Twenty-five years later, with over fifty chapters worldwide, Becky Brown has recently been inducted into the Leadership category of the National Motorcycle Museum and Hall of Fame.

Becky's mission is to promote a positive image, and educate and unite women motorcyclists. The humble yet ambitious lady with a sky-wide heart refused the position of international president and instead serves as the international secretary, treas-

urer, and spokesperson, promoting the integral success stories and sisterhood of the organization as a whole.

Women in the Wind is a key contributor to the nationally acclaimed Pony Express Run fundraiser for the Susan G. Komen Breast Cancer Research Foundation. All women and all motorcycle styles, makes, and models are welcome to join this riding sisterhood. National meetings draw riders from across the globe for a weekend of bonding, easy riding, and forgetting about housework, kids, careers, and husbands. "Shootin' the Breeze" is their monthly newsletter, which features the writing talents of chapter members. There is no strict initiation into this organization.

The women of WITW, though from a variety of backgrounds and cultures, unite their feminine spirit in the wind within such regional chapters as the Desert Curves, Ladies of Chrome and Leather, Lady Hawks, Sin Sity Sisters, Sisters of the Moon, Dame Yankees, Empowered Sisterhood, Iron Angels, Jersey Girls, Riding Divas, Wind Dancers, and so forth.

Leather & Lace MC

A Family Oriented Women's Motorcycle Club

In 1983, a little bit of leather and a little bit of lace came together in the vision of founder Jennifer Chaffin, who wanted to bring together women motorcyclists who had a serious passion for riding and making a difference in the lives of other people.

"Leather stands for the inner strength we possess as women, and the physical strength we demonstrate in handling our machines. Lace stands for our femininity, an intimate and important part of us all," states Jennifer.

A strong sisterhood and family respect is the hallmark of Leather & Lace MC. They share the wind, the asphalt, a purpose, and spirituality. The club has chapters and nomads across the USA, and potential members must prospect first. The women of Leather & Lace MC strongly believe in encouraging and empowering children because they hold the keys to the future. Community and charitable activities are regular events with this club. They also value raising the public's awareness regarding respect for motorcyclists. The women in this club are extremely committed to their common goals and visions. They take seriously the notion that Leather & Lace MC is more than a club; it is a sisterhood and trust is paramount. Also unique about this group is the Lace Investment Club, wherein members learn investment strategies and research techniques to develop their diversified portfolio.

"Leather & Lace is an amazing sisterhood and like everything in life, the level of

commitment is directly related to the benefits you will enjoy. Over the years, Lace members have seen each other through life's ups and downs, watched each other's children grow up, and even welcomed grandchildren into our sisterhood. We have supported numerous children's charities and we know that we have made a difference in many lives," shares Jennifer.

On the third Sunday in September, every member across the nation gathers in their respective locations for "The National Children's Run," a required event for all Lace members. All members start their engines at 10:00 A.M. and go for a 100-mile ride all in one spirit dedicated to their chapter's children's charity. "We are women working and riding together to make things happen, we are a force to be reckoned with." Leather & Lace MC is an international, family oriented women's motorcycle club, which welcomes all makes of motorcycles 550cc or larger.

> " *It is a bond that even the hands of time cannot tarnish.* "

The women of Leather & Lace MC continue to develop and evolve the sisterhood. The individual member lifestyles and careers may be quite different, but the women of Leather & Lace MC are accepted as family, as sisters, through their open minds and generous hearts, which extends into the community through their successful fundraising efforts. "It is a bond that even the hands of time cannot tarnish," says Jennifer.

Devil Dolls Motorcycle Club (DDMC), San Francisco

"No Chick Shit. No Issues."

Led by their ringleader, GOTHGIRL, members of the Devil Dolls MC ride American iron only. Interested in establishing a quality-vs.-quantity club, they intend to slowly develop membership like a good witches' brew. Known as the "baddest all-girl motorcycle club" the women also have huge hearts as a sisterhood and vehemently protect each other. They live and breathe the biker lifestyle and ride hard miles with engine-size smiles to prove it. Loyalty, honesty, and respect are their hallmarks. Their "No Chick Shit" means no dumb girl games, no gossip, no attitudes or jealous bullshit, no issues or victims here. Everyone's accountable. Everyone RIDES. Your bike runs. Suit up and show up. These women celebrate one another's strengths and support each other through tough times, which creates a very strong and sacred sisterhood between them. Humor is essential and these Dolls know how to have a good time. They embrace fun like a long-lost road. They sponsor the famous Girl Power Run that attracts women from around the country to the heart of San Francisco. Also of note are their infamous DDMC calendar and WORSHIP WEAR merchandise. The DDMC radiates with great energy, creativity, and GIRL POWER! While the club is friendly and outgoing, it is seriously private and selective of its members. Those interested in joining must prospect first.

Women on Wheels® (WOW)

Serving Women Motorcycle Enthusiasts Around the World

Founded in California by Arleen Ruby in 1982, this club boasts more than 3,500 members from around the globe and growing. Their mission: To unite all women motorcycle enthusiasts for recreation, education, mutual support, recognition, and to promote a positive image of motorcycling. The club welcomes all motorcycle brands, passengers, and riders as well as riders' families. Novice to advance riders, teen to octogenarian, women riders from all walks come together to enjoy extensive touring, chapter gatherings, rallies, and friendship. Families are invited to participate in events and club activities through a support membership, and children's memberships are available to encourage these easy ridin' younguns. Husbands and significant others joyously support their bikerladies' desire to live and ride free.

The club publication, entitled "Women on Wheels®," is a bi-monthly magazine penned by the members featuring new product information, industry news, and personal road stories and chapter events. "WOW members experience the fun and excitement of riding together, supporting each other, socializing, sharing adventures, and helping special charities—all while pro-

jecting a brighter image of motorcycling." The club's positive image of motorcyclists to the general population at large is high on their agenda. WOW was awarded with the Hazel Kolb Brighter Image Award in 1993 by the American Motorcyclist Association for their successful efforts.

The club's overall goals are to assist the motorcycle community and the public and to prove that women are serious motorcyclists and deserve recognition as such. They encourage the motorcycle industry to meet women's needs for equipment, clothing, and accessories; distribute safe riding information and encourage motorcycle safety courses; promote a positive image of all motorcyclists through educating the news media and the general public thereby challenging misleading stereotypes; and encourage women through the sheer enjoyment of motorcycling and the club sisterhood that they have limitless potential and can accomplish any goal or dream.

Speed Diva's MC, D.C.

Fast with Class

Speed Diva's Motorcycle Club hails from the metropolitan Washington D.C. area. The club promotes safe and fun riding and loves to plan rides and events for the entire female motorcycle community to enjoy. Formed in late 2000, the club rides hard, but safe, and part of the membership requirements is that riders must be able and willing to ride at least 150 miles in a day.

The SDMC holds an annual cookout with their "brother" club, Millennium Sport

Riders (MSR). The members also love to get together without bikes during the off-season. "We recently went to Ocean City for a divas' weekend away without the bikes. We shopped, went to dinner, hung out, and played games. We got to know one another better on a more personal note, which made the club stronger."

Women's International Motorcycle Association (WIMA)

Louise Scherbyn founded WIMA in the US during the 1950s and became the first international president of the association. During a magazine interview in 1952, she remarked when asked the reason behind WIMA "Why not unite as a body in exchanging ideas and opinions, problems, and advice?" WIMA has now grown to be the largest women's international motorcycle organization in the world with chapters in countries from the United States to Australia and New Zealand in the southern hemisphere to Sweden and Finland in the Arctic north, and from central Europe to Japan. After being dormant for a number of years, the U.S. association has recently been revived and is led by Alice Sexton.

Each country's chapter is assigned a captain who respectively leads the affairs of the organization. Membership is open to all women interested in any aspect of motorcycling, irrespective of age, nationality, race, sexual persuasion, religion, type of bike, or level of experience. Non-riders are eligible for membership, too. Major decisions of WIMA are approved by the International Committee, which consists of captains or representatives from each country, with each member country having one vote. There is an official International Rally annually in Europe during the summer. WIMA features rallies, rides, and events throughout the year in each participating country.

Moving Violations Motorcycle Club, Inc.

A small group of women who loved riding and sharing information about motorcycles gathered together in June 1985 to begin the Moving Violations Motorcycle Club, Inc. The experience of group riding, expanding knowledge, and developing friendships evolved into the club's philosophy: to enjoy safe, noncompetitive riding with other women motorcyclists.

Based in the metro-Boston area, members come from around the Northeastern region and as far away as Colorado. Candidates must prospect and be sponsored by a member, and prove good standing before being accepted into the club. Any size or style of bike is welcome. The club sponsors several official riders annually and members are encouraged to develop and participate in events. The club activities include maintenance clinics, motorcycle safety courses, fundraisers, leading parades, camping trips, and picnics.

Ebony Queens MC

To Promote the Joy and Pleasure of Safe Riding and Sisterhood

We've Joined Together to Try Something New;

If You're Eighteen to Eighty, We Are Looking for You.

We're Queens, Not Kings—Sisterhood Is Our Theme;

We're Looking for Women Who Share the Same Dream.

We Ride and Camp Both Near and Far;

But We Travel by Motorcycle—Not by Car.

We're the Ebony Queens, All Shades of Fine;

If Motorcycling Is Your Sport, Drop Us a Dime!!!

—Ebony Queens MC

Quality of Riders, Not Quantity" is the Ebony Queens Motorcycle Club of Michigan's motto. Formed in 1991 by the current president, Deborah "Pie" Autman, membership into the club is open to any and all females who own and ride a 500cc motorcycle or larger.

"We are more like best friends and real sisters, rather than a group of women who just ride motorcycles together," tells Pie. The Ebony Queens MC does gather for short monthly club meetings but members prefer to spend most of their time on the road traveling and exploring new horizons on two wheels. The Ebony Queens MC also helps other female clubs get started, lending their expertise in club development and business.

Sirens MC

Founded in 1986, the first Sirens Motorcycle Club was established in New York City. Now there are several more chapters around the nation. The Sirens have appeared in several media outlets based upon their support of women in motorcycling and their organized support of the Gay Pride marches. The club promotes motorcycling as a sport among women with an emphasis on safety, solidarity, support, and friendship. "We come in all kinds of shapes, sizes, colors, and personalities. We work at all different careers from carpenters to executives. Some of us are moms and grandmas. And yes, we ride all kinds of different motorcycle brands." The sisterhood embraces all women regardless of their sexual orientation. Truly the club celebrates the feminine spirit from all aspects. Every June the Sirens lead the legendary Gay Pride Parade in New York City as a show of support for their lesbian members.

The Sirens publish and distribute to the membership "SirenSongs," a monthly newsletter wherein they exchange information, and plan and coordinate group rides and activities including events with other clubs. Their goal, too, is to improve public acceptance of all motorcyclists—women motorcyclists in particular—and provide an opportunity for women to join together and share their passion for riding, fun, and freedom in a friendly setting. Member requirements include attending regular club meetings and requesting the sponsorship of a current member of the club. The pledge period is six months so the members can get to know the prospect.

Women's Motorcycle Foundation, Inc., and the Pony Express Run to benefit the Susan G. Komen Breast Cancer Foundation

Women's Motorcycle Foundation, Inc. (WMF, Inc.), is structured as a not-for-profit foundation in support of women motorcyclists, motorcycling in general, and to support the eradication of breast cancer through their highly praised Pony Express Run. The Pony Express Run, the largest female motorcycle–sponsored run, benefits the Susan G. Komen Breast Cancer Foundation. Male and female riders from around the country connect relay style from different legs of the carefully planned journey. "Regardless of how you participate, you'll be a part of a 'Journey of Hope down the Road to a Cure,' " declare the founders of WFM, Gin Shear and Sue Slate. Now in its fourth episode, The Pony Express Relay raises funds on both a national and local level to support the eradication of breast cancer. The first three national campaigns in 1996, 1998, and 2000 collectively raised $1,525,000. Every dollar is donated for breast cancer research via the Susan G. Komen Breast Cancer Foundation, the nation's largest private funding source for research. Twenty-five percent of funds raised by the riders is distributed to each participating local Komen affiliate.

While the WMF's main focus is using their motorcycle passion and zest for life to help eradicate breast cancer, it is not their only charitable concern. For the past twenty years, the foundation has sponsored track days in association with Reg Pridmore to improve the riding skills of women riders, including events that help women with mechanical applications and touring preparation. WMF was also instrumental in the planning and development of the Women & Motorcycling Conferences hosted by the American Motorcyclist Foundation (AMA).

WMF looks for opportunities to network with other organizations for the good of motorcycling in general and for women motorcyclists in particular. In 1996, founders Gin Shear and Sue Slate were presented the Hazel Kolb Brighter Image Award by the AMA for creating a positive image of motorcycling in the media. In that same year, The Komen Foundation awarded WMF with the Jill Ireland National Award for Volunteerism. The AMA named Gin and Sue as motorcycling pioneers and features the Women's Motorcyclist Foundation in its Women and Motorcycling Heritage Museum display.

Total Package MC, Los Angeles

Friendship, style, sexiness, and organization is what makes our club special. All female clubs stand out in their own way just from being female motorcyclists, especially riding a sport bike. Our club definitely comes in all shapes and sizes. We all have our own special careers and we share a common bond: our love for motorcycles and positive attitudes. A few of us enjoy drag racing and we're very competitive. We love the challenge.

It was very interesting and exciting to be a part of the *Biker Boyz* movie and see our club portrayed. Actress Lisa Bonet played a member of our club. We gave her a little insight about female motorcycle riders and what challenges we encounter. She was very into her role as a club leader and excited about the challenge. She had never ridden a bike before so it was definitely a new experience for her. We never expected to see much of ourselves in the movie, so the appearances they did show of us excited all of our members. Just seeing our club's patch on the movie screen made us scream each time.

Dangerous Curves, Hawaii

Dangerous Curves is an all-female motorcycle group, not officially a club, located on the island of Hawaii. "We welcome all female sportbike riders that enjoy riding in a safe manner and do not have a 'fast and furious' attitude when riding," states their website. In March 2001, two friends, Shannon Abrams and Shannon Wohlgemuth, were surfing the Internet looking for women's riding jackets and stumbled across "MissHell"'s personal website dedicated to sportbikes and riding. The gals sent Michelle Carrasca, a.k.a. "MissHell," an email about meeting and riding together. The three became instant riding pals. As word of the informal group traveled the open highway, more and more women united with the three. Dealerships

began referring female riders to ride with Dangerous Curves, a.k.a. "the all-gal group."

Dangerous Curves quickly caught the attention of local media, which catapulted the club's notoriety, and female riders reached out in droves to join. "We are more than just fellow riders. True friendships have grown. We get together for movies, dinners, horseback riding, beach days, and more. We have riders that range in age from twenty to sixty years old. We have single gals, married, some with children. Our careers vary from homemakers, medical, military, federal, beauty, finance, and corporate.

"When we ride, we have rules we expect everyone to follow for our own safety. We have sweepers in the back of the pack to make sure the group stays together. Since we are a 'new' group, we are learning as we go and have experienced some growing pains. Thankfully women are understanding and patient, even when we make mistakes . . . we learn from our mistakes and move on," explains Michelle, whose goal is for female riders to be able to ride together, respect each other, and enjoy themselves.

Spokes-Women Motorcycle Club, New Jersey

The Spokes-Women Motorcycle Club in New Jersey squashes misleading media stereotypes about motorcyclists and replaces them with a respectable image. Career women, retirees, homemakers, students and more are united through their common love of riding motorcycles within this club. In fact, their club gatherings look more like executive board meetings. Whether rider or passenger, single or married, mother or grandmother, women of all ages and backgrounds are welcome to join. Supportive husbands, fathers, significant others, sons, and friends are invited to become associate members once they are sponsored by an active member. Resembling a bike wheel spoke, their logo is a quilting pattern called the Mariner's Compass, representing the compass points to which they ride. The club engages in several fundraising efforts and encouraging safety is paramount for the Spokes-Women MC.

Voices from the Pack

Huggable Dee, California
Women in the Wind
1996 Harley-Davidson Softail Custom,
 "Purple Passion"

*T*here is nothing like riding with a group of all women. In early 1999, I formed the Riverside, California, Women in the Wind chapter of Ladies of Chrome & Leather. I'm 52 years of age and not skinny and to be quite honest, many of the ladies in my riding group are also not skinny and many are over 40. But, thank God, we biker-ladies are all ages, sizes, nationalities, some beautiful, some not, fat, slim, tall, and short. I love them all. We are definitely a force to be reckoned with.

A few months after my group was formed, *NBC Nightly News* included us in a segment they were doing on bikers. We had

34 ladies on the ride that day and we got plenty of stares. When people realized it was ladies only thundering down the highway their mouths dropped. It was a great feeling.

I love the camaraderie in the group. A ladies motorcycle riding group has problems mixed groups never seem to have. We are all strong women and because of that, there is some head-butting at times, but most of the time we are a loving group of ladies who support each other in any way we can. I am so very thankful that I formed the chapter. Many friendships have been made through the group with ladies who might not have ever met otherwise. I love being a woman and I love riding my bike "Purple Passion."

GOTHGIRL, California, ringleader,
Devil Dolls Motorcycle Club
1988 Harley-Davidson custom
Musician, ShoeShine Girl

*T*he whole Devil Doll MC adventure/journey has totally surprised me. I had no idea that the Dolls would ignite like they did, but then again I did not start the club or enter into it with any expectations along those lines. It has taken on a flow of its own—it touches and affects so many people, inspires them in a manner that humbles, awes, and moves me in such a strong way. I do not feel that we are doing anything that is that different, yet I love the path that the Dolls have taken.

There is a moment when I am riding alongside my Devil Doll sisters, a moment so cool, so pure and powerful, and just *fun;*

like when we are riding next to each other or takin' the curves side by side, it is this sense of union, of freedom but just in the *groove*. It is experiencing this rush of love and wanting to protect the girl next to you with every ounce of your being as you plunge headlong into the wonders and exhilaration of the road. When your eyes meet, it is a connection like no other.

Music and motorcycling to me are like a flow, a motion, like when I am riding and it is all happening: I am riding great and my bike beneath me is like a continuation of my body (without my human limitations), a flowing of muscle and machine, and it is the closest that I feel to flight, freedom and being one with the sky. When I am playing or performing music, and it is *on*, in the groove, my hands feel so strong and like birds flying upon the keyboard, it is similar to that sense of freedom and flying that I get when I ride my motorcycle. The power of when you are just simply plugged in and *on*.

Beth Takacs, Virginia
Women in the Wind
1999 Harley Davidson Road King
Criminal Justice Academy Video Unit

Riding has increased my friendships and acquaintances tenfold. It's bolstered my self-confidence and has given me a sense of physical and mental freedom. Living and riding free are my life. I've always gone against the grain. I've never fit the stereotypical female persona.

Riding a motorcycle is 90 percent mental and only 10 percent physical. You and your bike should feel like you're one

entity. You merely think about wanting to change lanes, look, and there you are. You shift gears without thinking because it becomes so natural.

I'm a member of Women in the Wind and have been since 1996. My two sisters are also members. Jeanne, the middle sister, was the first to join, followed by me, then our oldest sister, Marylou. Our mom is an associate member. She doesn't ride her own motorcycle, but she loves for one of us to ride her on the back. Her older brother is the one that got all of us interested in motorcycles when we were little kids.

Our chapter consists of a great bunch of women. You get to know a lot about a person when you go on road trips together. I've made so many new friends. The best thing about being in the group is that the women in my chapter are like me—they love to ride, go on long road trips, they're not afraid of a little rain, and they love to laugh and have a great time.

At 40, I've learned to like who I am and that it's okay to choose who I want my friends to be instead of trying to change myself to suit whomever I'm around. This is who I am. Take it or leave it. Either suits me fine.

Christine Nunes, New York
Women in the Wind
1971 Harley-Davidson Sportster;
1988 Harley-Davidson Sportster
Administrative Assistant

I belong to Women in the Wind and I enjoy it immensely. The camaraderie is great. I feel as if I'm part of something bigger, and

Ladies of Laughlin co-producer Randi Twells. "Motorcycle riding started out as a curiosity, progressed into a search for knowledge, evolved into a daily adventure; it became an obsession, then a sickness, and then a cure. It absorbed everything in my life."
Photo courtesy Randi Twells

Cheryl Rodgers
Photo courtesy of Cheryl Rodgers

Jenny Hahn Neely
Photo courtesy JHN

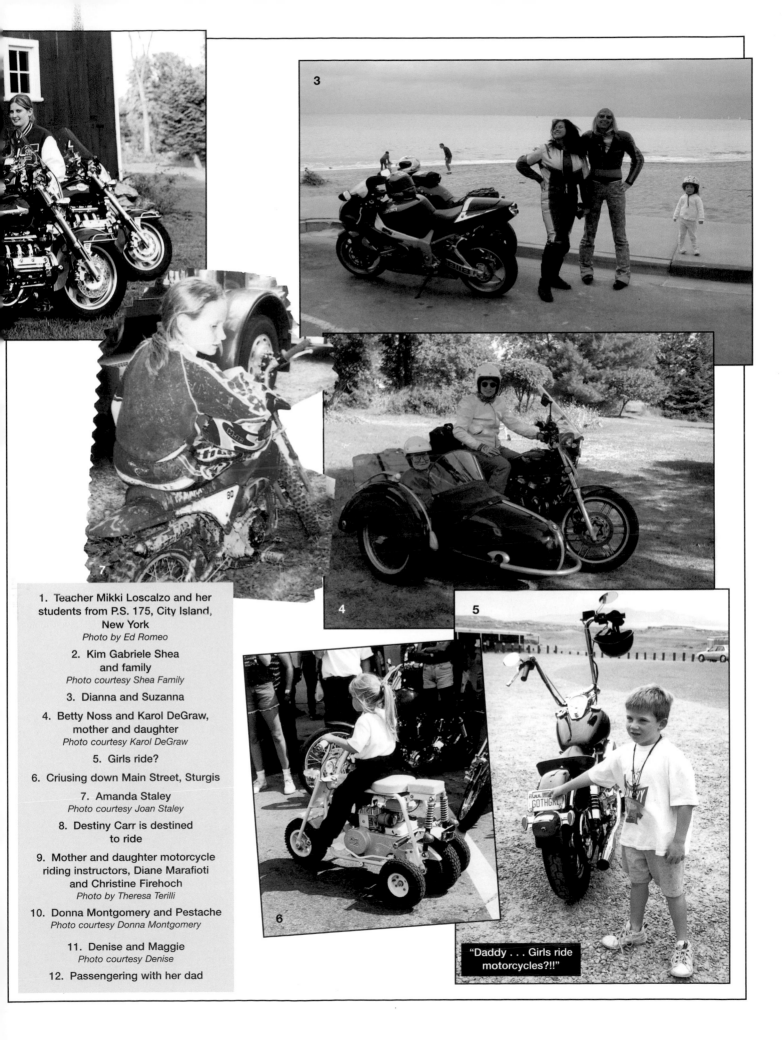

"Daddy . . . Girls ride motorcycles?!!"

Left panel (from top):
Jane Kern of Spokes-Women motorcycle club
Photo courtesy Walter Kern

Riding Rolling Thunder's Ride for Freedom in memory
of the veterans and to support veteran causes

Mary-Claire Burick built her own bike
© Doug Barber www.dougbarber.com

Jane Robinson has a need for speed
Photo courtesy Doc Robinson

Qian Ma kicks back on her custom Harley

Hardly Angels motorcycle "dance" team
Photo by Thru the Lens Fine Portraits

Pinky and Flybutter of the Bay Area Menstrual Cycle Club
Photo courtesy www.bamcc.com

" There is a moment when I am riding alongside my Devil Doll sisters, a moment so cool, so pure and powerful and just fun—like when we are riding next to each other or takin' the curves side by side, it is this sense of union, of freedom but just in the groove. "

GOTHGIRL, Devil Dolls motorcycle club
Christina Shook Photography ©2003

"Integrity. Love. Peace."—Jodie York
Photo courtesy www.jodieyork.com

Eliane Pscherer of Team OCTOPUSS, France
Photo by Gérard Delio/Photopress

Tiffanie Ragasa
Photo by Gary Rather

Writer Carolyn Boyce loves doing mechanical work on motorcycles. "My passion for riding—and being taken seriously for it—gives a wonderful sense of empowerment."
Photo by Peter Bierman

Freestyle competitor Heidi Henry does the "one-footed" cancan
Photo courtesy Steven Bonnau

Vicki Gray, of the Netherlands, on her Honda CBR600, races in the Supersport 600
Photo courtesy Vicky Gray

Jennifer Bromme in sidecar competition
Photo courtesy Jennifer Bromme

Drag racer Carina Sjutti
Photo by Bingo Rimér

Sandrine Dufils, Paris
Photo courtesy Sandrine

Judy Mirro test-riding the 2000 Honda 929 RR
at the Las Vegas Motor Speedway
Photo courtesy Honda Motorcycles

Vicky Jackson Bell, national champion
125 road racer
Photo courtesy Vicky Jackson Bell

Paula Strank,
AMA Hill Climb competitor,
in a timed uphill race
Photo courtesy Paula Strank

Motorcross racer Stephy Bau shows
"the sky's the limit" for women racers
Photo courtesy Steven Bonnau

Amanda Rees Tucker, Formula 125 racer
Photo by Peter Smakula

Claudia Glenn Barasch
escapes from New York City
into wide open country

anything that I give to the group is appreciated. I've helped different charities and worked on fundraising events, including an event for my fiancé who lost his leg from a motorcycle accident, but still rides. Belonging to a group makes you feel good, safe, and accepted. Everyone is welcome and accepted until they prove that they can't be trusted.

I always wanted my own Harley and at 35, I got my own bike. When my man goes to work, and the kids are at their dad's house, I'll hop on for a ride. All the worries, cares, frustrations go right out the window. I work for an uptight school district as a secretary. My co-workers think that my riding is "too dangerous and has a negative connotation." I've been told to "grow up," to "start living a normal life." But my one argument with most of these people is "if both of us died tomorrow, who can they say had more fun and got more enjoyment out of life?" The answer is always me.

I am no less feminine because I ride and I am a great inspiration for my daughter. She sees that a woman can support herself, can do what she's been told she can't do, and has the freedom to choose.

Jan Vargas, California
President, Sweet Evil WMC
1989 Harley-Davidson Sportster, "Baby"
Writer

I was inspired to create a women's motorcycle run, the Gathering of Women Motorcyclists, because nobody was doing anything like that for women riders. There was a real need for women to get together and bond over their own lifestyle and their own sport without the bullshit. I created the run with a friend Linda Chaput. We rode together to create a bond, to create a power among ourselves. Our first run in California was in 1994, and the women were begging for our runs twice a year!

"You are spirited, beautiful, strong, courageous, adventuresome. You are a woman who rides," is just one of the keepsake cards that we would distribute during our runs. It describes what is in our souls. The feeling at these rides was that everybody's souls were totally interlinked. It was incredible. We had women come from all over the country to participate in our ride. Can you imagine being in a pack of two hundred women riding motorcycles?

For that many women to ride together represented spiritual unity and healing for all involved. We all felt lighter on those days when the burdens of life were left behind to feel the wind in our faces and the love in our hearts. The joy I felt in being able to bring this together was overwhelming as I really felt like the catalyst in a power that was much greater than myself. It was the most wonderful feeling in the world.

Tracy Hennan, Texas
Leather & Lace MC
1996 Harley Davidson Sportster,
    "Purple Witch"
Engineering secretary

I finally started riding my own machine about two years ago after a long struggle to prove myself capable of handling my own bike. I've heard all the excuses known to man as to why I couldn't ride on my own. And of course, it wasn't the ladylike thing to do.

I've joined Leather & Lace MC and learned so much about the bonds of sisterhood that bring you together through the immense power of our inner strengths and femininity. I'm even forming a chapter in my area to promote women riders in North Texas.

In June 2002, I rode my Sporty to Hendersonville, Tennessee, for the Leather & Lace MC Midsummer's event. While there, I was able to ride with sisters from all over the country. There is nothing more awesome than to see a large pack of women with the Lace Angels patch on their backs moving down the road.

The National Officers of Leather & Lace MC have forever changed me. These ladies work together as an awesome team, promoting self-worth and the ability to bring women from all walks of life together to ride as one sisterhood. They demonstrate the qualities of leadership and skill in each of their roles to the betterment of our club as a whole. We all need role models to look up to and these ladies are top notch. They always seem to have the answers and always find the solutions. They are the true heroes to women everywhere.

Riding has made me face situations in life that have molded and shaped me into the person I am today. I feel now that I have the power to ride like a man, but look like a lady! I love the fact that I am in control of my own machine, my own thoughts, and my own destiny. Riding gives me that feeling of empowerment over my own life.

Jane Kern, New Jersey
Spokes-Women's Motorcycle Club
1998 Honda Gold Wing SE Motor Trike

*I*sn't the spirit of freedom in this country what it is all about? I have the freedom to make choices for me. I have earned the right to ride a motorcycle if that is what I want to do. I have been wife, mother, scout leader, little league mother, car pool mother. I've baked cookies for every one of my children's classes. Now it is time for me to just put on my helmet and go for a ride on my motorcycle.

I joined the Spokes Women's MC because I wanted to meet other women who rode their own motorcycles. I love every one of the ladies that have joined. No attitudes here. I am now the oldest member in the club. My husband, Walt, and I joined the Polar Bear Club, which rides all winter from the last Sunday in October to the last Sunday in March. I also belong to the Gold Wing Road Riders Association (GWRRA).

One of the things I like most about my motorcycle clubs is the work they do for charities. The Spokes-Womens MC makes and sells chocolate and gives the proceeds to the Juvenile Diabetes Foundation, the Women's Crisis Services, the Susan G. Komen Breast Cancer Foundation, Anderson House, and Rider Education of New Jersey. The Polar Bear Club gives toys to the Children's Hospital Burn Center. The GWRRA club gives money to the Rainbow Foundation for children with incurable diseases.

Riding gives me a feeling of freedom and independence. I just love riding. I love it that no one knows how old I am under my

Jane Kern of Spokes-Women motorcycle club
Photo courtesy Walter Kern

helmet. I can get out there and pretend I am 35 again. I love the shocked looks I get when I stop and take off my helmet and they see how old I really am. I always tell them it's never too late.

Riding has taught me that I can do anything if I put my mind to it. Nothing in life is impossible if you have the heart to try it.

Terry Haas, Pennsylvania
Leather & Lace MC
1988 C&D Chopper, "Billy-Bob"

*L*ace members call each other sisters. I am closer to some of my Lace sisters than I am to my blood sisters. Once I introduced my club sister to someone who knew my blood sister. After a moment of confusion, I clarified that she was my Lace sister. My Lace sister stated, "But I'd take a bullet for her." To this day that is the most profound thing anyone has ever said to me.

When the Silver Rose chapter president in Chester County was pregnant, and she rode till the day she delivered, I was the chapter road captain and planned the rides so that we all turned right as much as possi-

ble so I could protect her from being T-boned in an intersection. I would have ridden right in front of a car to keep it from hitting her.

The best part of being in a motorcycle club is the camaraderie. I know I am not alone; my sisters are beside me in spirit, if not in body. I know that I am not the only woman slugging it out in the trenches for a modicum of respect in my little corner of the world. We're all fighting the same fight.

The Make-a-Wish Foundation and Children's Mercy Hospital are the official Leather & Lace MC charities. The last weekend in April, we sponsor a poker motorcycle run that benefits the Johns Hopkins Breast Center. We solicit corporate sponsorships from area businesses and hold a poker run. The entry fee includes food, entertainment, and prizes. The purpose is to raise money and awareness about breast cancer.

We try not to dismiss members based on minor shortcomings like not understanding the sisterhood. We actively try to teach it to them. Some get it right away, some take longer. Some of them fake it very well and for a long time. I don't take a new member seriously until they've got five years of solid and active membership under their belt.

My life is motorcycling. If something doesn't pertain to motorcycles, I am usually not very interested. I love to learn new things, see new places, and meet new people, all of which I have done on my motorcycle. The motorcycle lifestyle is not something to be taught or learned. It is in your heart. You either have it or you don't. My motorcycle lifestyle taught me that I can do anything I want to, need to, or have to.

Loocie Brown, Massachusetts
Moving Violations Motorcycle Club
1995 BMW R1100R, "Sherpa"
Acupuncturist

I have been riding most of my life. I was a girl with a lot of dirt on her knees and now at 44, I lovingly wash that dirt off my bike. I've traveled to almost every state. I especially love the looks on the faces of the locals who can't believe a woman had ridden all that way just to visit their little town.

I belong to the Moving Violations MC, based in Boston. Back in 1985, when there were a few of us riding, we found a way to come together, ride safely, and most of all, to have a great time and share the fellowship of other woman riders. Together, we are a wonderful sight and a powerful presence. I think that fun is the key to keeping 90 women happy and to enjoying life each day. I have a good heart and a big spirit for adventure.

I have been a member for 17 years and joined the club in its infancy. I truly consider these women my extended family and would be there for them at a moment's notice. It is a wonderful bond built from daring adventures, a need to have lots of fun, and a love of motorcycling.

Wanda "Woo" Thomas, Maryland
President, Speed Divas Motorcycle
Club
2000 Yamaha YZF-R1, "Zeus"
Systems engineer

R iding is an extension of my state of mind: independence, power, versatility, excitement. I love it. I also love the fact that when our club rides together, people are surprised to see that all of the riders are women—especially because we all ride extremely well. Motorcycling is more than just a hobby. It is a part of my life. I love the adrenaline rush, the speed, the maneuverability, and the camaraderie with other riders.

I founded the Speed Divas Motorcycle Club with three other women. We are based in Washington, DC, but are always taking long-distance trips on our bikes. The club gives back to our community through fundraising for breast cancer and we provide mentoring and counseling for young teen mothers.

One of our most memorable trips was when my club and my husband's club went to Philly to spend the weekend with a few other clubs. On the way back everyone, about 30 bikes, decided to open it up. My husband and I were at the back but not for long. I was passing guys on bikes left and right at 140 to 160mph. Then I caught up to my husband and we continued passing people in and out of traffic. When we reached our destination, everyone was surprised that it was a woman passing them all. *That was a rush!!*

Charlotte White, Texas
Christian Motorcycle Association
2001 Harley-Davidson Low Rider, "G-force"
Customer service

I belong to the Christian Motorcycle Association. I wanted to ride with other believers of Jesus Christ, and we are out there as a strong union of biker men and women, prayerfully reaching out to other bikers searching for hope. [Based upon the brotherhood and sisterhood and this love within this lifestyle.] We have pamphlets that state, "Jesus would have ridden a motorcycle. If He were on this earth in the flesh, He would be next to you on His Harley telling you that He loved you . . . enough to die for you."

Motorcycles have opened doors for me to meet people that I normally may not have the opportunity to talk to. It has made me a more friendly person—not that I wasn't friendly before, I was just very quiet. But riding on my own, I've got to take charge. I like the new me! I like that I can do what others think I cannot do just because I am a "lady." If you have it in your mind that you want to ride, get yourself out there and do it. If you become intimidated, slow down and talk to yourself about what you are doing and why, and keep on keeping on. When you have the wind in your face, it won't be long before you wonder why it took you so long to get out there.

Betsy "Gypsy" Lister, Massachusetts
Various clubs
1997 Harley-Davidson Road King, "Gypsy"
Insurance agent

I'm a big biker's rights activist and am relentless about fighting for our right to ride free and make sure we're not discriminated against. As an insurance agent, I testified before the Commissioner of Insurance this year about motorcycle rates being unfair and discriminatory, which has resulted in some major changes in motorcycle insurance. There's much more to do, though.

I belong to the Massachusetts Motorcycle Association (MMA), Motorcycle Rights Foundation (MRF), American Motorcycle Association (AMA), Boston Harley Owners Group (HOG), Seacoast HOG, Bikers for America, and Highway Poets.

I love the freedom to experience the road, the wind, the outdoors, and being close to the environment I'm traveling through. My most memorable trip was to Florida. I rode alone, 4,050 miles, for two weeks—no one but me, my wits, my bike, and miles. My son admires all I do for motorcycling, but he hates bikes! Go figure! He's afraid I'll get hurt. There's been some bad experiences along with the good, but each bad experience I hope makes me stronger. I think it's rounded out my personality, too. I can handle my bike as well as any man can handle his.

I love the freedom to experience the road, the wind, the outdoors, and being close to the environment . . .

Vicki "Flame" Pearce, Washington Enforcer, Devil Dolls MC
2001 Harley Road Glide, "Roxy"

I'm a member of the Devil Dolls MC because they suit me better than other clubs. There are no chick issues, only a true passion for riding—with a healthy dose of humor. The focus is on riding; after all, it is a motorcycle club. It has been, and continues to be, the best journey of my life in terms of personal growth within a sisterhood that I never dreamed could really exist. We celebrate each other's strengths. We love and support each other. And we have a whole lot of fun. It is truly a gift to be a part of this Devil Doll journey. It's a privilege I'm thankful for every day.

Everything I do in my life I do to work toward the goal of spending as much time as possible on my bike, immersing myself in the culture and lifestyle of motorcycling. I have an artificial ankle joint (titanium) in my left leg from a motorcycle accident that has inhibited a lot of my other activities like snowboarding, skiing, and walking long distances. Motorcycling is something I do and do well. It makes me completely forget that I have a handicap. That's what makes it so powerful for me.

Riding has taught me to be more social. I have a strong sense of self and am at peace with who I am. Motorcycling has given me the confidence to try anything. It has taught me the power of conquering your fears.

Alice Sexton, California President, Women's International Motorcycle Association
1977 Moto Guzzi 850 Lemans 1;
1987 Cagiva 650 Alazzurra SS;
1993 Cagiva 125 Mito;
1976 Moto Guzzi 850 Lemans 1
Creative director

*W*IMA was originally formed in the U.S. and then faded away in the 1970s, while the European divisions gained momentum. I met Sheonagh Ravensdale, president of WIMA World, at the AMA 2002 Women in Motorcycling Conference, where she was recruiting to revive WIMA USA. At first I thought, "Another ladies riding group, so what?" But then I began to think about how most of my women friends also shy away from women's motorcycle groups. To me it seemed that there was no women's group that emphasized the *sport* of riding, racing, and touring; no group specifically committed to attracting the young sport riders and racers: street, track, or dirt, and no group with a totally international focus. At least that is my opinion, and I think there are plenty of others out there who agree. I am more a leader than a follower anyway, so I volunteered to give it a go.

WIMA USA is open to all women. We hope to create a dialogue with other women's motorcycle groups, initiating worldwide cooperation and a unified voice that utilizes the different strengths of all our groups to raise the visibility of women riders in this male-dominated industry. There are many different sub-groups in motorcycling. Don't assume we all wear fringe and ride cruisers.

A variety of circumstances were factors in the beginning of my motorcycling career. First, my car died and I needed transportation in a congested city. Second, I was turning 30 and thought, I'd better get busy and do something cool before I get old. Third, my then relationship was going badly and I thought for some crazy reason if I learned to ride a motorcycle, it might help. Well, of course the minute I bought the little Honda CM 200, my boyfriend decided that was too macho for a girl and he left. Fifteen years later, I own four Italian motorcycles and put on about 10K miles per year between touring and race schools.

Becky Brown, Ohio
Founder, Women in the Wind
2000 Harley-Davidson Heritage Springer, "Barney"
Industrial electrician and 2002 inductee into the National Motorcycle Museum and Hall of Fame

I decided to put an ad in the local newspaper to find other women who ride. I got quite a few calls. I took their phone numbers and came up with a time and place where we would meet to ride. Women in the Wind (WITW) wasn't meant to be an organization or a club. It was just a lady's ride. We did a nice ride along the river from Toledo as our first gathering. Then, someone at the local paper got wind of our ride so they wanted to come out and do a story about us. So, we had to have a name and that's how the name "Women in the Wind" came to be. We still do that same ride every spring and we call it The River Run. Spring

2003 will be our 25th Annual. We have over 50 chapters and 1,000 members in the USA and Canada. We have members as far away as Australia and England. I never expected it to grow like this and we have so many good memories. The one thing that really helped WITW in recent years is the Internet and e-mail. We have really used it to our best advantage.

Women in motorcycling has definitely changed over the years. When a woman would tell their husbands, "There's this group called Women in the Wind and I'd really like to ride with them," I think the guys would immediately think that we're a bunch of roughneck women. So in the beginning, when a woman would want to join or come check us out her boyfriend or husband would come with her! Then they'd see that we were all together having a good time talking about normal stuff; we were nothing like they thought we might be!

Sue Slate, New York, co-founder,
Women's Motorcyclist Foundation, Inc.
2002 BMW F650GS, "Pony Girl";
2003 BMW R1100S, "Morgan III"
Motorcycle Safety Foundation (MSF) instructor

*M*otorcycling is an edgy sport; it involves risk. My self-esteem, confidence, and sense of pure joy are continually enhanced by managing the risks while pushing the envelope to strengthen my skills and gain more experience.

As the national programs chair of the Pony Express Rides for breast cancer research and as a founding member of the Women's Motorcyclist Foundation, I have had the privilege of coming to know the finest women and men in the motorcycling community. Because motorcyclists recognize the risks involved with our beloved lifestyle, we understand both the mortality of the human condition and the immortality of the human spirit. Motorcycling attracts some of the most charity-minded people on the planet earth. My involvement with the motorcycling community and the diverse individuals it attracts has been life altering. So much of who I am has been influenced by sister and brother motorcyclists.

I belong to several clubs: Moving Violations Motorcycle Club out of Boston; Finger Lake BMW Motorcycle Club; Motor Maids, Inc.; Women on Wheels; Women in the Wind; Women's Motorcyclist Foundation, Inc.; and Women's International Motorcycle Association. Every one of these organizations has helped to promote our Pony Express Rides. Each is comprised of women and men who respect themselves and approach riding seriously. They encourage each other to push the envelope, improve their skills, and ride . . . ride . . . ride. I can't be as involved with each organization as I would like to be, but networking with the great diversity of riders represented by these organizations has enriched my life tremendously.

I have motorcycle-shaped corpuscles running through my veins. Motorcycling is an integral part of almost every aspect of my daily life. It has taught me how strong and independent I can be. Twisting along those roads less traveled, far from home, is my favorite aspect of riding. My most memorable ride includes riding up through British Columbia, the Yukon, and the Northwest Territories 175 miles north of the Arctic Circle to Arctic waters, and it was full of tales! Plus, this ride, billed Arctic Tour '93, raised $25,000 for breast cancer research and served as the launch site for the Pony Express Rides. I see myself as community servant. I've also experienced that what you give of yourself to others comes back a hundredfold.

Cynthia "High-C" Jones, North Carolina, founder, Soul Patrol Motorcycle Ministry
1996 Kawasaki ZX11
Gospel singer

I love the carefree feeling of being on the open road, just me underneath my helmet on my motorcycle. That's my best praying time. I know that motorcycles are dangerous, and I thank God for the ability to ride and for keeping me from danger. It's just me and Him. Riding is a spiritual experience for me, which is why I've incorporated that into my motorcycle ministry, the Soul Patrol. All the women are born again believers from different churches. The members ride all different bikes. We welcome all types of bikers.

I'm also the founder of the Ebony Angels in Raleigh, North Carolina, but I left to start my ministry. I've always loved motorcycles. I'm a firm believer in women being able to ride with dignity, grace and femininity. I go to the rallies and I don't believe there are any limitations to sharing the gospel of Jesus Christ. If I just want to free my mind I go for a nice country ride. I will incorporate my motorcycle into my concerts by riding on stage to start my shows. I'm working on a song now called "One Way" that will bring together motorcycles and the gospel. I live the life that I sing about. Some of my best songs have come to me while I was riding.

Soul Patrol goes to secular motorcycle rallies. We go outside of the church walls because to do the work of the Lord sometimes you have to go where the souls are: the fields, highways and hedges. The Soul Patrol receives a lot of e-mails from other bikers wanting to know more about Jesus Christ or they ask us for prayer because they see that we are there for them at any time. We get a warm welcome wherever we go.

Sheila McFarland, New York
Women on Wheels
2001 Heritage Softail Classic
Registered nurse, certified nurse
    operating room

I belong to various clubs and serve as the Women on Wheels (WOW) Lake Erie Chapter director. I first learned about WOW at Americade, the rally in Lake George, New York. I really loved what they were about so I started a chapter in our area. I was also a Ladies of Harley officer, whereby I created seminars to get more Ladies of Harley (LOH) members to move from the passenger to the driver's seat. I enjoy meeting others, sharing experiences, and encouraging other women to ride. The different clubs give me lots of opportunities to ride and learn from different, experienced riders.

I first started riding at 14. My sister wanted a horse but instead we got minibikes. My mother always thought my muffler burns were from the minibikes, but they were really from riding my cousin's dirt bikes. I especially liked off-road riding on my cousin's dirt bike but the mufflers didn't like my legs! After years of riding, my husband gave me money for our twenty-fifth anniversary. Instead of silver, the money was used for chrome: I ordered my new bike on our way to dinner, a brand new Harley-Davidson Softail.

I love to ride my bike or be a passenger behind my husband. (I used to be a passenger if there was a threat of rain until I bought the bigger bike. Now I'm rarely a passenger.) I feel that anyone on any type of motorcycle is unique. I love to see all the different styles and models of bikes. We all have common interests: the freedom of riding, feeling the breeze, seeing the country, and meeting other wonderful motorcyclists. We all love to talk about our riding experiences.

Kathleen Brindley, Toronto
Amazon MC
1985 Honda CB750SC
Professional painter and folk art sculptor

I am a member of the loosely formed Amazon Motorcycle Club of Toronto, Canada, which has been active since 1979. It was formed by four women riders, two of whom are still active with the beautifully kept original bikes they bought then. I am involved with them because the Amazons, for the most part, are politically aligned with my views; it is a mixed-race bike club of women riders. I promote safe motorcycling and feel very comfortable assisting younger members with my knowledge of bikes. Frequently we do Gay Pride days where we are invited as a group. These, of course, are usually a lot of fun. It is a wonderful group of women who show support and respect for other members where they can and who love to camp and party.

I got into riding when I saw my dad take off for a road trip on a motorcycle. He was the passenger. I felt a yearning for freedom but didn't decide to buy a motorcycle until I was safely past 50.

My favorite aspect of riding is the keenness I feel with my life and the skill it takes to ride a motorcycle—not to mention the closeness with nature and the openness. God, I am claustrophobic! I am exhilarated on the bike and feel very spiritual and excited with life when I ride. It reminds me of how small I am in this universe and it puts my problems in perspective. I can achieve what I want at any age, despite having had a stroke in the past and despite a lot of negative input.

Debbie "Pie" Autman, Michigan
President, Ebony Queens
1981 Honda Goldwing 1100 Interstate,
  "Pie's Pleasure"
Attorney referee, circuit court

My mother gave me a sound foundation and taught me that all things are possible if you believe in yourself and God. Motorcycles opened a whole new avenue of adventures and good times and making new friends. I love riding my bike and travel all over the country with her. I live my life embracing all things and all people. I am truly blessed to have been born a black female in the United States. I live my life drawing upon my strengths and always looking inside myself for the power and courage to live each day as freely and spiritually as possible. Riding with the Ebony Queens MC is to promote the joy and pleasure of safe riding and sisterhood.

Zenobia Conkerite, New York
President, Sirens MC
1996 Honda Magna 750, "Spirit Guide"
Radio producer

I had a dream that I needed something more in my life. Right after my fortieth birthday celebration, I started riding a motorcycle. I wanted something that I could call my own, something that would allow me to be free even while I had a day job. Rolling on the throttle and having the rubber meet the road is what I love most.

When I worked for a television talk show I was asked to go upstate and interview one of the future guests on camera. It was raining and thundering, but I made my way up there passing at least five car accidents, with the camera safely tucked away in my vest. When I showed up on this person's doorstep, he nearly passed out because here I was, a woman who had arrived on a motorcycle in this torrential weather.

Motorcycles taught me that I don't have to take crap from anyone. Through my riding at a later age, I am an example to children and other women that anything is possible. Almost like music, motorcycling can blur the lines of racism.

RaZor, a career woman, mother, wife, and a member of the Devil Dolls MC

Photo by Eddie Howells

**Cher Fialkowski of the U.K.
on her Honda in 1975**

Courtesy Cher

Betsy Huelskamp

Photo courtesy Betsy

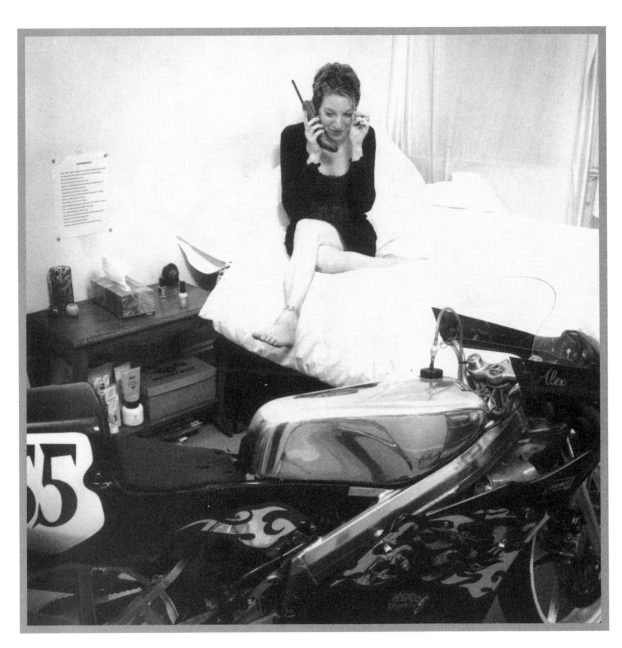

Alex Elinchoff

Photographer: Christina Shook © 2003

CHAPTER 7

Racy Ladies

She takes 3 deep breaths at the starting line

Revs on the throttle teases motorcycle

Shakes her leather hips and she's ready set go

Licks her ruby lips flag snaps down low

Knee draggin round the corner

speedo burnin up track

She says, "Baby, does this

bike make my butt look fast?"

> —from the song "Sonic Butterfly," written by Sasha,
> inspired by Melissa Shimmin and her Sonic Butterfly racing endeavors

The adrenaline is thick as a spoonful of syrup and waiting to become hyper energy, yet all is controlled and diligently focused on the speed track ahead. Drag the knee in the corner of a track, catch air on a motocross challenge, climb straight up a hill without falling backward, and imagine lift-off at the crack of a throttle. Motorcycle competition is wild, it's sexy, it's fast and it's stylish. It is the ultimate challenge. Racing is sugar and spice and everything nice.

The development of motorcycle sport largely paralleled and often coincided with the development of automobile sports. There was a class for motorcycles in many of the old town-to-town automobile road races, such as the Paris-Vienna race. The de Dion tricycle dominated the sport in 1897, but two-wheelers like the Werner soon set the stage for an entirely differ-

Clara Wagner, published by Blanchard Press, New York, 1911.
Photo only copyright by A. Loeffler, Tompkinsville, New York.
From the private collection of Jerry Hooker, www.motorcycle-memories.com

ent form of racing. In 1904, the Fédération Internationale du Motocyclisme (renamed the Fédération Internationale Motocycliste [FIM] in 1949) created the international cup, uniting five nations: Austria, Denmark, France, Germany, and Britain. The first international cup race took place in 1905 at Dourdan, France. The race for the Tourist Trophy (TT) became the most famous of all European motorcycle races, however. The first TT race took place in 1907 on the Isle of Man, on a course that was the world's most famous for many decades thereafter.

Motorcycle racing in North America began in 1903 with the formation of the Federation of American Motorcyclists in New York City. By 1924, this society evolved into the American Motorcycle Association. Since 1937 the Daytona 200-mile (320-kilometer) race has been the leading U.S. race.[18] Now

competition is fierce in several race clubs and organizations and in all manner and style of motorcycle competition. Happy to toss aside the restrictive clothing and label of "weak" that plagued women, the first documented female participating in competition in America was Clara Wagner in 1910.

Check out the racetrack pits and you'll see women poured into tight body armor leathers looking like characters straight out of a James Bond movie. The racetrack is a controlled environment. The rider is completely free to focus on the activity at hand: riding. There are no pot-holed roads, cars, pedestrians . . . the track belongs to rider and motor-cycle. It's the best place to develop awesome riding skills free from the street's unpredictable obstacle course. It's brilliant to see riders leaning their bikes so deeply into the turn that their knee guard brushes asphalt.

On the earthen motocross, enduro, hill-climb, or trials courses the bike and the body are put through demanding tests of rider skill. To see riders handle their motorcycles with such finesse on challenging terrain makes the competition look like art. Race schools and organizations are dotted throughout the country and special seminars and sponsored classes are held at nearby racetracks. There is a unique camaraderie among women racers because, while we are a fast-growing community, we seek

Here are a few different types of racing in which women compete. Further explanations can be found at www.bikerlady.com.

Drag Racing	Trials	Baja
Motocross & Freestyle	Dirt track	Vintage
Roadracing	Speedway	Sidecar
Enduro, Hare & Hound	Ice Racing	Supermotard
Hill Climbing	Paris-Dakar Rally	Iron Butt—Endurance

to become the best and share ambitious efforts and knowledge with others. The racetrack is a fun place to share the common experience of diving into the twist and turn strategies. The energy is high octane and everyone shares the same exhilarated spirit. The sound, the scent, the visuals—all entice the rider into a landscape of riding freedom where it's just asphalt, rider, and machine.

Motorcycle racing is enjoyed by professionals and amateurs alike. Women are still racing hard to raise manufacturers' awareness and support of their passion for the sport. The industry is just beginning to accept that women are serious competitors with the need for proper coaching and development, and serious sponsorship— the same as male racers receive. Without appropriate support on all levels, achieving professional racing status is very difficult for females.

Voices from the Track

Angelle Savoie, Louisiana
2001, 2002, 2003 NHRA Pro Stock Champion
  Drag Racer
Owner, Angelle's Motorsports

I started drag racing as a hobby and the hobby got to be quite expensive. The first race I ever won was the most memorable. We had trained really, really hard and so many people told me that I'd never make it; I'd never do it. Getting that first win under my belt was awesome. It was September 1996 in Reading, Pennsylvania. That race was only four races and two months from the day I first started and we won it.

In the beginning, it was very difficult to race without sponsorships. I had to sell my home and move away from my family, then we were getting paid really well, and then we lost our sponsor. It's such an up and down thing. It depends on whether you can keep a sponsor and keep winning. You've got to have a really strong passion for racing to be able to put up with what we put up with. I just want to race and enjoy the competition and get to ride the motorcycle. I just want to be the best and I don't care about being the best female. I just want to be the best racer.

We reach 190 miles an hour when we drag race. It's the acceleration that's the big deal. We experience 3Gs off the starting line. We go from 0 to 100 mph in two seconds. You're literally trying to stay on the bike. The acceleration is really tough, but the speed is nothing because you're getting up to that speed and you're shutting down right away. It's not like you're traveling 190 mph for a long period of time. It doesn't even feel like it. When I ride my street bike and I'm doing 90 mph it seems like it's a lot faster.

There are parallels between life and drag racing. It's definitely something that you can beat yourself at if you think negatively, because you win and lose the race on the starting line. You have to have a powerful motorcycle, you have to have a great team, but you don't have to have the fastest bike to win. I think the same thing goes for life. You don't have to be the richest person, you don't have to be the best at what you do, you just have to have the right attitude and think positively. As long as you believe in yourself you can make things happen.

My husband gave me a sticker that's on the dashboard of my bike that says, "Believe in Christ, all things are possible." I see it every time I'm on my bike. Several times when I started to have some doubts, I look down at that sticker and say, "Okay, you can do this."

Debbie Matthews, California
1995 Kawasaki KX250
Owner, Women's School of Motocross (WSMX); DMSPORTS, management for race events and promotions

I love racing. I love the excitement, the rush, living on the edge, making split second decisions that decide whether I win, lose, or crash. If we are honest with ourselves, this is probably why we all race. Each race is different with new challenges. There are new faces, different conditions, and your mental state and those of your competitors changes. You plan, but along the way come surprises. You must adapt quickly. Analyze the situation, make fast changes and decisions. These learning experiences make us risk takers and help us to excel in life and in business. We are not afraid to let it all hang out, because deep inside we *know* that we can do it. We are the adventurers, explorers, and inventors of the past generations.

For me, even now, winning still involves sacrifice, dedication, long hours, and hard work. Winning is also being able to get up every morning and be successful in raising my family; being able to still ride although not as fast or stylish. Winning to me now is finishing a moto without getting hurt and going out for pizza after the race with my racing buddies; helping others experience the joy and confidence that riding offers. Winning to me is making a difference.

Winning means evolving. Rising up to meet adversity head on. Winning means picking ourselves up when we fail, dusting ourselves off, and going forward. It means never giving up, despite the hand we are dealt. This is winning. No, I may never do a triple again. But I can teach. I can give back. I can mentor. I can be an example.

Vicky Jackson Bell, California
2000 Honda RS 125
125 Grand Prix National Champion
  Road Racer
Co-owner, with Anthony Bell, of Spectrum
  Motorsports

I love any kind of competition. Having good balance skills and the will to win a competition, great hand-eye coordination, and the ability to see ahead of where you are contributes to good racing. I've raced against men all my life. I think most men are a little more aggressive, which makes you more aggressive.

The starting line is always one of my favorite parts. The tension is boiling, the adrenaline is flowing, the waiting an eternity then *bang,* all hell breaks loose. The rider next to you has the same amount of power, but will your bike accelerate faster? Then as you approach the first turn it's who has the balls and the right line? Who will stick their wheel in there? You have, so far, won the first third of the battle, the start, then the race is the next third and last third is the finish.

The race is always more fun if you are battling with one or more people, swapping the lead two or three times a lap. The race goes so much quicker like that. If you are on your own leading, you have time to think about doing everything right, it should be natural and effortless. On your own it's a

relief to see the checkered flag whereas if you are second or third when you see the last-lap flag you always want two more laps not one, so you can catch the draft and catch up. The last part is the finish, the home straight, and the finish line and the relief you did it or the disappointment you did not.

Motorcycle racing relates to life and its principals because like life it is full of emotions. The joy and happiness, the fulfillment, disappointment, depression, anger, and sometimes embarrassment. Everything you have to deal with in life is part of racing. The best thing is it has its own life. You live in a fantasy world, the race is like an adventure, its real but unreal and has danger and pain; it's like crossing over into a dream for twenty or thirty minutes, then back to the real life. It is an addiction, like many parts of real life, a drug if you wish. It is hard to quit or retire for anyone who has enjoyed the thrill of danger and the quest for competition. Racing is not like golf that you can do your whole life; the mind slows its pace as life goes on, but the pace of racing stays the same or gets faster.

I love the feeling of freedom, seeing and feeling everything around you, and being totally in control of what's going on. When that happens you have synergy with the bike. That's the problem with teaching. Students tend to ride the bike and not let the bike do the things it's naturally supposed to do underneath. When you let the bike do what it should, you become one and it's amazing. All the different styles of racing that I've done contributes to my success in road racing. It's like cross-training.

Lucie Stone, United Kingdom
1995 Honda Fireblade RRT 900 on the road;
1998 Aprilia RS250 on the track;
1989 Yamaha Serow in the dirt
Electrical testing engineer

The bike is a way of expressing yourself, a way to release all the pent-up energy and aggression you collect during a hard week at work. Some people might go and have a hard workout at a gym. I put on my leathers, fasten my crash helmet, and head out onto the open road or race circuit and get ready to wind that throttle for all I'm worth. There's no better feeling: the howl of a big engine just underneath you, the wind rushing all around you, the power you have over this great big, threatening motorcycle just cannot be beaten by anything else, ever! It's complete freedom from everything else. Your mind focuses solely on you and your machine working in harmony. Nobody can disturb you in your little world. It's hard to understand if you've never ridden a bike before, but there's just no feeling like it.

I love taming the bikes—jumping on something completely alien to you first time, and learning how to make it work and go as fast as it possibly can. I get so much joy out of learning about new bikes, it brings a huge smile on my face as I start to work it out and get used to it.

My only real hobby is biking. I love the social scene that comes with bikes. I'm a real people person, so I get very lonely very easily. Sitting around with a group of like-minded people chatting about your favorite subject is great—even better when you've got a few girlfriends who are into it, too.

Motorcycling has made me who I am today. All my experiences of travel have been on my motorbike, a majority of my friends are bikers, and my family is into them. If you've ever had that urge to get on a bike and try it for yourself, do it! You'll wonder why you wasted so many years thinking about it instead of just doing it.

Zina Kelley, California
2000 Ducati Monster 900i.e.; 2001 Ducati
    MH900e; 2002 Suzuki DRZ400S;
    1999 Aprilia RS250
Racing editor, Ducati.com

Looking back on my first few track days, I think "Wow, anybody can race, because if I went that slow and I'm going this fast now, there's no reason why anyone couldn't do this." I was crawling in the beginning. I think expanding women in racing is just a matter of making women aware that they can race. Take a track day, take classes, ask questions, learn from other riders.

Once you begin racing you learn one of two things about yourself. You're either adrenalized by it and you become a different person when you race, or you try it and realize it's really scary and you fight demons all the way. You don't know until you try. I get on the track and that's the only moment in time where I lose all my fear. Only when the starter throws the flag and we're off, for some reason all the fear goes away and I can turn it on.

There's this real high-speed sweeper at Willow Springs that we take maybe at 100 mph and you just drag your knee for the longest time through this turn. It's a beautiful thing. It's almost like a watercolor, and I'm painting this beautiful line through the turn. It's like an artistic event for me. It's also one of the places where I pass a lot of men.

Sarah Whitmore, Michigan
Yamaha YZ 125
Motocross Racer

My life revolves around my bike. Everything I do has something to do with racing. I like riding because it gives me such a great high, a feeling nothing else in the world can achieve. The thrill of competition, overcoming fear, and seeing the look of pride on my parents' faces is the best feeling in the world.

I race professionally in the Women's Motocross League (WML). I currently ride for AGP Race team with my teammate, Tania Satchwell from New Zealand. We don't make very much money, but it's growing fast.

Motocross has mostly taught me determination and independence. Almost every day since I was eight, someone has told me girls can't ride. Whether they're joking or not, it still hurts. Motocross has taught me to not pay any attention to them and keep on riding, because that's what I love to do. Motorcycles aren't just for outlaws or daredevils, they're great for women and families, too.

Kris Becker, Washington
2003 Harley-Davidson SuperGlide on the road; Custom Pro Fuel, "Wildkat," on the track
Pro drag racer, AHDRA and CMDRA; co-owner, Northcoast Thunderbikes

I am currently ranked third in the West Coast Division of the AHDRA (All Harley Drag Racing Association) and third in the CMDRA (Canadian Motorcycle Drag Racing Association). In order to ride this bike, and my previous Pro Dragster and Pro Fuel bike, I started working out with a personal trainer until I became extremely muscle-bound. It was very strange to see the numbers on the scale be so high. I have a much healthier self-image about my body than I did when I was 17. I am much more comfortable in my body now.

It takes a lot of focus to get on that bike and try to crank out a seven-second pass, knowing that pretty much everybody is watching, especially the other fuel bike riders. Our lives depend on being able to handle a 600-pound monster traveling at 180 miles an hour and faster, so in addition to working out, I also have to be mentally capable.

I thought about drag racing for many years before I actually did it. In August 1990, I took my stock 1979 Harley-Davidson Lowrider down the track in Sturgis and ended up winning the event. My first race experience was really pleasant and made me want to go back again and again. In 1995, I won my first fuel event, becoming the first woman in the history of the AHDRA to win a professional fuel class event.

What is it like to race one of these bikes? When we finally get to the starting line I'm pretty pumped. I'm focused. I've watched the other riders go ahead of me and I try to concentrate on what they are doing on the track. When the race begins, I get this incredible sense of calm—it's like I know what I'm doing and everything is fine. I can't hear anything but the loud motor and that's all I need to know. I can finally breathe a little but to be honest I don't know if I breathe or not until it's over.

Susanna Schick, California
1999 Aprilia RS250, "Kate Moss";
1997 Ducati M750, "Fred"; 2002 Yamaha R1
Roadracer and patternmaker

I believe that I embody freedom and feminine energy in everything I do—like riding to work in stilettos, racing in pink leather, just being my own freaky self every day.

The coolest thing about riding is never being trapped in traffic. My most memorable ride is when I got arrested for speeding on the way to racing school. My co-workers find the fact that I ride entertaining and some have been inspired to ride themselves. I work in fashion, race at least once a month, and ride every day.

Riding has helped me to conquer fear in all aspects of my life and given me a stronger sense of self, of independence. When I started racing, it was a big ego boost to tell my friends that I was racing, as it never failed to impress, but the reality of it was that I was dog-slow, and I had to become okay with that in order to continue racing and therefore improve. For the first time in my life, I allowed myself to be involved in something at which I didn't excel. I'm still one of the slowest people on the track, but a lot faster than most street riders, and constantly improving.

Vicki Gray, The Netherlands
Ducati 600ss and 1992 Honda CBR600
    on the track; Ducati 900ss, "Gianni," on
    the road; Husqvarna 250 off road
Road racer and Account manager,
    telecommunications; motorcycle riding
    instructor

I entered this sport without a male figure setting the example for me. I just purely wanted to race in my heart! I'm the director of a foundation I created called RaceGirl MotorSport, which has two purposes: 1) to encourage women in MotorSport (circuit, off road, or street); and 2) to enhance the skills of the already-licensed rider (men or women).

I strive to do what is in my heart: riding and racing! No matter the challenge, I will not give up or deny this passion. In all I do—relocating to other countries, changing career paths—it's the courage to realize my dreams and my desires that provides the freedom to be me.

I love everything about riding my motorcycles, but the best thing is the *sensation* and the motion. When I race there is no other adrenaline rush! Speeding through the corners, the acceleration, the feeling after I race when I get my helmet off. I'm totally high and on top of the world especially when things go well. I get an extreme kick out of it all, the mechanics I do, the preparation, the paddock, I love the fact that there is so much input required: mastery of riding skills, timing, judgment. . . . Motorcycle racing is a totally embracing and consuming sport of the mind and body. My motorcycles fill me with extreme pleasure, thrills, and ongoing challenges! I've met some super people in all facets of riding who share the passion or the fear! Motorcycling has become a way of life for me—something I shall not ever be without.

Katja Poensgen, Germany
Suzuki GSX R1000, "Baby"
World championship GP 250 racer

Living and riding free applies to 100 percent of my life. I live for today and nobody knows what tomorrow brings. My favorite thing about racing is the speed and competition. My most memorable ride is when I scored 2 GP points in the GP 250 in Mugello in 2001. This was the first time that a girl made WM points in the 250 class. Riding motorcycles is my life. I am a real racing rider and my life revolves around everything to do with motorcycle riding. The most important thing that I learned from riding motorcycles is that everything is possible for girls.

Carina Sjutti, Sweden
Harley Davidson Drag Bike, "Belzebub"
Drag racer in the Harley Drags; taxi, limousine, and truck driver

I think one of the most powerful things you can do is ride a motorcycle. I feel excited every time I start the engine because I know that it's all up to me and that no matter what, I can handle it. Riding a bike tells others about the strength and power within a woman. I love to feel like a queen of my life and my racing within my own perfect world.

I love the speed, the adrenaline when racing. It's so nice beating the guys! When I am alone on my bike, I am so completely free! It's the best part of riding. I also adore the family feeling with all the other racers. We call this the racing circus because you live rather budgeted during racing season. People who ride motorcycles are wonderful friends. They remind me of the saying "Friends are like stars. You don't always see them but you know they always there."

Barbara Toribio, New York
1998 Yamaha YZ125
Motocross racer and music recording company executive

I organize women's motocross racing for the American Motorcycle Association (AMA) District 34 in New York. I'm not afraid of being labeled a bitch for asking for what I want and refusing to take no for an answer. After a lot of campaigning and networking with every other female motocrosser that I met anywhere in the region, I established a core group of girl racers. Now that group has taken on a life of its own and is growing beyond my wildest dreams, with less and less effort on my part to find more women.

A couple months ago, we had a full gate of my fiercest competitors. Going into about the sixth turn, neck-and-neck with three other girls, I slid out and dropped the bike. I jumped up and got going fast but at least ten riders passed me. I don't know what came over me but I poured it on like never before and started picking off riders one by one, and some in clumps of two and three. I had no idea that I had won, but the look on my husband's face said it all. I've never seen him so thrilled in my life. When I cleared that last jump and came down the other side of it, the first thing I saw was him jumping up and down and screaming.

Marie Whittaker, Ontario
1975 Suzuki GT750, "Water Buffalo," as a
    sidecar passenger, also known as the
    "swinger" or "monkey" position
Racer in vintage sidecar competition and
    elementary school secretary

I am an ordinary, middle-aged woman who likes to go fast and loves motorcycles. Racing sidecar is a team sport, which makes it unique in the world of motor sports. Being part of that team is much more exciting and satisfying than sitting on the back of a bike.

I got involved with racing because my husband was racing when I met him. He already had a sidecar passenger and women

were not on the track at that time. It was something that I always wanted to do. In the spring of 1999, a friend and I took part in our first race. We finished second.

What I love about riding, next to the racing itself, is the camaraderie. The people I work with think their secretary is "cool" and just a little crazy. My children don't say much about my passion for sidecar competition, but our youngest child is also a sidecar passenger. He enjoys it very much, which makes it a family hobby.

Jane Robinson, Australia
1991 Harley-Davidson FXR,
    "Scarlett O'Harley"
Drag racer and receptionist

*M*astering a heavy and powerful motorcycle has taught me that I can achieve anything if I put my heart and mind into it. Riding is the essence of freedom—woman and machine combining as one, leaning into corners and curbs, defying gravity at extreme angles of lean, and finding the rider's "sweet spot" with a perfect bisecting of the apex.

My first real experience of riding in heavy, and I mean heavy, rain occurred while I was coming back from an overnight trip. I was properly attired so I was warm and dry. I found myself laughing out loud at the ridiculous conditions, riding through blinding, torrential rain with sheets of water washing across the road, and thinking, "You wouldn't be dead for quids!"

Riding has increased my self-confidence and allowed me to make new and different friends, both male and female. And an accident I once caused taught me not to be overly cocky.

Debbie Knebel, South Carolina
1984 Suzuki GS1150/1327 race bike;
1998 Honda Hawk on the road
Drag racer with Team Vanson: SuperGas
 and Hot Rod Cruiser/ProStar 2002

I encourage people to strive to achieve whatever their desires are, regardless of what obstacles they believe are in their way. Obstacles should be viewed only as stepping stones to success; and of course, success is what you make of it.

I began my bike riding at age 37. After riding on the back of my husband's bike for about eight years, I decided to take a Motorcycle Safety Foundation course. Immediately after returning from my day-two lesson, I took my husband's Honda out for a ride. In 1994, two years after the MSF class, I attended my first drag race and was hooked. I now spend most of my two-wheel time on the track. Our off-time is usually spent preparing our equipment and catching up around the house. We both miss the road riding and hope to return soon!

Drag racing requires a certain amount of physical ability, but in the world of competitive motorcycling, drag racing would be the least demanding on the body. Therefore, I believe that any woman who passionately rides a bike and is skilled on the road will be capable of drag racing. Most local tracks are great places to learn; however, there are several motorcycle drag racing schools that will get you started.

Riding my motorcycle has taught me that God is awesome and that nothing compares to His love. He has allowed me to use my passion to show others His love.

Kerry Watson, Texas
2002 Kawasaki ZR-7
Car racing instructor

I am all about living and riding free. I'm now 45 years old, but when I was a teenager I met an old lady on a bus who told me she had always done everything people expected of her and never anything she wanted to do. She made me swear that I'd do what I wanted to do and I always have.

What I love about riding is how you are just right inside nature when you are riding; you feel the wind on your face, pushing your body. Riding has given me a lot of confidence, especially from motorcycle track school. I understand now how just a twitch or nervousness transmits immediately to your bike, and that is how life is. As I have learned on a bike, one mistake and your body suffers; in a car one mistake is just a spin or small car damage.

Jessica Zalusky, Minnesota
2003 Suzuki GSXR 750 and 1999 Ducati
 748s on the track; 1999 Yamaha YZF-R6
 on the road
Roadracer—AMA Pro Thunder and AMA 600
 Supersport

I got into racing after watching all the pro racers race at Brainerd and thought, I could do that. Then all the guys I was riding with on the street started to race and I thought, I can do that. So I converted my bike into a race bike, and on I went!

When you're at the starting line, your heart starts to pound fast. You have to relax because the guys around you are just about to jump the gun and you don't want to follow them. Also, you have to relax so that you don't take off and wheelie. You just want to be smooth on the start, try to get to the front of the pack and stay there.

I don't know why there are not more women on the track. It's a tough sport but I have found that most guys are accepting of me. I hear a lot of women say the opposite. I just try to be myself. At times I know I have had to prove myself to the guys. I have also tried not to let what everyone else thinks about me get to me. I have had a lot of critics who thought I was not ready to race, but critics will always be there. Personally, I enjoy racing with all of the guys and would not want it any other way. I'm not a complete tomboy. I just like having fun on the track and dressing up at night to go out if I want to! Riding and racing is a way for me to experience my life to the fullest.

Stephy Bau, Italy and Florida
2003 Honda CR 125 (3)
Professional Motocross champion

I started racing at six years old in my native country, Italy. My parents were always big fans of the sport. The first time I ever competed, I was the only little girl. I had no experience at all racing and I finished third in the first race in my life. After that race, I won every race that year. I was

hooked on the sport and have been racing ever since. I came to America four years ago and I'm the only woman right now to have a professional license to compete in the professional Motocross events with the men. We have a big enough league for the women, the Women's Motocross (MX) League, and we are considered professional, but still we don't get the money that the guys get.

I'm trying to break down barriers and it's so hard. Being a professional in this sport for a woman is still really tough. We put in the same energy and commitment as the professional men but we don't get paid the same. The best men get millions of dollars per year, the best women barely get by. The industry said that this is because the women are only 5 percent of the market for this sport, but if that's true, the number-1 woman should have 5 percent of the money that the number-1 man makes and that's a six-figure check.

Miki Keller from the Women's MX League is trying to make this change for the better for us, and I will keep pushing and trying to win titles to make this happen. Motocross is my life. Everything I do revolves around it. Sometimes it is sad that I don't have the true recognition that I deserve, but I think that if I keep working hard things will change. I will never give up! We are the best! It's a struggle. I love Motocross so much and want to be able to get paid fairly so that I can make a living and do what I love. I race all over the world; it is a job. You have to train hard, be healthy, and travel to the races. All of these expenses are on ourselves.

Eliane Pscherer, France
1998 Kawasaki Tomcat "Black Rocket";
2002 R1 Yamaha, " Pépette"
Road racer with Team OCTOPUSS
 and makeup artist

How cool to be a woman and live your passion for racing. I love to be energetic, to have the power of life, and to share this passion with others. I decided to create my moto-club, Team OCTOPUSS, in 1996 with a friend of mine who was dying to race too, Miss Fabienne Lerousic. Now we are thirteen women who compete in different championships. We organize free practices around French racetracks. My team helps the ladies learn the best solutions in motoracing. We help them with the first step on a racetrack, without fear, providing good advice on how to start racing if that is what they wish to do. On a track it's recreation time and you are finally allowed to go fast without fear of the police and other obstacles. It's not a shame to love the speed. You just have to choose the right place to speed so you can enjoy it, like on a track.

My most memorable race was when I took my first departure in the twenty-four hours of Le Mans and the Bol d'Or; my dream come true. My favorite part during such a long race is the nighttime because it's magical with the lights, and how the turns jump up into your face with the speed! WAHOU! Riding promotes the continuous way I enjoy living my life, free! Women need emotion, sensations, and respect, and the motorbike is a good answer to that, you'll see.

Judy Mirro, Vermont
1996 Ducati 900ss, 1986 BMW R80/1050
 on the road; 1996 Honda RS125GP on
 the track
Road racer, motojournalist, MSF instructor,
 track day instructor

I'm a self-taught, single rider who has always thought of myself as a motorcyclist first—and a woman second. I do not want to give you the impression that it has been stress-free—over the last 27 years of riding I have had my fair share of idiot encounters. I still hear the same one-liners I have heard since I was 18: "Aren't you a little small for that big bike?" "That your boyfriend's motorcycle?" "You gonna ride that all by yourself?" I have chosen to combat the occasional pig-headed attitude against women in my own way, with my own style. I prefer the one-on-one approach. "Kill 'em with kindness," I say. Smile a lot and pretend none of what they say matters. Maybe one day it will go away.

Not all encounters have passed quietly. While mingling among the mortals of the Midwest, I encountered a man [Judy now bites lip] who literally jumped out into the street and shouted, "You're not thinking of parking your motorcycle next to mine! You'll drop it into my bike! You're just a woman." I did park my motorcycle next to this man's bike, but not without a nasty exchange of words after he tried to grab my handlebars to take control of my machine. A few of his friends gathered around to apologize for his behavior and the next thing I knew he was trying to buy me a beer. I could have refused, but I knew that if we made peace, the next woman might park next to him without circumstance.

I can tell you many more of these stories, but why bother. They all sound the same. What really upsets me is the continued prejudice and discrimination against our younger women. When I hear professional racers talking about their sons being schooled for racing, but not their daughters, it bothers me. Why can we not all keep an open mind and allow our sons to be the future umbrella boys and our daughters to be the racers if that is what they choose? Would that be so terrible?

My old riding companion Bud once gave me a coffee mug for my birthday. I still use it daily, and it reads: "Whatever a woman does, she must do twice as well as a man to be considered half as good. *Luckily, this is not difficult.*" While the message is amusing, I realize that Bud was also trying to empower me, knowing the kind of prejudice I have had to endure. So what is all the fuss about? Women, men, motorcycles, it's all in the attitude. I look forward to the day I do not have to work so hard to help the world take notice of the fact that I am a motorcyclist first and a woman second.

Judy Mirro

Paula Strank, Pennsylvania
1998 KTM 125 SX
2001 and 2002 AMA District Five HillClimb champion and medical assistant

I take control when I'm hillclimbing my dirtbike. For those few seconds it's just me against the hill and whether I make it or not is entirely up to my own skills I have learned throughout the years. I work as a medical assistant during the week, living by someone else's rules. On the weekends when I race its all about going out and riding to the best of my ability, hoping to come home with that number one trophy. The feeling you get from riding your bike and conquering a hill is such a rush— knowing that you just made it to the top and got a fast time and hoping it was good enough to beat all the guys. I am one of only a few women that hillclimb and I race against the men.

I met my fiancé, Casey Kimble, through hillclimbing. He competes in the 251cc open ATV class. I got involved in hillclimbing because my father and brother raced. My parents didn't want me to ride because I was their little girl. I always loved hillclimbing and thought if the guys could do it then I could, too. My dad has since retired and my brother is National #2 in the Pro Hillclimb 800cc class. He was champion last year and lost the title this year by one point. I am an amateur hillclimber. He races for money. I race for trophies.

Nancy Montgomery, racing instructor for Keith Code's California Superbike School™

Photo: Ken Ryder

Mariola Cichon finds solo motorcycle travel a spiritually enlightening experience.

Photo courtesy Mariola

CHAPTER 8

Long-Distance Lovers

Man, the road must eventually lead to the whole world.
Ain't no where else it can go—right?

> —Jack Kerouac, *On the Road*

Those early mornings tearing up and down mountain passes as the sun
glares and fades, those late nights across the cooling deserts, the smells
of pine and wildflowers, are all why I ride. But the sharing around the
campfire at the end of the day with like-minded riders is what makes it
so much sweeter. Even if it weren't for the intense feelings I get from
riding, those totally alive and in love with life feelings, I value the
people I've met through the miles, and sMiles.

> —Voni Glaves, tour leader, Ayres Adventures

Long-distance lovers. It's about the romance of the road, between
rider, motorcycle, and road: the perfect ménage à trois. My shero, Fran Crane,
God bless her and rest her soul, was testimony to this statement. Fran was an
explorer and completely seduced by the road's magic. She was a beautiful
iron Godiva with her waist-length hair dancing in the wind as she charged
along on her chrome horse through twists and turns as if she were dancing
on air. Fran lived by the credo "The greatest pleasure in life is doing what
people say you cannot do." And she rode her motorcycle in testimony to that
statement by getting into the *1988 Guinness Book of World Records* for riding

from New York to San Francisco in a record 44 hours and 29 minutes.

Fran was a very active member of the Iron Butt Association and would regularly participate in their butt-burning marathon rides, which included three Iron Butt Rallies riding 11,000 miles in 11 days. The Iron Butt rally is particularly grueling because one must arrive at specified check points at a certain time or be penalized, and collect bonus points by riding to obscure locations, proving their presence by taking a Polaroid photo holding their official Iron Butt rally flag. She was a tough competitor and will be remembered forever among women riders as a true pioneer of the motorcycle lifestyle and sport.

The lady long-distance lover adores destiny, adores the journey. To her, it's not about the destination; that's just a cherry on top of a gigantic banana fudge road. It's the ride. During her voyage she welcomes the unknown, the unpredictable, that which is out of her control. Wide-open spaces and the whole world are her asphalt playground. Twisties and canyon carving are chances to intimately deep-tango with the road.

The journey is a place to lose and find yourself. The highway beckons the rider to travel its endless ribbons. According to Mongolian Shamanism,[19] which focuses on personal power and inviting good fortune, "Everyone has their own universe, everyone has their own path." The road is a path to reinvent one's self and abandon the draining rigors of everyday life and responsibility. What better way to do this than on a motorcycle, where one cannot help but open up to the supernatural circumstances that

happen on long-distance rides. The "wind horse" is one's personal psychic power and a prayer offering to the wind according to Shamanism. "By being conscious of wind horse . . . one can walk one's life path in power, in safety, and with good fortune. This attitude toward life creates self-awareness in one's actions and consciousness of how individual actions shape one's own fate." Sounds like wind horse attitude is a breed kindred with iron horse attitude. Extreme self-awareness and indescribable elation is what occurs mile after blessed mile on a motorcycle.

For me riding distance is the perfect zen. I enter into that joyous contemplative place akin to a sweet daydream. It is the moment of complete union: body, mind, soul, emotion, which equals perfect liberty for me and wide-open fun. The art of travel is accepting the journey that lies ahead that belongs only to the rider, the one who is in perfect agreement with embarking upon the voyage of abandonment. When the rider embarks upon a long-distance journey, she invites life transformation and this promotes clarity and awareness for untold miles as landscape reels by the rider and morphs with environmental transformation.

If I didn't have to stop to fuel the scoot, heck, I'd just keep on riding. A few times I've ended up sleeping on my bike, parked under a safe, cozy canopy of trees. Riding long distance entices the road magic to occur on many levels.

One of the greatest gifts that a rider can allow herself on a journey is to release all fear and inhibition and allow the opportunity for adventure to work into her life while on the ride. Many people are surprised when they learn that I often ride extreme long distances "soulo." It's great fun for me because it's so unpredictable and it's a great adventure at every turn. Anything can happen. That adventure is the ultimate opportunity for me to let go and let God because I can't control everything that will happen on the road. I simply must let the magic happen.

Whether trotting the globe, gypsy riding, or entering Iron Butt competitions, there are many women who abandon life as they know it for a little while as they venture out free and uninhibited, satisfying their wanderlust and enjoying the endless adventures on the open road as long-distance lovers.

Voices from the Distance

Airyn Darling, Washington
1993 BMWK1100RS, "Grak"
Student and writer

R iding has had a huge impact on my life. I've never been short on confidence in general, but until I began riding motorcycles, I didn't understand how capable I am of handling pretty much anything life throws in my direction. The knowledge that I really don't need to rely on someone else for my own well-being is incredibly liberating! Further, when riding, I largely leave schedules behind. The only things to worry about are gas stops and the next curve in the road. Getting away from stress and frustration on the bike is absolutely invaluable, and I'm free to set my own pace, ride my

own ride, and operate entirely on my own terms.

There isn't a particular "lifestyle" that comes mandatory with riding—anyone can ride, from the tiniest, quietest young woman to the elderly great-grandmother, and everyone in between. Just be yourself, ride your own ride, and don't feel the need to justify yourself to anyone! Keep your own lifestyle, or choose any elements of other lifestyles as you desire—we're all part of one huge, diverse family, and as Sasha likes to say, we're all sisters in the wind. Get out there and go, girl!

I belong to the Iron Butt Association, because that's where the long-distance touring/competing lunatics congregate. I've completed single- and multi-day rallies, and a bunch of solo endurance rides, and I've met the kindest, coolest, most generous people in this community. These are great folks, and even without the riding, I'd want to spend time with them.

The guy I was dating in 1996 rides, and for a while I rode pillion. I have always been interested in motorcycles, but labored under the delusion that there was virtually no margin for error in terms of stability, and that I would kill myself inside of two weeks. Riding behind him, I quickly realized that riding was a lot less dangerous than I previously believed, and I said, "Screw this—I wanna drive!" With bike ownership came addiction, and it hasn't released its grip yet.

Motorcycle riding has given me more confidence, and a sense of satisfaction that I can get out there on my own, forge through life's complications, enjoy the good times, weather the bad times, and come through it all without fear. It's put me in touch with some of my best friends, and they have enriched my life immeasurably. Riding has made me a better person on numerous levels.

Linda Babcock, Colorado
1998 Yamaha XT 225; 2001 BMW 650GS; 2001 BMW R1100RT
International tour director for Ayres Adventures

I can't believe how a decision to ride a motorcycle has changed my whole life. My husband and I are now motorcycle tour leaders. We are on our way to South America for two months to help pre-scout and finalize routes in six countries for our upcoming South American tours. I still have to pinch myself to make sure it's not all a dream. But then, that's what started it all!

I am involved in several clubs, some of which are local and some national. I began by joining the BMW Club of Colorado. From there I discovered and joined the BMW MOA, BMW Riders Association, the Oilheads, the Chain Gang, BMW Riders of Pikes Peak, Edmonton Black Gold Beemers, and the Iron Butt Association.

I became involved with motorcycles when I dated someone who had a BMW motorcycle. I knew I was hooked the first time I threw my leg over the saddle. I totally fell in love with riding. After we parted ways I knew that I wanted to continue riding, so I decided to buy my own bike and take the MSF course and I started visiting motorcycle dealerships.

Once I bought my bike and after a lot of practice and a few tip-overs, I decided it was time to strike out on my own on a solo early morning Sunday ride. I figured there'd be little traffic, so I gathered up as much courage as I could and breathlessly launched into my new life. It was great! One thing led to another and eventually I met more motorcyclists. Before I knew it, I was on my way to Sturgis. Even though I had only ridden a couple of months, never been on an interstate, and accumulated a grand total of 800 miles' riding experience, I was eager. I consider that trip my right of passage! Since then, I've ridden to the Arctic Circle, done numerous Iron Butt Association long-distance rides, participated in a couple of Canadian long-distance endurance rallies, ridden to the bottom of Mexico's Copper Canyon, spoken on panels, and had articles written about me.

My fellow employees were skeptical of my love for motorcycles at first. They thought I was crazy, but the more I rode to the different places I was always going to on weekends, the more questions they started asking. Finally, it became the norm to say, "So how many states did you visit this weekend?" My children were very concerned at first, too. They thought it was too dangerous for me to be riding. They tried to discourage me as much as they could. It was as if roles had reversed. "Where are you going? What time will you be back? Who're you going with?" It was quite amusing.

Riding has given me more confidence in myself, a broader view of life, and a huge cross-section of friends. I'm less judgmental;

more loving and more forgiving. What I learned from riding, too, is that if I really want to do something, I mean REALLY want to do something, I focus on it and never give up. If you're passionate about something, then follow your dream until it comes true.

Carol "Skert" Youorski, Georgia

2003 BMW K1200RS, "K Dancer";
1998 MuZ Baghira 660, "Mardi"
Surgical assistant

Riding my "Dancer" through the twisties is my free dance. My bike leads me into a wild dance. A dance that is exciting and one of a kind, at least until the next one. I follow my bike's every motion, holding gently to the throttle, clutch, break, and hugging the tank with my thighs. What an incredible feeling to have so much power leading me to ecstasy.

I am a member of American Motorcyclists Association (AMA) because AMA is working to support my rights as a motorcyclist. I am a member of the BMW Motorcycles of America so I can hang with other BMW riders around the country. I am a member of the BMW Motorcycles of Georgia to contribute to my own state's club. I am a member of the Swamp Scooters of Louisiana because I love the way they party and cook, and my best friend is president. I am a member of the Twisty Sisters in Georgia and Two Wheels Only Motorcycle Resort.

When I was 20, a man said I could ride his dirt bike if I could pick it up. I, a strong tomboy kind of girl, could not budge that bike. I figured I could never ride a motor-

cycle because I just wasn't strong enough. Years passed and it wasn't until I saw a BMW K100 that the fever for a motorcycle first caught in my mind.

While at an open air concert with one of my best friends we talked about some of our life's dreams. I said I'd like to go on one of those motorcycle camping trips. She said there is one problem, we need some guys to take us. *Not!* I said let's go take one of those MSF courses and learn to ride our own. The rest is history.

I have ridden nine years now and well over 200,000 miles. I have dedicated my trips to sharing with other motorcyclists, especially women, a simple way to pick up a bike if you drop it. I hope no woman ever goes 20 years thinking she can never ride a motorcycle because she can't pick it up.

Almost all the people I work with live vicariously through me for their adventures. I can't say how many people, especially women, say to me they wish they had my nerve. My kids think it's cool that I have a passion for motorcycles. I have taught my daughters to ride, and my son is next. They are used to hearing from me well over a thousand miles away in one day.

Motorcycling has made me so much more independent, so much more confident, so much more in control of myself. Being a woman who rides her own has given me the idea that I can do anything I set my mind to. I travel all over the U.S. to encourage other women to do the same. I have learned to trust my instincts, and to believe I really do know how to do something and do it well.

Erin Ratay, New York
1997 BMW F650
Professional career counselor

My husband, Chris, and I were former New York City dwellers for whom life was going pretty well. We always enjoyed motorcycling and traveling, and slowly realized that our annual two-week summer vacation just wasn't enough. So, we quit our jobs, sold our apartment (huge profit) and our furniture, donated most of our clothing, and became instant minimalists. And now we're traveling around the world on our own tour. The best experience on our ultimate journey has been meeting so many great, generous, friendly people all over the world, from all walks of life. We started this trip dreaming about all the wonderful things we would see and thought that that would be the ultimate experience. Now, it's not what we've seen (which indeed has been spectacular), so much as, who has touched us. It's given me a whole new perspective on the positive nature of humanity.

My advice to any female rider who wants to take a long trip is don't hesitate, do it. I've met several solo female motorcyclists on the road doing what we are doing. I admire them most for their courage to travel by themselves. Once you commit to the idea, then everything else falls into place. The logistics of it are like anything else. Finally, you are never alone. There are many other travelers out there doing this (it's not a boys club!), and millions of people are available to help you when you need it. No matter what country we've visited, everyone loves motorcycle travelers!

It's extremely liberating and a whole new way of living to just abandon life as you've known it and just head out on the open road. Our day is our own, which means we work or play when we want. Every day is not a holiday like most people would think. Just the daily act of navigating from one place to another, asking directions, getting lost, finding a place to stay and decent food to eat can be a real chore in a country where you don't speak the language. We've spent seven to ten days at a stretch repairing the bikes when they've broken down, searching for parts on the Internet, working with local mechanics. But it is always our choice; no one is standing over us telling us what to do.

Traveling on our motorcycles has opened me up to the diversity of the world and taught me to appreciate that everyone is generally good, but that we all have differing opinions. We were in New Zealand on 9-11-01 and were comforted by all of our friends both there and around the world. We got e-mails and phone calls of support from every corner of the earth. Not everyone agrees with the policies and actions of the U.S. government, but our international friends were there for us during that tragedy. It made me look at the world more like one big family rather than a world made up of different nations. I hope I carry this feeling with me always and look at everyday things through those glasses.

The old saying "You only live once" is a deeply meaningful statement. One should always try to follow their dreams. Don't let anyone dissuade you from following your dreams, because you only have one life to live. Have the courage and confidence to live it the way you want to live it!

Dee Gagnon, Colorado
1986 Honda Interceptor 500, "Red Pony";
   1987 Honda VFR Interceptor 700
Motorcycle traveler; journalist; author
   of *DeeTours*[20]

I basically bought a motorcycle for cheap transportation and had no idea the life-changing impact it would have on me. It's been cool to be a role model or inspiration for others because I ride alone long distances. My journeys make people think about their own lives and what they dream to be doing.

DeeTours happened because I had been in a job where morale had gone down due to corporate downsizing and I had had a very bad motorcycle accident, so I was out of work for months and had to reflect and think about my life. I read travel dialogue books about traveling through small-town America. Those books really inspired me, so I thought, I'm going to go back to work, save up as much money and time as I can, and instead of getting laid off or transferred, I'm going to take things into my own hands and take a trip on my motorcycle like never before.

I didn't set out to write a book, but as the trip unfolded day by day, I realized the possibilities. I was making an impact on people everywhere because I was inspiring them! I was having the time of my life doing what I wanted to do, riding my motorcycle and having new experiences.

Going the distance on a motorcycle brings out all the human qualities like strength and bravery. At times, I feel very brave, like when I ride in bad weather using every ounce of strength and concentration to stay on the road; but when I'm in a situation like that, I haven't got a choice. You can't pull over to the side of the road and wait it out when the wind is so bad that it'll knock you right over if you slow down or try to stop. The more faith you have the more you're able to recognize things, like when coincidences happen. When you have to draw on your inner self to survive, it's a very spiritual experience. My books are a legacy that I'll leave behind and my motorcycle has enabled me to do that.

Freedom on a motorcycle is like freedom on a horse. At the tips of my fingers I hold enormous power, speed, and I'm in control of that. I realize that in the blink of an eye I can lose everything or gain everything. At the end of every long ride or harrowing ride I hug my motorcycle and say, "thank you, Pony, for bringing me home safely." My "Pony" has over 150,000 miles and I bought it brand new.

Mary Sue "SuzyQ" Luetschwager, Indiana
1997 Ultra Classic Harley-Davidson,
   "Black Beauty";
1997 BMW R1100R, "Butt Buster"
Truck driver

I was the first woman to finish the Iron Butt Rally on a Harley and I was a grandmother when I started riding a motorcycle. I don't sit home and bake cookies anymore! Learning to ride took courage, strength, and determination. It hasn't always been easy, but the rewards are pretty neat!

When you ride you are usually admired in one way or another. Some people have never been to 49 states and other countries. I have, and 48 of those states were visited on a motorcycle. The energy that allows me to do this is my female spirit, set free. The birds flying in the sky couldn't enjoy that any more than I enjoy my ride.

After a broken engagement, I rode off to Sturgis, South Dakota, as a passenger on a Moto Guzzi with two truck driver friends for a "getaway" adventure. One of them let me ride the Guzzi around the campground a couple of times, and the other told me after the second try that I was a natural. I came back home, bought a new bike, and after a scary first 500 miles, took an MSF course. I've been riding ever since!

I love the way that riding clears my head. I like the feeling. It's euphoric! Inner peace! A feeling of total accomplishment. One with the machine. I love the way total strangers come up to you and want to take a picture of you and your bike. The feeling of respect from total strangers. Their envy. The beauty of the ride. I love everything about motorcycles.

My fellow employees and my friends admire the fact that I ride. One of them read the book Ron Ayres wrote about the 1995 Iron Butt Rally, and said, "*You* were in that book! You are a famous person!"

My daughter's husband had a fatal accident on a motorcycle, just one year before I started riding. I was afraid to tell her that I had bought a motorcycle and was riding. However, I rode the BMW to one of her

son's graduations, and he said, "Grandma, you made me the envy of all the graduates, riding up on the motorcycle. I was so proud of you!" My children all accept the fact that I ride, although at first I believe they thought I was crazy. Now, four of my children ride, some more than others, and one still rides as a passenger occasionally.

From riding, I have learned that if you want to do something enough, and have enough patience, you can usually accomplish it, if you are physically able to do so.

Nicky Austin, England
1987 Suzuki GT550; 1998 Suzuki GSF
    1200S Bandit
Motorcycle courier

I love riding anywhere anytime. Touring and rallying are how I spend most of my time on the bike. I do not have a car driver's license so my bike is also my transportation to work. I like the absolute freedom I have. I can go anywhere and do what I want anytime. I do a lot of camping when traveling on the bike. An important thing I learned from riding is that the only limits we have are the ones we give ourselves.

Camping on a motorcycle is fantastic. The best thing in Australia has been falling asleep under the stars. It's hard not to become complacent about it. When you get to do something wonderful every day and night for a long period of time, it is easy to forget how lucky you are. Generally speaking, though, I love having everything I own and need on the back of the bike. I can be totally self-sufficient. As long as I take plenty of water I don't need to stop in caravan parks.

Many people, both men and women, often question me about my solo wanderings. Most of the time there isn't anyone available to come with me. I tend to do things on a whim without really thinking.

It's absolute madness to be a motorcycle courier! It was fun filtering up through the middle of the traffic, but it can be pretty dangerous. We had a lot of laughs on the two-way radios. I was on the same channel as the push bike couriers and those guys are crazy. There is a great support system, though. If anything happens to anyone they just get on the radio and within minutes there's couriers coming from every direction to help sort out whatever the problem is. It's hard work, too.

Having my own bike certainly gave me an independence that many people never get a chance to have. I often wonder if I would have gotten into bikes if Dad hadn't been a biker. He has a photo of me at three using a paint brush and petrol to clean engine parts. He also used to take me everywhere on the back of his bike. I can remember my parents buying me my first helmet. I was seven years old. In the bike showroom they had a big turntable in the window showcasing a bike. I sat on it going 'round and 'round and I could hear Mum saying to Dad, "But what if she doesn't like it, it's a lot of money to spend." Dad just laughed and said, "Of course she'll love it."

There are so many trips I want to do. My dream is that I can continue to do all these wonderful things. The ability to go somewhere is more important than where you are going. Just go for it. If you don't, you'll never know if you could have done it or not.

Susan Johnson, Washington
1986 BMW R80/GS, "Beemerbago," a.k.a. "The White Elephant"
Business and technology consultant

I don't drive a motorcycle, but I navigate as a passenger. My husband and I have traveled around the world from north to south, to over 26 countries in Europe, Africa, and South America, successfully completing an odyssey that only a few hundred people in the world have accomplished.

While still traveling, we published our travel stories and photos on our web site, which we have now expanded to become Horizons Unlimited, the largest, best-known, and most respected motorcycle travel information site on the web. Horizons Unlimited is a global motorcycle club, with 172 Horizons Unlimited Motorcycle Travelers' Communities in 58 countries. The Communities enable motorcycle travelers, both those on the road and those at home, to meet up with like-minded people.

Some destinations require a greater degree of rider attention than your hometown does, but so does the big city just down the road from your home. You simply need to be alert, and use common sense. Remember, home will still be there, unlike the wild animals in Africa, the fascinating culture of the people of Bhutan, and the unspoiled beauty of places like Sipadan or Namibia.

Our lifestyle has been determined by our desire to travel the world by motorcycle. We work and save, then travel and spend. We have no children, and until we finished our first round the world (RTW) in 1998, all of our possessions fit into a storage locker. We expect to continue traveling as long as possible, both for a second RTW, and to return to favorite places, such as Africa. For me, the best thing about traveling is not knowing what's around the next corner. For some people, that would be the worst thing about traveling, but I love surprises!

I was scared at the beginning. But each country that we visited gave us the confidence to take the next step. And people are people, all over the world. Newspapers and TV like to emphasize the worst aspects of every country; that's how they sell papers. Use common sense, put yourself into other people's shoes, stay patient and keep smiling, and you can get through almost anything.

Patty Meehan, Louisiana
2002 Harley-Davidson Heritage Softail
  Classic, "Baby"
Speech-language Pathologist

As I've grown older, I have become more and more aware of my spirit and its need to be free. I suppose that's why I've been in love with bikes for as long as I can remember, and that's why I'm happiest when I'm riding. Riding is the epitome of freedom, having all that power under me, belonging just to me, to fly wherever I want to go; and the freedom to be out there on my own, taking in all that is around me, the sights, the smells, the sensations. My mom, an incredible lady, taught me that I can and will do whatever my spirit leads me to. Being female is irrelevant. I know that.

I've been drawn to motorcycles since I was I kid. I don't know why, as no one in my large, middle-American, Catholic family rides. Motorcycles have made my heart thump for as long as I can remember. As a kid, I rode the neighbor's dirt bikes. Then in college, I hung out with the local bikers and learned about the mechanics. I love mechanical things and things with motors that go fast. I've wrenched on my own bikes as much as possible. Bikes have always been in my heart and my spirit. My favorite aspect of the ride is the freedom and strength that it gives my spirit, and the brotherhood and sisterhood shared with other bikers.

I just returned from a 3,500-mile solo trip from home, Louisiana, to Colorado, to visit a dear friend. It was an incredible trip and one that I will remember forever. I can't wait to head out on my next great adventure.

Riding allows me to be who I am and has taught me that I am a complete and whole person in and of myself, and that I am responsible for my own happiness.

Doris Maron, Canada
2001 Honda Magna 750, "Untamed Spirit"
Retired financial advisor

I made the decision to travel around the world in December 2000, to put my working life on hold and experience the freedom of living. Many of my well-meaning friends and family tried to discourage me with their own fears, but I kept my focus on the goal.

I started riding motorcycles in 1989 after taking the motorbike safety training course. The first year took me south along the Oregon and California coastline to the Mexican border. What an experience that was, riding the curves along the coast! I certainly felt my inexperience as a rider. Coming back through Arizona I saw the Grand Canyon for the first time. Another great adventure! In 1992, I bought a Tiny Mite tent trailer and traveled in luxury. It was a real treat not to sleep on the ground. This year was my first trip to Sturgis for the rally and my first trip to a GWRRA Wing Ding, which was held in Madison, Wisconsin. In 1994, I went to the Wing Ding in Albuquerque, New Mexico, with other members of the GWRRA Chapter in Edmonton.

One of my older brothers came home with a motorcycle one day and I knew right then that I wanted one. I didn't get one, though, because when I was growing up, girls didn't do such things as ride motorcycles. It wasn't until I was married and divorced that I pursued my dream. I was 41 when I took the Motorcycle Safety Training course and bought my first bike. I have been riding ever since and enjoying every minute of it.

My favorite aspect about riding is the freedom I feel when I'm on the road. The open air, the rain, the wind, even the snow and hail on occasion. I look back on each experience as a wonderful adventure. The people I have met since I started biking are also a favorite aspect. Many are great friends and some are distant acquaintances. More are strangers waiting to become friends.

Many people are surprised to find out I ride a bike—both fellow employees and new acquaintances. My children are very supportive of my riding passion. They were young when I started riding and often one of them would accompany me. I took them on long trips as well as short ones. My grandchildren love my bike also.

I used to be a shy person with very little self-confidence. Over the years I have worked hard on changing my life. I am a completely different person now than I was ten years ago—even one year ago.

Take the motorcycle training course and learn to ride safely. Then find a true friend to ride with and experience the road and nature. Don't be in a hurry. Take time to enjoy life. Enjoy today and don't worry so much about tomorrow. I have found that the things I worry about usually never happen so when I catch myself worrying, I remind myself of that.

Phyllis Lang, Pennsylvania
1999 Harley-Davidson Dyna Super Glide, "Traveler II";
BMW Funduro F650, "Pumpkin"
Motorcycle insurance agent and motorcycle safety instructor

What I love most about long-distance riding is the feeling of accomplishment. I love the freedom of the open road and it's important that I ride the most miles that I possibly can. It gets to be almost an obsession. When I ride alone, I can ride as far as I want, stop if I feel like it, or not stop at all. I am free with the wind in my face and the scenery flying by. I compete in the Iron Butt Association's long-distance endurance rallies because I adore riding long distances.

I love the challenge of riding the Iron Butt Rally—11,000 miles in 11 days. It's a wonderful adventure and special because my husband, Fritz, and I both love to ride the rally together on our own bikes. It's challenging and we enjoy spending time with the other members of the Iron Butt Association (IBA). The best aspect of the IBA is the attitude of all the other riders. People whom I considered my heroes talk to me and give me pointers. Ardys Kellerman is one of my sheroes in the IBA because she's an excellent rider, doesn't quit, and she's a great friend who shares the same passion for motorcycles and long distance.

Carla King, California
1984 Yamaha 650 Maxim;
1994 Ural Tourist Sidecar 650;
1985 Chang Jiang Sidecar 650;
1999 Royal Enfield Bullet 500;
2000 Moto Guzzi EV California 1000
Travel and technology writer and author,
   motorcycle travel journalist

I grew up in rural North Carolina and my family always had vehicles around— tractors, go-carts, and such. There was an old Honda 75 dual-sport rusting in our shed and my dad said that if I could fix it, I could ride it. So at 14 years old I learned something about the mystique of motorcycle mechanics and was soon zooming, bumping, and crashing through the tobacco fields and the woods, thrilled with my vehicle of escape.

All these years later I still find that motorcycles make the perfect traveling companions. They give me the independence I crave and help me to immerse myself in a journey, connecting me to a place in a way that traveling by car, bus, or train doesn't provide. I prefer to ride the indigenous motorcycle of a country when I travel: an Enfield in India, a Chang Jiang in China, a Moto Guzzi in Italy. Each machine is a representative of the culture, and I love the reaction I get from locals who are pleased to see me touring on their country's machine. By riding it I am less a tourist and more an ambassadress of the United States. These motorcycles have served as my entrée into the lives of people who rarely interact with outsiders and the experiences on both sides have been overwhelmingly positive.

Motorcycle travel has taught me many lessons about the inner and the outer world. It has taught me to be alert and absolutely present in the moment, that hurdling fears brings great reward, that engine troubleshooting is an extraordinarily creative process, and that independence is as much about your reliance on others as it is about self-sufficiency.

Elsie Smith, Maryland
1985 BMW K1000RT
Business Owner

Personally, I think riding a motorcycle has nothing to do with the female spirit set free and all the other "feminine" stuff. I think it has to do with the *human* spirit, male or female.

I belong to BMW Bikers of metropolitan Washington. It's nice to be part of something, and to serve the membership. I've been on the board most of my ten-plus years of membership. I have a design firm and work with friends to advertise their motorcycle-related products.

My youngest brother and his friends rode, did motocross, skydiving, and other "fun" stuff. I wanted to join them! That's how I got interested in motorcycles.

I am pretty straightforward, common sense, but I like to have fun. I like to travel, and motorcycling has allowed me to meet a lot of people in different areas of the country (and world) that I might not have met in some other sport. One of the most important things that I learned from riding is that God watches over me.

Mariola Cichon, Illinois
1998 Kawasaki KLR650
World motorcycle travel photojournalist

I find inspiration when I ride all around me . . . in the eyes of an elderly woman fascinated by my bike and by what I do . . . in a sunrise over the jungle . . . in the thousands of e-mails I receive from people all over the world from my website . . . in my children and millions of other young people who are so desperately searching for a reason to live.

Life is just a breeze. I do not want to just pass it. I want to experience, feel, love, cry, laugh, get angry, and then love again. The world is huge, but is it getting smaller and smaller, and more and more polluted by chemicals as well as by what we call civilization. To see it before I close my eyes has

always been a dream of mine ever since I can remember.

Above all I have learned from motorcycle riding that feeling young has nothing to do with age. Even though I am 42, I feel younger than ever. I have changed a lot since I started this journey nearly two years ago. I became more open to people, I have no trouble communicating with strangers, which is another thing I learned. There are no real boundaries between people. What we perceive as boundaries exists in our own minds. I used to wait for others to approach me with friendship and now I am usually the one who extends it first. I have learned to trust my instincts and my angels. They have saved my ass from trouble on countless occasions. I learned there is nothing impossible, really, I just have to keep my eyes and heart open, that is all.

My favorite thing about traveling the world is learning about different ways of life, and riding by motorcycle is by far the most favorite aspect of wandering the earth for me.

Please do not believe in boundaries. Women are strong, if not stronger, than men. We can do everything! All it takes is a bit of imagination and courage. The farther you go, the more courage you will have. What seems to be impossible at first turns out to be child's play from another perspective.

Erika Lopez, author, actor, and artist, adores her motorcycle and incorporates it into her creative works.
Photographer: Christina Shook © 2003

CHAPTER 9

The Bikerlady Artiste

wind in her face

springtime has a particularly sweet smell.
so sweet, you can almost taste it;
certainly, you can feel it,
when you ride with the wind
in your face.

the anxiety pours away
like water down the back of a swan.
listen.
the freedom of the open road beckons.
answer,
and it comes back to you
like a dear old friend,
happy to see you again.

you swear the hummmmmm of your motor
emanates from deep within your soul
and it does.

—Rose "Bams" Cooper

All women motorcyclists are poetry in motion. Some choose to take their gifts and infuse their free spirits into their artistic performances and presentations. The result is the bikerlady artiste.

Motorcycle riding inspires all of my artistic endeavors. My songs are filled with lyrics about riding and the music is composed based upon the rhythms and grooves of the road. My writing always seems to parallel the metaphors of riding a motorcycle: the road, the journey, the signs, the destiny, the independence, the reflection, the family, the cycles, the wheel, the landscape, the distance, the inhibition, the freedom.

Well, you can see how motorcycle riding can be so incredibly inspiring not only within everyday living, but in the world of art and performance, too. I hope that you, dear reader, see the true art of the motorcycle and how it affects the rider and inspires the artist. It has changed my life on many levels, but mostly it has opened the door to my creative spirit. I have discovered the breadth and depth of my personality as a work of art. I have unearthed my purpose in this lifetime as an artist and writer all through riding many miles on my motorcycle, which ultimately unleashed the power within me to come forth and present this book to you.

Voices from the Boulevard

Catherine Bell, California

2002 BMWR1100S; 2002 Honda CBR600F4i; 2002 Honda RC51; 2001 Yamaha R6; 1965 Honda Dream; 1978 Honda Hawk w/Hondamatic engine; 1965 Lambretta Scooter

Actress, star of the television series *J.A.G.* as Lt. Colonel Sarah (Mac) MacKenzie; co-star with Jim Carrey in Universal's feature film, *Bruce Almighty*

When I was 18, my cousin had a Honda 125cc street bike. I thought it was so cool. I asked him to show me how to ride. I totally loved the freedom and exhilaration that I felt being on a motorcycle. So I went out and bought a Honda Rebel, then a Yamaha YSR-50 and used it to commute to UCLA. I loved the reaction I would get when I'd take off my helmet (even though it wasn't a law back then, I always wore one and other protective gear: boots, gloves, proper clothes). People would always be in total shock that I was a girl and I thought it was so cool to shake up the "norm" like that.

What I love about motorcycles is the freedom, the open road, feeling the wind, and the air. Seeing the scenery without feeling closed-in like a car. Using your body to steer and move the bike. A lot of people think it's cool that I ride, though a few are worried, but I tell them I've been riding for over 12 years and never had even a scrape! They're definitely surprised. I'm expecting my first child and my husband and I plan on getting her on a bike as soon as she's ready!!

Riding has made me more in tune with other drivers because you're *hyper*-aware of your surroundings on a bike. I've developed more confidence to try new things, to do things that may originally have scared me. Motorcycle riding taught me that I'm braver than I thought and can do more than I thought I could. I tell women who are interested in learning to ride to take the safety course. It's vital! And the course gives you all the tools you need to feel comfortable starting out as well as the tools that will keep you safe.

Melissa Holbrook Pierson, New York
Author, *The Perfect Vehicle: What It Is
About Motorcycles*[21]

For me riding is a physical and emotional freedom. You're really mothering yourself on a motorcycle. The idea of doing something that is really only for your pleasure, it's not where you're giving pleasure to anybody else, you're not taking care of anybody else but yourself, is enormously freeing.

The big thing for me that motorcycles did is open a door and I looked through that door and saw that there was a whole other world on the other side of it, with people who were bound together by a passion for one thing. And that passion is really a passion for passion.

> " *I feel erotic while riding a bike . . . because it's such ecstasy.* "

You can't compare motorcycle riding with anything else. It has to do with the motorcycle's history and the role that it plays in our society and what it represents. Sitting on top of a motorcycle is a way of saying all these things: I'm a human being, I want to protect myself but I'm also willing to go up to the edge and look over it.

Life is a little bit about letting go and saying I can't hold on to everything. I cannot control everything and if I want to have pleasure or live, essentially, I'm going to have to say I'm willing to have a certain amount of faith. Riding is a faith-based occupation.

Stephanie Finochio, New York
2001 Suzuki GSXR 600
Professional stunt woman, actress, and
pro wrestler, "Trinity"

When I got my first bike and rode it . . . that was truly my spirit being able to fly. Motorcycles have been and always will be a part of my life.

Riding my bike is the essence of me, it's that little child, the woman, the tomboy all wrapped into one; it's elegant, yet macho; playful, yet dangerous; which equals excitement and freedom.

When I see my motorcycle or any motorcycle, for that matter, I zone out and there is no distracting me. I am drawn to it like a magnetic force and the energy is indescribable. Besides just loving bikes, I also wanted to make riding them one of my stunt specialties: trick riding, crashing, and maximizing my riding skills. I ride all types of bikes.

I feel erotic while riding a bike . . . because it's such ecstasy.

Lynelle Corbett, Colorado
1997 Harley-Davidson Dyna Super Glide
Founder of the Hardley Angels Motorcycle
Drill Team

I love music and I listen to tapes frequently when I ride, especially on group rides. I love to position myself last in line and watch the bikes gliding along curvy mountain roads as a unit. We live and ride in some of the most beautiful country on earth. With a backdrop of majestic snow-capped peaks, lush forests, clear lakes, and brilliant blue skies, those orchestrated group rides inspired me to start choreographing routines so more people could appreciate the beauty and grace of dancing motorcycles.

You'd think that riding skill would be at the top of the criteria list for being on the team, but it's not. More important to us are attitude, cool-headedness, and commitment. That's what makes people like it and stick with it. We like for potential members to approach us rather than us trying to talk someone into it.

After eight years, we've built our repertoire of maneuvers, stunts, and routines so that as the show changes each year, only a few new elements are added. Through this unique form of entertainment, the team educates audiences in motorcycle control and rider safety, promotes goodwill between motorcycle riders and their communities, and encourages women to step outside of a comfort level for challenge, personal growth, and achievement.

Brenda Fox, California

2000 Harley-Davidson Softail Deuce
Model, stunt woman, actress, spokesperson,
  host, Baja 1000 off-road racer

Motorcycling adds a sense of adventure to life. Riding breaks down barriers and opens up opportunities to meet incredible people from a wide variety of backgrounds. It has enhanced my life and it sure

makes getting to your destination point a lot more enjoyable. Jumping on my bike, riding down the open road, brings me to the present moment. I find it excellent for relaxing my mind, releasing stress, and finding parking in Los Angeles.

I have always had a passion for custom bikes, and riding with master artist builders like Arlen Ness and Jesse James probably directed me to find motorcycle-related work. For fifteen-plus years, I've had the opportunity to work with incredibly creative, talented people in the motorcycle business and I've enjoyed working with legendary stunt coordinator, Gary Baxley. Out of all the bikes that I enjoy, riding an awesome chopper is my absolute favorite.

Maria Willers, Nevada

1972 Harley-Davidson FLH, "Harlet";
1987 Harley-Davidson Heritage Softail,
  "Misty Dragon";
2001 Suzuki Intruder Volusia, "Ms. Smoking
  Hottie";
1971 Honda dirt bike, "Grey Lady"
Performer, The Victor McLaglen Motor Corp.
  (VMMC)

I'm the first woman to ever join the all-male motorcycle stunt and drill team The Victor McLaglen Motor Corp., which has been in existence for almost seventy years. I've been a member and have traveled all over the country for over two and a half years now. I needed a challenge in my life after I almost lost it three years ago due to illness. I thought trying out for the Corp would force me to improve physically, something I needed badly. I got that, but I also gained a family and pushed myself past anything I have ever tried to do before.

My most memorable ride has been performing with the VMMC as a woman rider for the first time in the corp's existence and in the event's history, at the Love Ride. Riding motorcycles has opened up a whole new world for me. And it's taught me that I'm never too old to learn something new or to experience something different or to try something people say I can't do because I'm a woman.

What you read negative in the newspapers or see in the older biker movies is *not* what motorcycling is about. Some of the most amazing people I have ever met ride motorcycles, and they are usually some of the nicest people, too.

Cris Sommer-Simmons, Hawaii

1988 Harley-Davidson Heritage Softail
Singer, songwriter, award-winning motorcycle journalist, columnist for *Hot Bike Japan*, and author of "Patrick Wants to Ride"[22]; co-founder of the former *Harley Women* magazine, 2003 inductee to the National Motorcycle Hall of Fame and Museum

My first memory of getting hooked on motorcycles was at age 9 when my stepfather took me riding with him. He says he couldn't leave the house without me. I fell in love with motorcycles then and have been involved ever since. I rode as a passenger until I learned how to ride dirt bikes at 14 and got my own first street bike, a Yamaha 100, at age 16. I got my first Harley, a 1977 Sportster, at age 22 (in 1979) and have had at least one Harley ever since.

In 1983, my best friend, Jo Giovannoni, and I started the second chapter of Women in the Wind, an all-women's motorcycle club. A few years later, after feeling a huge void in the industry for the woman rider, we founded *Harley Women* magazine. It became the world's first motorcycle magazine for women. The magazine was sold twice, withstood two name changes, and is still going strong, being publisher today as *Woman Rider* magazine.

My first time riding to Sturgis was in 1981 where I only saw one other woman rider. Back then, there were very few women riding their own bikes. It was nothing like it is today. One of my most memorable rides was when I crossed the Big Horn Mountains in Wyoming on a summer night in 1982; I had no idea what the sign "Open Range" meant. There were more animals in the road than I have seen in my life. Two giant beef cattle ran out in front of me and I had only a second to react. Instead of hitting the brakes, I had to speed up fast and ended up going right between the two huge beasts. My life flashed before my eyes that night. I learned a valuable lesson that stays with me to this day: Do not attempt to cross the mountains at night!

When my older kids were small they were so used to seeing me ride with my girlfriends, they thought everyone's mommy rode motorcycles. It's not really a big deal to them. Their friends seem more impressed than they are. All my kids, Lindsey, Josh, and Patrick Harley, know how to ride dirt bikes.

Riding motorcycles hasn't really changed my life, in the sense that it has always been a big part of my life. I can't imagine where I would be without them. I have so many wonderful memories from riding and have met most of my best friends through motorcycling. And through my passion for motorcycles is how I met my husband, Pat, at the Sturgis Motorcycle Rally in 1989, a defining moment in my life.

Sam Morgan, Florida

1929 Indian 101 Scout, "Lily";
1931 Indian 101, "Bess" (wall bike)
Motor Drome trick rider with American Motor Drome Company's "Wall of Death" (Wall is owned, built, and ridden by Big Jay Lightnin')

I ride a 1931 Indian 101 Scout motorcycle, performing tricks and fancy acrobatics while riding up on the side of a 90-degree (straight up and down) wooden barrel wall. Sonny Pelaquin, my mentor and "dad," took me off the streets and showed me how to ride the drome. Here I was 15 lying for 18. I learned to ride the wall on an Indian 70. Not much power so you had to throw yourself up onto the track then throw yourself up onto the wall. Sonny was an excellent teacher. He gave me my great life and taught me how to be a trickrider and showman.

There's four of us in our crew right now. I was the only woman rider here for most of my life, and still the only trickrider. In the old days there were many women show performers. They did their acrobatics on the bikes all made up with their lipstick and painted fingernails. They were very feminine, gorgeous women who climbed all over the motorcycles—strong, awesome women. Sonny used to call me "The Mile-a-Minute Girl" after Alice Brady, a famous rider from the twenties. His mother, Viola, rode with his dad until she had her first child in 1929.

Motorcycles are my life. It's like breathing. When I go up on the wall, I ride by the odds. I try to keep my odds down. It's like drawing. When you create something, it comes from within. . . . Nobody can ever take that away from you. Everything you do

Sam Morgan, renowned trick rider blissfully engaged in her passion, riding the wall.
Photo by Don Daniels

up on the wall is all yours. There happens to be extra adrenaline there (goes with the G-force), as well as a mental discipline, which makes one stronger. It's a gift.

Christina Shook, California
1980 BMW R100S, "Bing";
1978 Yamaha XS11, "Wells";
2001 Suzuki Bandit, "Candice"
Motorcycle photographer

I love the power, energy, and strength of the bike. I love embracing this traditionally male world: the danger, the physicality, the mechanics, the grease, the sweat, the helmet hair, the leather and heavy boots. I make it mine, and therefore, feminine.

Each of the women motorcyclists that I have photographed have served as an inspiration to me. I feel a portrait is a two-way proposition between photographer and subject. There is some affinity I feel for these women that I am able to capture their character and spirit. Their passion for bikes shines through and even the shyest woman will open up when it is about her and her bike.

Through my forthcoming photojournalism project, *Truth & Beauty: A Portrait of Women Bikers*, I have learned to delve deep into a subject and take a single topic to new levels of insight and purpose. I have been fortunate to find subjects that hold so much appeal and mystique. Within the topic of women bikers I have been able to study endurance, beauty, perseverance, and the influence and interaction of the traditional male and female roles.

Meredithe "Shorty" Freidel, South Dakota
2001 American Ironhorse Ranger T
Model and spokesperson

*M*otorcycles let me express that we may have tits, but we can get on the bike and ride it as good as and sometimes better than any man! We can do this while looking beautiful, being pregnant, and at the same time know how to cook and clean! No man can say he can do that!

I enjoy doing motorcycle promotions and poster modeling because I can ride my bike, party, and meet some of the coolest people in the world, and make a bike payment all at once. I love it when I'm admired for being a good-looking girl, but when they know I'm a good-looking girl who can ride, well, better watch out. I love the respect.

Rose "Bams" Cooper, Michigan
2001 Buell Blast, "Hot Sauce";
2003 Harley-Davidson Heritage Softail Classic, "Centurion"
Poet, movie critic, and co-author of *3 Black Chicks Review Flicks*[23]

*T*ruly, you meet the nicest people on motorcycles. One of the reasons is because riders have a love for being on a motorcycle; this feeling extends through most of their lives especially when we congregate with other like-minded people. You have this great joy when you ride that's incomparable to almost anything else.

Michigan to Atlanta was my first long solo ride, riding my husband's 1997 Harley-

Davidson Ultra Classic. I love riding that bike and you can't help but smile when riding that big "bagger." The funniest reaction I ever got was when I was rolling into one of the local grocery stores and this guy saw me pull up, put the bike on the side stand, take off my helmet. I'm walking toward him and he says to me, "Did you ride that bike all by yourself?" I said, "Oh no. My husband's at home with the remote control to the bike and he'll let me know when it's time to go home and then he'll steer me home." And the guy believed me.

The term "cager" makes perfect sense when you're in the car. You have this strange feeling like you're caged in and you don't really know that you're caged in until you're not caged in anymore. When you ride a motorcycle for the first time and you realize that it's so open, you can't ever go back to feeling comfortable in a car again.

Molly Culver, New York
2002 Ducati 998; 1999 Harley-Davidson
  Fat Boy, "Barney Bad Ass"
Actress, co-star of the television series *V.I.P.*,
  "Tasha Dexter"

A few years ago I went to Ducati Revs America in Las Vegas to try the new bikes that Ducati had to offer. I was with all the top racers on the track and they showed me how far you can lean a bike over. By the second day of riding, I was absolutely dragging my knee in the turns.

Not a lot of people know what it's like to go 140 mph through a turn. When it's right and it's perfect, it's magical. Riding motorcy-

cles is the closest you can come to flying.

What's awesome about being a woman rider is that I don't have the ego that men do. I don't have to get out there on the track and beat the guy. My goal is to beat my own time, take that turn better, or known my line better. I'm definitely an advocate for women in motorcycles. I think that women take comfort in seeing a girl like me get on a bike. Anybody can do it.

I like who I am when I'm on a motorcycle. It feels like I do better for myself. It feels like I give myself a gift when I'm on a bike. When I think about the purity of riding, like on my Harley or on a dirt bike, it feels really close to something very natural. I'm more peaceful. My disposition is right on. When I'm on a bike it doesn't feel like I should or could be doing anything else but what I'm doing.

Ann Ferrar, New York
1993 Yamaha Virago 1100;
2002 Kawasaki Voyager XII
Author, *Hear Me Roar: Women, Motorcycles
  and the Rapture of the Road*

When I learned to ride, I went through the same metamorphosis as most of the women that I wrote about in my book. The confidence building, and learning to master the machine really did transfer into other aspects of my life. That was a wonderful experience. The motorcycle changed my life. With it, I became a more open person, not to mention a more mobile person. Living in New York City, I'd never owned a vehicle before. I went from walking to riding a motorcycle on the streets of Manhattan.

The inspiration for the book came from when I went to Sturgis in 1990. While there, I met Becky Brown and Women in the Wind, and I heard all the stories of adventure and freedom from these powerful women. It was thrilling. Seeing these women riding in a pack with their hair flowing, they were like Goddesses. Their exuberance was so contagious. That was a life-changing experience for me. I realized there's so much more *history* here and that this is a book after hearing all of these wonderful stories. And so I delved back to women at the turn of the century and researched the progression of women riders to the present day.

My book became an odyssey. I rode 30,000 miles over a six year time frame all over the country with my camera and my laptop computer on the back of my bike, a 650 Honda Hawk GT. It was a labor of love and I met so many powerful women. One of my great experiences was meeting Bessie Stringfield. She had a profound influence on me.

Over the years, I've come to see how my book has influenced the lives of so many women. It broke ground and covered a facet of women's history in America that no one had ever really looked at before.

Gevin Fax, California
1982 Harley-Davidson FXWG, "Shadowfax"
Musician, actress, model, artist

I've been completely infatuated with motorcycles since I was young. Bessie Stringfield is my idol. I wanted to be like her, a black woman who rides the hell out of a motorcycle, does stunts, carries herself really well, and is a professional!

I'm what I call a floater. I used to try to fight against things, got to do this, take care of that, stress out. But, when you're a floater, you have to live in the moment and only move when you're passionate. Riding a motorcycle taught me how to be. Simply be. Float from moment to moment.

My most favorite time is when I've been on the road for three hours straight, nothing around and not a lot to focus on at that point. Desert riding does this for me. It's long and tedious, but I don't have to really think. Thoughts just drift in and blow right out. I sort things out in my mind until there's nothing. It's all blown away in the wind.

My art relates to the motorcycle because it takes on a life of its own. I create spiritual Black Native American regalia pieces. The best ideas for my art come when I'm thinking about nothing. All the decorations on my motorcycle have meaning. The mural, all the colors, all the animal pieces, and the beads have meaning. My motorcycle is a work of art for me.

It's a power staff as well as a spiritual staff, too. It's not just a motorcycle. It's like a spiritual animal. I refer to my motorcycle for peace. When I meditate in the morning, I go for a ride on my black stallion in spirit.

HONDA

Melissa Harris, Ohio
Artist and founder, Cycle Portraits

I find the biker culture fascinating and filled with all kinds of wonderful stories and colorful characters. And each bike is as unique as the rider. The women and men I paint appreciate that my work is clearly about their relationship with their bike and not about illustrative style or melodrama.

I passenger on motorcycles with my male buddies from time to time. I do find however, that the independence of spirit and character that a woman rider carries with her—*this* commands respect from me as a human being.

I really enjoy painting motorcycles composed *with* the human form. Both fit singularly together and the contrast of machine and chrome with the organic (human form) is a perfect match.

Painting portraits of bikers and their motorcycles has created the biggest transformation in my life, a kind of spiritual/social change. I've found that bikers and their hospitality, their willingness to share with me—well, it's life-affirming.

Carré Otis, California
Actress, model, fundraiser, speaker, author, entrepreneur, activist

A motorcycle represents an unbridled joy. It matches my personal sense of adventure and I've always felt like a gypsy. It's very liberating to head out on the open road. Riding taught me how to be very present, very well prepared, and very practical. You can't just get on a bike and go. You need to be practical about a lot of matters. You need to be prepared to face the elements and the terrain. The most enjoyable ride for me is heading up Route 1 along the Pacific Coast.

What do I think about seeing Rubenesque women at the rallies wearing what they want, comfortable with themselves? I think it's great and we need to see more women accepting of themselves. Strong women can find a sense of pleasure and empowerment through a variety of activities other than focusing on their physical body. Plus you're a lot stronger and sturdier when you're a bigger gal. We need to strengthen our sisterhood and support one another as women.

Dr. Barbara Joans, California
1995 Harley-Davidson Low Rider, "Lady" Anthropologist, Ph.D., and author of *Bike Lust: Harleys, Women, and American Society*[24]

I study people. I study communities. Bikers were the very first group that I studied where I actually fell in love with the people. I had known some people who rode motorcycles, but not until I actually started hanging around with them did I get a sense of that community. I found it to be a very distinct and important group of people.

The most important aspect that I discovered was that bikers comes in all different colors, sizes, genders, ages, classes, and every other notable quality. It was myth shattering. There are many types of bikers and they are not, as the myth tells us, all outlaws. Although the outlaws are certainly there, and in many ways they are role models for survival on the road, they are not the only type of rider.

You can be what you want to be within the biker's community! You can truly be who you are. As long as you're honest, plain talking, straightforward and real, you can be yourself. There are so many interesting people in the lifestyle.

I love the Redwood Run. That's my favorite gathering. When I first went, it was very wild, and lawless, but it became much more tame as the years went on. But that wild, lawless time was extraordinary. It was there that I discovered so many truths about bikers. They are, in general, the very best of folks.

Quelix "Q", New York City

Honda CBR RR900, "Pink Panther"
Stunt street rider with the Brooklyn Black
  Dragons, affiliated with the NY Ruff Ryders;
  field tech for telephone, cable, Internet
  companies

My fiancé, Sidest, inspired me to ride. I was a passenger at first. Most of the time I'm the only female in our stunt group. It's fun. I do all kinds of stunt riding in the streets, burn-outs, wheelies, endos, all kinds of stuff. It's like dancing on the bike. It's an art form. We get permits so we're safe, but sometimes we'll just do our stunts when there's no traffic. We like to gather out at Fountain Avenue in Brooklyn to do our riding. My posse is filled with riders from all walks in life. Our children ride also.

When you ride, you're in control, you're free. I'm a very powerful and strong woman and love to ride my motorcycle. My motto is you don't have to look like a man or act like a man to ride. You can be 100 percent woman, sexy, and ride a bike. My bike is bright pink because when I'm riding 150 mph past someone, I want them to know, yeah, that was a woman on that bike.

Joan Brady, California

Author, *God on a Harley*, and *Heaven in High Gear* [25]

The inspiration for my first book came when I was working as a nurse. I envied my patients who believed in God. These people who were so sick had such peace. I really wanted to have peace. I thought, "If I were God how would I get to me?" I thought, if God was really smart, he would come to me as a really good-looking guy and he would ride a Harley. I think it came from years of being so repressed in parochial school that when I would see people on the open road riding Harleys, doing whatever they wanted to do, that just screamed independence to me which is something I have always cherished.

Then I thought, God on a Harley? That's a catchy title. So I spun a little fantasy from that. I wrote the whole book in longhand on a yellow legal pad. I didn't even have a computer. I had so much fun with it. I had no idea how the book would end. A lot of it is autobiographical. Before I knew it, it was done. But it took six years before it finally got published.

I had to have the courage to walk away from everything that was hurting me in my life and journey into the unknown and I did. *God on a Harley* changed my life.

Madusa, Virginia
1992 Harley-Davidson Softail;
2003 Harley-Davidson V-Rod
Professional wrestler, monster truck racer

My grandma, Violet, rides a motorcycle. She's 80 years old. She inspired me to ride. When I was a kid, she'd take me for rides. She's gone all over the United States and Canada.

As soon as I got my Harley I rode everywhere. I've toured all over the country. I travel so much for my job that when I get a chance to ride my Harley I get to clear my head. And I hum a lot when I ride. I've overcome a lot of things, situations and relationships, in the wind. It's a healing therapy for me. I may be in front of 60,000 people each weekend and it's great, but I like being alone, too, because I'm always in the public eye. The motorcycle is a part of me and I can be by myself when I ride.

You have a different meaning of life with the bike when you're a hardcore biker. There's a certain respect. When you've sometimes never had anything except you and your bike, that bike means more to you than a lot of things. Sometimes your bike sits in your kitchen. Sometimes your bike gets parked in your bedroom. When I ride cross-country, my bike parks in the hotel room with me. I don't let anyone ride my bike. My bike is my body and my soul.

Debbie Evans, California
2001 Ducati Monster 1996, "Matrix2"
Hollywood's top stunt woman
U.S. Motorcycle Trials champion, 2003
   inductee into the AMA Motorcycle Hall
   of Fame

I've been riding motorcycles since I was six years old. Motorcycle riding has always represented freedom for me. I'd get on my bike and basically all my problems and hassles that I got from other kids not liking me when I was little would go away. It was a great thing for me. Motorcycles was an area where I excelled and it gave me a sense of being free, having control, and being able to express myself.

I have been competing in motorcycle Trials riding since I was nine and got a trophy for third place as a kid the first time I rode. I love the challenges of Trials because you don't necessarily have to compete against anybody else. You can go off by yourself and pick out a rock or a log or something and ride up it. You work at it and work at it until you can conquer it. It seems like once you get it, you consistently are able to go over it without too much trouble and then you move on to the next obstacle.

Having no fear is something I learned as a small child. I was a little afraid of the motorcycle, but it was something that I could walk through. I think that people get paralyzed with fear because they don't know how to walk through things. Very early on I gained a healthy respect for what I was doing because motorcycles are dangerous and you need to respect that.

Trials riding taught me tremendous focus.

Trials is like golf in that you go from section to section. You get to a section and you have to stop and plan and figure out where you're going to go and how you're going to do it. You're scored against. That's segued into my stunt work, my job, and my life. I'm able to analyze things, take things apart, and focus when I do stunts—it's like riding a section in Trials. There's cameras and lamp stands in the way and a light shining in your face. If you go too fast, you're going to overcook the corner and take out a camera. If you go too slow it doesn't look good. When I do a stunt I walk it like I walk a Trials section and it's really helped me in my stunt career.

I do a balancing act on my motorcycle where I balance the bike standing still with no kickstand and I stand on my head on the seat. I picked up that trick when I was fourteen. After seeing someone else do it, I wanted to give it a try. Balance is a very important part of life because without balance you cannot truly be happy. I have lots of balance. I have my career, my family and my faith, my relationship, and all of that is a lot to do! I've learned to set my priorities. My three kids and family come first. And faith gives me a great amount of peace in my life. Without my faith and trust in Jesus Christ, I wouldn't be able to do the things that I do. I have a tremendous amount of faith and my husband and I share that faith.

Just recently I learned how to do moving tricks on my motorcycle for the movie *Torque*. I had to learn how to stand on the seat and ride the bike at about 35 miles an hour. Then I learned how to stand on the tank with my arms out. I learned rolling burnouts, moving slowly and getting the rear tire spinning in 360 circles. I learned how to do crossovers where you're sitting on the tank with your legs over the fairing and do a nose wheelie like that. I was on a Triumph TT 600. It was funny because the guys who were professionals couldn't believe that I learned all of these tricks in such a short amount of time. I've done a lot of really cool motorcycle stunts over the years of my career.

Sometimes people tell you that you can't do something or that you shouldn't do something because it's something that they don't understand or can't do, from their perspective. Motorcycles have taught me not to be limited by other people's opinions.

Feeling Free
And hookin' it on
I feel the wind in my face
The travel is tough
The terrain is rough
I feel like I can do anything

—Debbie Evans

JoAnn Ransom
9/9/61–4/18/98

"too short of a road"

Photo by Stephen Ransom

CHAPTER 10

Healing Winds

Four wheels move you, two wheels move your soul.

> —Tom McIntyre, fellow rider

Winds of change—direction

lead me

To

inner reflection

Take from me troubled tales

Lead me to

where I will prevail

> —Sasha

Sitting lonely, heart is heavy, or maybe disease ravages? What can whisk you away from that which ails you? Seems like nothing, but one thing can: the Motorcycle.

Sitting patiently, awaiting its partner, full of love, nil of hate, ready, willing and able to provide the great escape: the Motorcycle.

God uses metaphors. God is a storyteller. God communicates through the wind, whispering. The road is the journey of evolution to joy, peace, and pure love. Riding is floating on the wind . . . flying free. Riding brings us to that extraordinary, perfect, still place in our hearts, in our minds, in our souls—united with our perfect purpose. The most beautiful and stirring metaphor that God has so graciously blessed us with in recent decades is the Motorcycle, a representation of personal freedom and free will: living and riding free. It has brought great joy and has led us to brotherhood, sisterhood, love, camaraderie, family, respect, trust, and made dreams come true. Most of all, the motorcycle has brought peace and healing, and unfathomable bliss truly unexplainable because it so deeply stirs the spirit.

My motorcycle consistently delivers me into bliss carrying me away from the heavy yoke of life. I feel like I ride directly into the palm of God's hand—an inner sanctum of peace and healing so joy prevails and love reigns. Prior to that roar away from whatever's bugging me, yeesh, I want to ride away from myself sometimes! I'll get my 'tude face on and ride off and when I return, I'm s'miling because the mind's cobwebs have been blown away into the vapor. Without my chrome, PMS (Parked Motorcycle Syndrome) can really cramp my lifestyle.

The most blessed healing I have received is peace with my lost motherhood. Yeah, I can be a motorcycle mamma if I can't be a real mamma with my own kids because of my infertile condition. Motorcycles teach you the ultimate mothering for yourself because you must be completely resourceful to ride the distance in life. You've got to accept situations beyond your control, because there are many that happen on the open road.

My motorcycle keeps the path to my inner beauty clear, genuine and preserved.

Riding keeps me on the path of my purpose and what better joy than to be who you love to be in complete freedom. This is very therapeutic. It's a total embracing of self, environment and the moment. Riding is utter awareness of sweet life, which brings deep gratitude for our Creator's thoughtfulness. And this is perfect healing peace found only in the wind on two wheels.

These are the profiles of very brave and courageous women who overcame serious adversity to find indescribable peace in the wind on two wheels.

Voices from the Healing Highways

This chapter is dedicated to the late JoAnn Ransom, beautiful wife of Stephen Ransom of Tampa, Florida. For several years, Stephen and JoAnn Ransom made the Black Hills and Sturgis Motorcycle Rally their annual romantic destination. They were a well-known, fun-loving couple who lived and breathed the quintessential free-spirited lifestyle.

But the romantic dream tragically ended on April 18, 1998, when Stephen's beloved wife of sixteen years lost her sudden battle with liver cancer at age 36. Before dying in her husband's arms, JoAnn whispered her last wish: to ride their favorite motorcycle trip to Sturgis just one more time and release her ashes into the wind to fly free with the eagles.

She made their home an artistic statement of their motorcycle lifestyle. "I'd come home and there'd be all these creative things around the house," Stephen said with a chuckle. A macho Harley-Davidson gas tank mounted upon the pretty gray siding of their home holds a bouquet of flowers. A glass table pierced with a Springer front-end is topped off with a lamp. She was an all-around arts-and-crafts guru who could show down Martha Stewart—the difference being that most of JoAnn's artistry was centered on Harley-Davidson motorcycles and the open road.

JoAnn shared Stephen's passion for building motorcycles. She proudly helped build and detail her custom '45 Flathead. "She only weighed ninety pounds and she'd kick start that thing and get it running. We worked on so many projects together. She was my right-hand partner, my truth, and my lover. She was so talented," said her husband, "We had fun and never tired of each other."

It took Stephen a year and a half after her death, at the 59th Sturgis Motorcycle Rally, before he could attempt to fulfill his wife's last request. With her ashes carefully protected and strapped to the passenger seat of his Harley-Davidson Softail, Stephen reluctantly made the journey to lovingly fulfill JoAnn's last wish . . . and now she truly soars free with the eagles.

Carol Groves, Michigan
2000 Harley Sportster 1200, "Sweet Madness"
Retired and a graduate student

I have had gas in my blood and exhaust in my hair forever. Motorcycles have been in my life since I was a freshman in high school. I breathe a sense of freedom with every mile. My husband, Michael, and I had the same passion for motorcycles. He had a life-threatening illness and we could no longer travel from border to border and coast to coast in our motor home, so we bought two motorcycles. On the motorcycle, Michael gained a sense of freedom from his medical situation. He also gained dignity and a feeling of control that he had lost because of the illness.

One night while riding, he had a freak accident that claimed his life. I was devastated. With the help of some key people at the Harley-Davidson dealership, I had my husband's motorcycle rebuilt. I had it custom painted with an eagle and our initials. I made a decision to ride his motorcycle and I sold mine. The day I picked up the bike is one of the most important days of my life. Every time I ride, I feel my Michael's presence. I am happy. I am free. I am peaceful. I am me.

One of the hardest things I ever had to do was get back on my motorcycle and ride away from the accident. I did not have a choice. I knew if I didn't get back on, I would never ride again. When I rode away from the accident, I had to go get my Jeep to go to the hospital. On the way, I had no choice but to go back by the accident scene. You can't imagine what that was like. I knew my husband's motorcycle and his blood were lying in the street. There was a big dark spot in the street for a long time after.

As Neil Young says, "Sometimes what you love will kill you in the end." I know Mike died doing what he loved to do: riding his beloved motorcycle. He lived in grand style and died the same way.

Because of the relationship Mike and I had and the activities we enjoyed together, I knew it would be a slap in the face if I didn't ride again. My husband taught me to live life instead of letting life live you. Another thing that I learned from the death of my husband is that you never know when your life can change. Enjoy life, live, and love.

Patricia "Peachesz" Zukowski, Pennsylvania
1997 Yamaha Virago1100
Jill of all trades

During the daytime, I sold flowers on the side of the road in Port Jervis, New York. I was the Rose Lady. With two children and a house to support alone, I had to work hard. From the mainstream clubs to the more obscure and bizarre independent bikers, all the motorcyclists cruising along the Delaware River would stop by my stand and talk to me. I found them to be refreshing and honest. I was going through a bitter and brutal divorce during that time, and the bikers protected me from an abusive husband.

Riding teaches me to be aware of everything around me. My reactions are quicker, I see more, feel more, absorb it faster, and appreciate it longer. My children love bikes and riding. I think they worry about me sometimes but they understand what passion is.

Early on in my life, I had allowed someone to make me forget who I was. I was a tragedy because I permitted it to happen, thinking I had to be less so another could be more. Biking has allowed me to understand in the deepest core of my being that I am as fierce and strong as the roar of a motorcycle barreling down the open road alone, that I am as gentle and sweet as the perfect curve on the perfect day. The road is ever before me. The direction I travel is always my choice. I know I am never alone, my brothers and sisters are only over the next hill. And the ride to get to my destination? Well, that's the fun part and the hardest part at the same time.

Brenda L. Bates, M.A., C.Ht., California
1995 BMW R1100R; 2000 Aprilia Pegaso; 1979 Yamaha YZ250
Master of psychology and clinical hypnotherapist; author, *Back in the Saddle Again: How to Overcome Fear of Riding After a Motorcycle Accident*[26]

Motorcyclists are unique people. Never before has the psychology of the motorcyclist been studied by a professional psychologist who is also an avid rider, until now. In my book, *Back in the Saddle Again,* I help post-accident riders understand the psychological issues behind their passion, which aids in overcoming their fear of riding; thus helping them to decide whether or not to return to motorcycling. Often the answer is yes. Beneficial to all motorcycle enthusiasts including nonriders, my book sheds psychological and philosophical light on the rider's extreme passion for motorcycles.

Through much research into the psychological collective unconscious and symbolism, I regard the motorcycle as a metaphor for life. Motorcycling embodies the spirit of living: passion, motivation, skills, a direction, and courage. People attracted to motorcycles tend to have personality traits that coincide with the archetypal symbols of the Centaur and the Wheel. Riders possess a deep need to be released from the boundaries of the human body and to express the self as powerful and independent, almost animallike, thus the Centaur. They also tend to relate to the collective unconscious symbolism of the Wheel, which, historically, has represented the psychological or spiritual attainment of feeling centered while simultaneously being in motion. This explains why riders often report feeling that motorcycling is a sort of Zen experience for them.

My favorite aspect of motorcycle riding is the personal experience of self-sufficiency and enjoying the scenery in an open, unbound way. I also love the challenge/danger mixed in equal proportion with the graceful dance of riding and experiencing the beauty of our world.

Shelly Denny, Minnesota
1999 Harley-Davidson Dyna Lowrider
Student

I was once a drunk and a drug addict. It wasn't until I got clean at eighteen that I was able to have the dream, the cash, and follow through to get a motorcycle. I've seen many people lose their bikes to addiction, and I see many people riding today because they are clean. I thank God that I am one of them! I thought that if I quit using I would have a boring life and turn into some religious nut handing out Bible literature at the airport, but the truth is, I got to become the person I always wanted to be and I get to ride a Harley!

Growing up in a biker family has given me a unique perspective on life. Riding my own bike is what I needed to do to know that I don't have to be limited by anything. It has also made me sort of a celebrity in my town. A lot of people want to know "Who's that biker chick with the long dreadlocks?" Riding a motorcycle taught me that I can do it. Other people don't know what I am capable of. Maybe riding is not for everyone, but a lot of people won't know until they try it. I've had many women tell me that they are scared to ride on their own, but when they see little me riding a full-size Harley, they know they can ride, too.

C. Cecelia Ariaz, California
2002 Suzuki Volusia
Paralegal/LDA/Real estate agent

Riding allows me freedom. I spent twenty years in a wheelchair due to MS and was restricted in my movements by the chair and the expectations of the general public of those in chairs.

I was offered freedom from my chair by a crazy wonderful doctor that had an idea to release the spasticity of my legs. I took the offer, and my legs are now free, as is my soul, and I have never looked back. I had dreamed of walking and I now am able to walk. Then I dreamed of riding a motorcycle again and now I'm riding again. It's great to get out on the open road and experience the world around me as I ride through it. My life is limitless and I can do anything that I want. I'm in control.

D.J. Jones, New Mexico
1999 Honda Valkyrie Tourer, "Big Bertha"
Owner of DivaSkinZ, motorcycle and casual
    fashions for women and little divas

As we know, sudden curves in life can happen when you least expect them and I confronted one of those sudden curves while out for a short fall ride. The sun was shining, and the temperature was about 60 degrees—the perfect fall day. Remembering the importance of wearing the proper protective riding attire from the safety course, I had taken the time to gear up. The extra time was well worth it. My helmet, jacket, gloves, chaps, Levis, and boots saved my life.

DJ of DivaSkinZ
Photo by Eric Putter
©2001

I had been out for a couple of hours with the crisp air wafting through my helmet. I was thoroughly enjoying myself when I came upon a car preparing to enter the highway. My hands were poised ready over the brake and clutch, my headlight was on high beam, and I was honking my horn like a mad woman. I was sure the driver saw me, but when I reached the front of her car, she abruptly pulled out and struck me and my motorcycle broadside. I was thrown 120 feet, landing face first and skidding on the pavement. It wasn't until I finally stopped sliding that I realized my right foot had been crushed between the car and bike.

After I was told I would never walk again and may loose my foot, I chose to take that as a personal challenge not just to walk but to thrive!!! It took two long and extensive surgeries to save my foot from amputation. My first thought was to walk again, because the possibility was great that I would not. Hour after hour, day after day I worked endlessly through the pain. After two months of hard work and rehabilitation I was walking.

After getting back on my feet in two

months, I not only drove my bike through all the lower 48 states but I have also completed all the Canadian provinces alone! The accident changed my life and so has riding. Now I never take anything for granted and I make sure to live life as if it were my last day, because it just may be.

When I'm in the saddle, I feel free, I feel complete. Other than my marriage of 18 years to my wonderful husband, Mark, nothing has filled my heart with as much happiness as riding my bike mile after mile after mile. Motorcycle rides are very therapeutic and spiritual to me. That's why I share my passion with as many people as I can. Organizing Diva motorcycle runs for women and writing positive stories are a couple of ways I have found to share and hopefully inspire others to live their lives to the fullest.

The open road for me is not only freedom but is my church. I feel closer to Mother Earth more than any other time in my life. We don't realize what we have until we almost lose it so we need to get out there to live, love, explore our souls and the world; it's up to us and we can do it!

Lisa Marschall, Illinois
2003 Harley Davidson Heritage Softail
    Classic, "IProwl"
Wireless industry executive

Being set free in the wind while riding my motorcycle has given me the courage to take other risks in life, knowing that if I set my mind to something, that this free-spirited lady can do anything that she believes in. One of my strengths is my stubbornness and after a serious knee injury

from a spill while riding in summer 2002, I was not afraid to get back on my bike. I love the camaraderie when I ride with other ladies. We all seem to understand the relationship with our motorcycles and the road. There is a feeling of God all around you when you ride. The spiritual journey of riding a motorcycle is unbelievable.

Everyone thinks I am crazy for getting on a bike again after my accident. What do they know? Certainly not what it feels like to have the wind in your face, and hear your heart sing a song.

Tammy "Gypzy" Eshelman, Ohio
2003 Harley-Davidson Heritage Softail
    Classic
Psychiatric-care registered nurse

There were no role models in motorcycles when I was growing up. I have always had a free, adventurous spirit. And I have always struggled with limitations that are placed on women merely because we are women. So, when I started voicing a desire to ride a motorcycle it was met with the normal criticism: "You can't do that, you're a woman." No one ever encouraged me.

I made a few mistakes growing up. I became a rebellious teen, always getting into trouble. Then I became an alcoholic and drug addict. At 23, I hit bottom hard. I lost all my teeth, was a size one from anorexia, and had a life-threatening liver infection. I needed to change. I worked hard for nine years putting my life back together. It was then that I decided to learn how to ride a motorcycle, so I took a rider's safety

Gypzy strikes a pose!

course. Three days later, I bought my first Harley. I have been in love with riding ever since.

Because of my love for riding the distance, my nickname became "Gypzy." Riding a motorcycle, feeling the wind in your hair and experiencing the freedom of the open road gets into your blood. It became my new drug of choice.

During the years of my adventures, I became an inspiration to women and men to follow their dreams and learn how to ride. One such woman, Clare, became my closest friend. After a long time of mental anguish, she finally bought herself a motorcycle. We would ride together and talk of our dreams. In 1999, she was diagnosed with cervical cancer. As she became progressively ill, we still rode as much as her health would allow. A week before she died,

she told me how much she admired my courage and strength and that I was the woman who gave her the courage and desire to ride a motorcycle. I was blessed to have her in my life and grateful to have inspired her to follow her dreams.

The more I ride the more I wish I could do it all the time. Riding a motorcycle has given me a reason to live and love life.

Xochi Hughes-Madera, Washington
Kawasaki Vulcan 1500, "Beautiful"
CEO of CancerGifts.com and CEO
  of Madera Woodworking LLC

When I ride, I am set free from daily cares and concerns, with nothing but me, my bike, the road, and the wind to focus on. My goddess within awakens fully

The beautiful and spiritual Gevin Fax on her motorcycle, Shadowfax
Photo by Richard Aramas

Clockwise from top left:

Top Hollywood stunt woman and U.S. Trials champion Debbie Evans on the
Ducati given to her for stunt work in *The Matrix Reloaded*
Photo courtesy Lane Leavitt, www.stuntrev.com

Carla King is a motorcycle travel journalist, too
Photo courtesy www.carlaking.com

Pro wrestler and monster truck driver, Madusa
Photo by Robert Erdman

Lou George loves photography and her American IronHorse motorcycle
Photo courtesy Lou George

> *"My bike is my body and my soul."*
>
> —Madusa

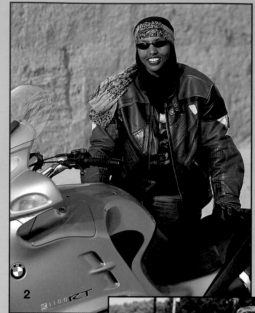

1. Diane Howells, founder,
Motorcycle Safety School,
New York
Photo by Matt McDermott

2. DJ of DivaSkinz
Photo by Eric Putter ©2001

3. Beth Walkington on her
"Road Couch"
Photo courtesy Beth

4. Skert teaches riders how to
pick up any fallen bike,
all by themselves

5. Cris Sommer-Simmons
Photo courtesy Cris

6. Karen Thompson, "Queen of
the Tire Burnouts!"
Photo courtesy Karen Thompson

Linda Beasley is Queen of the Road
Photo © Linda

I will not pass the boys
I will not pass the boys
I will not pass the boys
really...I mean it this time

Lipstick before a Main Street stroll

Iron Butt rider Phyllis Lang
Photo courtesy Immortal Image

Author Dee Gagnon gets ready for the road

She Is Art: a woman and her motorcycle
Photo by Betsy Huelskamp

Gypzy's goal is to be a gypsy and travel the globe

Leah Whaley shines on her ride
Photo courtesy Leah Whaley

Actress and stuntwoman Brenda Fox, with the "Blue Flamer" bike by Bandit
Photo by Randall Cordero

**Rose Andrews at the AMA Women
& Motorcycling Conference**

**Peggy at the AMA Women &
Motorcycling conference**

**Judy Wheelihan,
co-owner of Harley-Davidson
of Greensboro, North Carolina,
at Daytona Bike Week**

"Many life challenges have come my way—and in fact, there are many now facing me—but my motorcycle will always be there to help me through."

Cathy Gonzalez
Photo by Grookett Photography

Watching the world ride by at Daytona Bike Week

Dee Modglin, motorcycle clothing designer, Femme Gear

Shirley Davis hangs out on Main Street, Daytona

BBC Rock deejay and TV host Mary Anne Hobbs
desert riding in the U.S.
Photo courtesy BBC Photo Library

Camryn Manheim, Golden Globe and Emmy Award–winning actor,
and star of ABC's The Practice: "I ride a bike for three reasons. You
always get there on time. There's never a parking problem. And
who wouldn't want something that powerful between their legs?"
Photo by Mimi Craven/Icon Int'l

Cher with darling young biker Robbie at the
Children's Craniofacial Association motorcycle
fundraiser event at Sturgis
Photo courtesy Buffalo Chip Campground,
Sturgis, South Dakota

Catherine Bell, star of CBS TV's "J.A.G."
Photo courtesy Catherine Bell

charged, healthy, strong, and powerful as soon as my feet leave the ground and I twist the throttle! I forget that I am fighting cancer. As the wind flows through me I am at peace with the cancer and everything is right with the universe and me. I know that the Great Creator has blessed me with the ability to ride and therefore the ability to be who I am, an intelligent, beautiful, strong woman who is not afraid of life.

When I was diagnosed with cancer, my world as I knew it changed forever. Knowing you have no control over your mortality is a hard pill to swallow. I felt helpless and weak, but I am not a weak spirit. I researched to find out what to do for treatment because the type of cancer that I have is very rare. There have only been three dozen cases ever reported worldwide.

I found comfort, serenity, and safety in my husband's arms. But I found strength and courage while riding my motorcycle. I could think, make plans of action, and make decisions that would mean the difference between life and death. Riding in the wind gives me the "place" to let my higher self be heard. It also gave me the chance to hear what the Great Creator was trying to tell me regarding my life purpose and the lesson of cancer.

As I continue living with cancer, riding my motorcycle is the very best medicine I have found. When riding I am in control and immediately the feeling of helplessness disappears. When I twist the throttle and feel the power of the engine it sends power and energy throughout my whole body, mind, and spirit. I feel strong, healthy, and full of life. I'm here to *live* out loud!

My illness has taught me many lessons:

1. Do not take your life for granted.

2. Live each day as if it may be your last— in a healthy and positive way.

3. Take time to smell the roses, talk to your loved ones, and listen to what they say with love and compassion.

4. Help others in need, for some day you could need help.

5. Do what you love and the universe and the Great Creator will provide what you need.

6. Pray—if only a humble "Thank you for this day of life"—to whomever it is you pray to.

7. Live, love, and *ride!*

Sue Simmons, Kansas
1998 Harley-Davidson Sportster
Nurse in a drug and alcohol
   rehabilitation unit

What I love about motorcycles is that I'm in control of this heavy, powerful, fast machine all by myself and riding has taught me that I can do anything I set my mind to do. When I turned 50, I started belly-dancing lessons; I bought a Harley at 52. I don't think my grandkids will ever forget this grandma! With anything you want in life, go for it now, because you don't know what lies ahead.

When my husband and I divorced, I bought a Harley and was moving on, until he told me he had lung cancer. He moved back in with us and I took care of him. The cancer eventually spread into his spine and he died in my arms.

He showed me how to not be afraid. How to roll with the punches and to live and have fun while you can. I painted my bike this year with one shooting star on each side of the tank, one for him, one for me, and then a star on each fender for our son and daughter.

Patty Brassfield, California
1997 Harley-Davidson Heritage Springer
Manager, car wash/gas station

Breast cancer forced me to drop all the balls I was juggling. It made me want to stop and concentrate with all my senses and to experience the world I lived in and feel it before it ended. On my motorcycle I could do this. My sense of sight became very keen, indeed. Following the Salmon River in Idaho, I wondered if I was the only one in the world who sees God's wonders and handiwork the way he intended them to be seen and appreciated. I know that prior to living with cancer I did not have the same appreciation for living life that I do now. I don't believe people do unless they have faced their own mortality. Only then does every little thing become so very precious.

All my life I followed the rules and still, cancer came to visit. My Harley is pretty much my only rebellious behavior. Having lived through cancer I have nothing to fear. When I am riding through the mountains in a particularly scenic area I feel very close to God and I'm not afraid because every day I live, now, is a bonus day.

Michele Flowers, California
1996 Honda Shadow 1100

After many years of addiction and single motherhood, I found spiritual recovery in 1995 at age 29. This new freedom empowered me to achieve many lifelong dreams that seemed impossible to reach.

First I worked on my spiritual relationship, my relationship with my beautiful teenage daughter, and then myself. Through self-discovery I realized my motorcycle dream! It was amazing how easy it was when I decided to learn to ride and to do it responsibly.

This simple act and my eagerness to talk about it brought into my life more women with similar desires. One after another we were all getting motorcycles and riding everywhere together. I have learned more about honor and respect through my relationships with these women than I could ever have imagined. Over the years we continue to ride together and encourage new women to follow their dreams.

I continue to honor my spiritual growth and my many relationships. I never tire from the freedom I feel in life and especially freedom in the wind. I had always been "the bitch on the back." After years of being single and not getting to ride, recovery from active addiction gave me the courage to seek out my own license and motorcycle. Learning to ride was the first dream I had that I was able to set my mind to do and did it. It empowered me to follow all my dreams and be successful.

Riding Motorcycle

Every ride reminds me of death,

The two of us, a drunken pickup,

errant deer

Something explodes, slow flight after impact

A flash of time and then the fall

A branch in the throat, a leg turned wrong

Darkened shreds of skin—

Let this machine pass powerfully through me.

My body is the engine

His body is the fuel.

We rule our gears and mirrors and chrome.

Our leather stories are mortal sketches

We swallow the horizon

—From Linda Back McKay,
Ride That Full Tilt Boogie[27]

Diana Coopersmith, welder on the Golden Gate Bridge

Photographer: Christina Shook © 2003

CHAPTER 11

The Motorcycle Lifestyle

I contradict myself. I am large. I contain multitudes.

—Walt Whitman

Motorcycles are spiritual, emotional and physical liberty. They are a way of life that defines personal style, shaped by truth, cultivated from liberty. Motorcycles mean riding on the winds of change and having fun doing it. Freedom is the foundation upon which this lifestyle respires, transpires, and inspires. There are different variations on the lifestyle theme within the motorcycle culture. However, every variation offers the rider a unique definition and outlet for personal reflection. To outsiders evaluating a rider on a machine, it offers an imaginative canvas on which to paint their opinions and judgment.

Riding a motorcycle is the expression of personal freedom, personal existence, embodiment of spirit, a release of or voyage into a satisfying mind trip—like a mind spa that blows out the cobwebs and cleanses away stale personal refrains. It's an opportunity to enjoy silence on every level, a quiet mind, a quiet heart, a quiet soul that all settles into a quiet peace. Zen. The lifestyle is an opportunity to commune with other people and nature, and thus simply embodies the three hallmarks of essential human nature to commune with self, be with community, and become one with the natural environment.

Take a culture of like-minded individuals, each drawing in a breath for freedom's sake and exhaling anything that suffocates freedom, and you've got a mighty force of fun-loving people. There are subsets within the culture that define the alternative biker lifestyles, ranging from those who simply use motorcycles as a form of cheap transportation to those who base their very existence on this earth upon the possession of their two wheels— an extension of their souls.

Most of us identify our very existence with the motorcycle, and this establishes among us a strong basis for extreme camaraderie. While we are interconnected in our passion for motorcycles and freedom and the open road, we are individuals on a quest from mediocrity, which, in turn, creates an interesting discovery. Working in the motorcycle business exposes us to another dimension of "family" within the lifestyle.

The motorcycle lifestyle developed into a community of people with the same passion for adventure, discovery, and good times. This established the foundation for the motorcycle clubs and organizations to begin. The riders within the motorcycle lifestyle become an extension of family and sometimes more like family than a rider's immediate kin. I've never known the meaning of deep laughter, altruism, love, commitment, and extended family until I discovered the motorcycle lifestyle. Perhaps it's because we experience a spiritual, emotional, and physical liberty from being in a constant state of awareness that opens up our entire being to embrace others, the environment and ourselves. Clanlike, we want to protect each other.

One of the coolest things about riding a motorcycle is the wave, a total connection with another human being that you don't even know—or do you? Bikers wave to one another while riding as if greeting the free spirit in the other: "Hey free spirit . . . isn't life great?" Gas stations and food stops are the greatest opportunity to meet folks, which often results in lifelong "familyships."

We connect readily as we recognize the passion in another rider's soul. Those who are not of the lifestyle and have nothing to do with even riding a motorcycle, those people who haven't judged us as threatening, approach us as if we wear a friendly welcome banner. Those who have poorly judged us (usually influenced by shallow media cues) and don't understand this treasured lifestyle perceive a distorted picture of who bikers, motorcyclists, enthusiasts, whoever rides a motorcycle, represent. They see us as merely shady characters. Just what evil do they see inside the dark crevices of our free-spirited, fun-loving, slap-happy, trustworthy, deliriously peaceful, self-accepting, altruistic selves?

The hardcore clubs prefer to be left alone by curious mainstream society and other biker subcultures. It's like poking a stick in a hornet's nest; it's none of anyone's business what goes on in there and if you stir the nest, you'll get stung. They are busy with the inner workings of their own culture. Sure, they would readily reach out a helping hand to a stranded club outsider. But the more private hardcore clubs keep a tight clan so that they can protect and uphold their code of honor and loyalty.

Yes, we are interconnected, but we are also individuals with a purpose that contributes to the betterment of mankind. Our quest for continuous spiritual, emotional, physical, mental evolution, and fun is beautiful and the only way in which world change can take place. The true nugget within the motorcycle lifestyle is the treasure that every spiritual and religious organization or individual teaches. That is *awareness*. The act of riding a motorcycle opens up the rider's senses to a height of awareness on many levels that is a meditative state. It is entirely zen.

> People are looking for relationships that can be characterized as kind and understanding, but it is growing harder and harder to find open and expressive relationships. There is a basic human need to belong, which includes the need for frequent personal contacts and for bonds with others marked by stability and emotional concern (Baumeister & Leary, 1995). Unfortunately, an increasing number of people do not have this bond with others in their lives; these socially isolated people tend to be unhappy.
>
> —Leonard A. Jason, *Community Building: Values for a Sustainable Future*[27]

In his book, Mr. Jason describes that community-building is a must for world change. He goes on to say,

> From a western perspective, a healthy individual should have sturdy foundations in four areas: the body, which should have strength and endurance; the mind, which should be adept at creativity, problem solving, and accruing knowledge; the spiritual domain, which should have goals and visions that help direct and focus life; and the social arena, which should have strong connection with family and friends. I suggest that these four domains can be richly expanded upon by borrowing from other wisdom traditions. Using this broadened perspective, one might strive to inculcate the following features: a balanced and flexible energy field within the body, long posited by Eastern yogis as a source of health and well-being; a peaceful and quiet mind, advocated by meditators from a variety of religious traditions; a spiritual sense of interconnectedness and oneness, supported by those who live within a variety of mystical traditions; and a reverence for nature and others, a social domain advocated by a number of cultures, including that of Native Americans.

The act of motorcycle riding embraces all four of these areas, which in turn provides the foundation for a strong community. And this is the motorcycle lifestyle. On the other hand, riding solo is still very much a part of the culture. However, this lone rider will always greet another rider with that wonderful clanlike familiarity.

Working in the lifestyle is a blessing that can only be described like this: wild, fun, loving, familial, adventurous, transformative, enlightening, romantic, altruistic, purpose-filled, happy, unpredictable and balanced, and that's just a start.

I began in this lifestyle as a young woman infatuated with motorcycles who displayed nomadic tendencies very early on. I would wander off into the woods just outside of Woodstock, New York. My mother screamed at me from a distance to get my ass home, but I would be a tiny speck far away, wandering with no real purpose. I would learn in my adult years that wandering is one of the most purpose-filled activities that I could do. So my parents had to deal with this wanderlust in a child who loved leather, hippies, motorcycles, nature, music, people, and had quite an imagination—and who was far away from their comprehension and the familiarity of their lifestyle. A feisty spirit that needs to manifest can never be suppressed in the end, so, all of the dynamics of my personality, the people I chose to commune with, and my antithetical lifestyle would exist because it would be for my greater good and for the good of those with whom I chose to connect. The key was to be aware of the opportunity to simply be.

> " *Bikers are the most altruistic bunch I've ever known.* "

That opportunity to work in the lifestyle manifested itself during my passenger days. I loved writing and decided one day to write an article about my passenger experience at Sturgis. I sent in the article to one of the motorcycle magazines and it was immediately snatched up. From there, my love affair with writing about the lifestyle began and I developed a wonderful fan base to support my creativity. I can tell you, too, that I don't like to go around patting myself on the back for garnering such notoriety; I like to pat others on the back for their incredible accomplishments by virtue of discovering motorcycles and thus making beautiful changes in their lives.

My talent as a writer and all my creative talents as a multifaceted artist stems from that beautiful life force within me that drives my motorcycle-riding soul into a state of higher consciousness. That life force, to me affectionately known as God, the Universe, Mother Earth, Father Sky, Son of God, Jesus, Madonna, Mother of Christ, Goddess, Cosmos, Consciousness, the Magdalena, the Awesome Groove, is what gives me the talent to do what I do. I am just a being that allows the gifts to move through me, these gifts that were brought forth and implemented because of my participation in the biker lifestyle and passion for motorcycles and the road. I love the motorcycle lifestyle because it defines living and riding free and living on the edge away from the false safety of mediocrity and, thus, stunted evolution. It gives me the authentic outlet for my creativity. Motorcycles are my creative lifeblood.

Bikers are the most altruistic bunch I've ever known. If someone ever did a survey they would realize that most money generated for fundraiser events comes from the generous and passionate hearts of the biker men and women. We have that urgency in our souls to help one another, which is the reason why we would drop everything to help a brother or sister. That same urgency and passion transcends into our fundraising events. There isn't enough we can do to orchestrate an event. We go the extra mile in all facets of our life to serve another.

There are several thousand well-attended motorcycle events around the world where bikers commune with one another and completely engross themselves in the moment and the lifestyle. Motorcycle rallies, events, fundraisers, charity runs, races, social watering holes, club activities where people from all walks in life with common interests join together. Can you imagine what it is like to celebrate this common bond? It is a party 24/7, lasting the duration of the event dates and longer. Then it continues on the road. Men, women, and children join together with others to bond as family in the wind. Every time we straddle our rides, we're setting out to celebrate an adventure, entertain ourselves, and drive away from mediocrity.

Mediocrity. To settle. To become or mimic others around you. The motorcycle culture is being threatened by newcomers who do not understand the lifestyle: the soulfulness of the motorcycle and honoring the brother- and sisterhood as a whole. The wannabes can step right in and purchase the image and pretend to be a part of it, and this gives those who don't know anything about the lifestyle the idea that the wannabe is an example for all of us. It also threatens the uniqueness of the lifestyle as a statement of personal freedom to be lessened to mediocrity. Mediocrity from trends threat-

ens the inherent and mysterious values of riding. Living the lifestyle is all about authenticity, respect, and heart.

Yasuhiko Kimura was quoted in the magazine *What is Enlightenment?* with reference to the world paradigm shift for soul searching as saying: "Authenticity is fundamental, more fundamental than spiritual enlightenment." Authenticity of self gives the person a holistic approach to viewing the truth in all things. True authenticity cannot exist in mediocrity. The majority of those in the biker lifestyle are authentic, true-to-self people with a vehement sense of community and the ability to trust and establish lifelong friendships that become an extension of family.

Rallies

I love going to the rallies. That's where all the families come together for days of riding, partying, communing, and reconnecting. They may be folks you only see at the events, but they are family, just the same. Shirt off the back? Oh, heck, they'd give you their house, anything you need, true bros and sisters. My favorite of all the rallies is Sturgis because I love the journey to reach the sacred Black Hills. If I'm coming in from the east, it's cornfields and farmland and such. If I'm coming in from the west, it's the rugged earth, mountains, plateaus, deep forest, and desert. Heading in from the West is by far my favorite and satisfies my wild chrome cowgirl nature.

At the rallies, riders unite as one large community, all from different walks of life

Sturgis motorcycle rally

and subsets within the culture. Ah yes, another misconception that nonbikers have is that we're penniless. That's not the case. Motorcycles cost as much as a new car these days and we'd buy a pair of "sneakers" for our bikes before we'd buy a pair for our feet. Bikers contribute to the economic development of many towns and cities across the nation from our attendance at motorcycle events and rallies. We love to buy and support anything that has to do with our passion. Relationships between city officials and bikers were always strained until officials realized just how much money these bikers were spending. We've helped save many towns and cities from otherwise bleak financial status.

Besides, most townsfolk love to experience the high-throttle energy and friendly, carnival atmosphere when bikers are in town.

My "family" extends to those who work in this glorious lifestyle. We reconnect at all the major rallies and shows. Sturgis, to me, is the most special. I think it's the aura of the beautiful Native American spirituality within the earth of that Wild West town that makes it so special to me. The lush landscape that melts into harsh terrain, the townspeople, the pioneer energy of that breathtaking place is precious and conducive to a bunch of asphalt cowboys and cowgirls gathering together to share the spirit of adventure.

Pearl Hoel was the strong lady who

stood behind her Jack Pine Gypsies club man, J.C. "Pappy" Hoel, who organized the first Black Hills Motor Classic, now known as Sturgis Bike Week. The club sponsored a "Gypsie Tour" through the Black Hills. Pearl and the wives of other club members fed the entire Sturgis motorcycle rally—about 100 men, women, and children—back in 1938. A free picnic of weenies and Sloppy Joes was served in a tent behind the Hoels' Indian Motorcycle dealership. Folks camped on the Hoels' lawn at Junction Avenue. The main event was a half-mile dirt track with twelve riders and lasted all of a weekend.

"I have wonderful memories over all the years," says Pearl, 98 years old, who still opens her home and property to many annual visitors who adore her and shower her with gifts. "There are people that we have known for years and have known long before they were married and now their children and grandchildren come. I've got a fellow that sleeps in the garage. I don't know what I'd do without them. They're like family. People always stop by to say hello. I've made so many wonderful friends over all these years."

The rally has been an annual event, except for two years during WWII. As the years reeled by the event grew substantially, attracting a bevy of vendors, other race organizations, high-profile entertainment, major corporate sponsors, and almost every motorcycle manufacturer and after-market company. The rally that began as a small family-style gathering has evolved into several hundred thousand attendees and has spread out to surrounding cities, like Rapid City, Hill City, Keystone, Spearfish, Custer, Deadwood, Belle Meade, and Wyoming, with the little town of Sturgis nestled in between. The riding is spectacular and well worth the trip.

Daytona Bike Week represents the kick-off of riding season and it's party time. Many from the North trailer their bikes because of inclement weather or laziness. But, of course, when it's time for the annual Iron Butt Association Pizza Party in Daytona, or the Motor Maids' gathering, all riders ride in no matter what. No trailers, no matter the weather.

Daytona becomes a motorcycle town for an entire ten days, featuring beach, sun, sand, bike shows, tons of music, and unique attractions. This rally stretches across Volusia County and into New Smyrna Beach, with riders venturing to nearby Orlando and far away Miami or Key West. Daytona, more so than the other rallies, has a high attendance of sport bike riders. This is more of a hang-around-town-and-party kind of rally because the riding is not that spectacular except for the Volusia County Loop. Besides, Bike Week traffic is thick and steals time away from leisurely riding anywhere. It also is a racer's rally, featuring many different motorcycle competitions.

A beach race in January 1937 launched the Daytona 200, sanctioned by the AMA, also known as the "Handlebar Derby" by locals. The course was a 3.2 mile stretch of beach and road. Starting times were dictated by local tide tables. In 1942, the Daytona 200 was postponed due to the war. The official race activities did not resume again until 1947, but enthusiasts still gathered every year for an unofficial "Bike Week." When the races resumed, the city fathers of Daytona asked residents to open their homes to motorcyclists since nearby motels and campgrounds were filled to capacity. The new beach race featured a 4.1 mile course and ran until 1960 when it was moved to The Daytona International Speedway. Year after year, more and more bikers would visit Daytona and today the number of attendees for the event approaches well over half a million each year. Because the spring event became so popular, the tourism board decided to hold Biketoberfest to close the riding season.

Laconia Bike Week in New Hampshire is the oldest running motorcycle rally, as well as one of the big three, with attendance reaching 375,000. Nestled on Lake Winnipesaka, Weirs Beach is host to the thunder of Harleys and whiz of sport bikes that ride in nationwide and from Canada. The rally spreads far into the wilderness of cabins edging the lake and features the famous AMA Gypsy Tour that oftentimes runs through two or three states. Treated to New England's lush green scenery carving through the mountains, riding is the big draw for this rally, as well as the motorcycle race competitions.

Americade, held in Lake George, New York, is considered the largest multi-brand touring rally in the world and tends to attract those with a penchant for extreme distance riding, cruising, sport touring, and traveling with their families, including children. Born in 1912, Emily "Dolly" Jackson

Ronda Oman, Sturgis Motorcycle Rally Committee
Photo by Ronda Oman

was celebrated as Americade's oldest-riding motorcycle passenger. She rode up until age 90, sadly meeting her death when a deer collided with the motorcycle she was passengering on. Americade awards their attendees with accolades including the royal treatment given to the king and queen of the rally. Loud pipes are not welcome from any bike at Americade. The organization supports the AMA's motto, "Loud Pipes Risk Rights," and is not too accommodating of outrageous characters. Honda motorcycles has the largest presence at this rally, overshadowing Harley-Davidson riders. Americade is a mild-mannered, family-friendly gathering featuring a tour expo with vendors that sell items for serious travelers. A large contingent of Christian Motorcycle Association members (and other religious groups), and law enforcement and rescue clubs like the Blue Knights (police), and Red Knights (firemen) enjoy this rally. "The common thread running through the fabric of Americade is the level of responsible, respectable, mature behavior by the attendees," explain rally officials. Lots of riders hit Americade on their way to nearby rowdy Laconia Bike week, which begins a week later.

Hollister Independence Rally in California, coined the "Birthplace of the American Biker," earned its reputation back in the late forties when some mischievous members of the Boozefighters Motorcycle Club had a bit too much to drink and got out of hand. No real big deal, but the media decided it was their immoral duty to sensationally inform the nation with the hyped-up news that bikers had wreaked havoc, pillaging and destroying the hamlet. That and a few other harmless mischievous antics set the stage for the negative media portrayal of bikers. Nonetheless, the Hollister Rally, held the first full weekend of July, is still a super popular destination for bikers celebrating independence. Although it's an adult-oriented party, they host activities for wee bikers, too. Also based in Hollister is the Top-Hatters motorcycle club, one of the oldest motorcycle clubs around, which sponsors a high-octane poker run—a motorcycle run where riders participate in a game of poker, stopping at locations along the route to play their hand.

Charities

Bikers love to give. We will gather near and far to benefit charities, families, and individuals in need. We become elite event organizers, bringing together the community, townsfolk, and attracting major sponsors and celebrities for a charitable cause. We're almost superhuman in our ability to manage and organize an event for the needy. In addition, tapping into that "lean on me" nature encourages a tight run ship as bikers cruise in the name of benefiting another.

The following charities represent just a peek into our philanthropic behavior.

The California-based Love Ride brings together over 20,000 riders each November for a charity run to support the Muscular Dystrophy Association. A favorite charity of the official corporate sponsor, Harley-Davidson Motor Company, the Glendale Harley-Davidson dealership developed this event in 1981 and over the years recruited several celebrities to support the ride. Jay Leno has participated in 17 Love Ride runs, now serving as the grand marshall. A familiar face on the scene is the beloved Peter Fonda with his happy, life-is-divine wide grin.

What better person to play Santa than a biker? With a host of naturally burly gray beards, giant hearts, and ho-ho laughter, regional Toys-for-Tots runs and other holiday benefits across the nation hosted by bikers fill the November and December activity calendars. Strapped to fenders, handlebars and empty pillions, toys and food arrive in droves for needy children and families across the country. Faces of children light up as they're scooped up by men and women motorcyclists embracing the tiny beneficiaries in a leather scented hug. Afterwards, watering holes and culture clubs swell with bikers celebrating the season of giving.

Established in the early 1930s, the Old Time Newsies of Ohio have sponsored an

Paula Gray
Photo courtesy "Skip" MacLeod

annual charity weekend that features a professional motorcycle race benefiting the Big Brothers/Sisters of Greater Dayton since 1971. Started by Harry "JR" Kelly, former AMA president and board member of the Motorcycle Industry Council (MIC), the charity motorcycle race and relative charity efforts have raised several hundreds of thousands of dollars over the years.

The Ride For Kids® raises donations for pediatric brain tumor research. The organization also serves as a nationally recognized educational and patient support program for patients and their families, and the medical community. Of course the program was started by a compassionate motorcyclist—is there any other kind? Mike Traynor, a newspaper executive, had a friend whose child was stricken with a brain tumor and with great urgency, he began The Ride For Kids® in 1984. Legions of manufacturers and motorcycle organizations gathered to support this cause, operated by the not-for-profit Pediatric Brain Tumor Foundation of the United States. "Every motorcyclist that I have met at a Ride for Kids® event over the past several years is someone who loves life and lives it to its fullest. And every child that I have met at a Ride for Kids® event has demonstrated that same zest for life," explains Mike Traynor in his letter to registrants. Currently, the Foundation is expanding programs across the country and invites all motorcyclists to participate in the ride events held nationwide.

Childrens' Craniofacial Association (CCA) "envisions a world where all people are accepted for who they are, not how they look." If you remember Rocky Dennis in the movie *Mask* then you know the devastating effects that craniofacial complications can have on the patient and their family. Cher became involved with the association after portraying Rocky's mom, Rusty Dennis in the movie. Cher dedicates a significant amount of her time and resources to empowering the organization's forward movement and the children's self-esteem. Cher's genuine adoration for the children and concern for their parents led to an annual retreat weekend in her name where stories and experiences, self-renewal, and acceptance are the healing essences. The Association holds an annual charity run at Sturgis Motorcycle Rally each year featuring a Harley-Davidson motorcycle autographed by Cher as the raffle prize.

Bikers are extremely patriotic and many have served our country and continue to do so. Rolling Thunder® Ride for Freedom is held every Memorial Day weekend in Washington, D.C. Hundreds of thousands of men, women, and children from around the world attend this ride in remembrance of our veterans, POW/MIA and to support veteran issues. Thousands of motorcycles roar through the capital to remind the government and the American public that these heroes and sheroes will not be forgotten. Talk about a show of brotherhood and sisterhood—biker veterans bonding together to support one another, to laugh, to cry, and ride their motorcycles in the name of freedom to memorialize brothers and sisters who gave their lives for freedom.

Everyone participates in this healing memorial weekend, which also features a haunting candlelight vigil at the Wall. "We wanted to shake the hell out of the United States government and expose the cover-up, lies, and the corruption of this great government that destroys trust. Ray Manzo came up with the idea to do a motorcycle run for the issue," explains Sgt. Artie "Dictator" Mueller, who is president of the national chapter. Rolling Thunder has several chapters throughout the country, which sponsor a variety of fundraiser events during the year. This national organization is also active in lobbying and other political endeavors to benefit veterans. I can't think of a better way to spend Memorial Day weekend than rolling for freedom to celebrate our veterans and in remembrance of those POW/MIAs. Because of these selfless, honorable souls, we can live and ride free!

Bikers also come together to help private families who are plagued by tragedy whether it is illness, death, or some other misfortune. United as brothers and sisters who fervently protect "family," motorcyclists will do anything to help a friend in need: raise money, repair a home, provide food, help with personal tasks, or mother someone's child.

Motorcycle clubs have preferred charity organizations that they support. Year after year the event organizers tirelessly give of themselves and their talents to benefit the needy, the destitute, and the fallen. Bikers from all subsets within the lifestyle selflessly fill their calendars with charity activities year 'round.

Working in this lifestyle has rewarded me with lifelong friendships, a career beyond my wildest imagination, and a life journey filled with childlike wonder, wanderlust, and enormous gratitude for every blessed moment. Love, harmony, adventure, individuality, community, good times, and heart are the fringe benefits of this lifestyle and career choice. So I'll take living on the "fringe" of society any day. There's nothing like saddling up on my motorcycle and heading out for a journey because I have to; it's my job. That's truly my kind of living and riding free.

That's truly my kind of living and riding free.

Voices from the Road

Leah Whaley, Wisconsin

2003 Harley-Davidson Heritage Softail
   Classic;
Custom Shovelhead Stroker
Harley-Davidson Motor Company, H.O.G.
   event coordinator

I am who I want to be when I ride. It's me, my thoughts, my dreams, my wishes. It's spiritual. It's my place to be with God and to find my peace. It's me, the bike, the road, and all the wonder and beauty of the world.

I was hooked on motorcycles immediately through a blind date on a 1984 Harley-Davidson FLHS. About three years later, I got a 1975 FLHS in purple and have been riding ever since. I love the sense of self, of independence, of freedom, and especially the sense of community! I belong to the Central South Dakota H.O.G. Chapter 4854, of which I am a past director. Being a member of H.O.G. is a means to share the camaraderie of the road, to meet others who share a passion for the sport of motorcycling.

Riding has taken me to more places than most people only dream about. I have met the greatest people in the world, thus creating the most awesome family of friends. Riding a motorcycle is the best way to experience America. I love the looks I get cruising down the road, in the middle of nowhere or in the middle of a town. The looks of longing I get from people crammed in their SUV's all caged up in the air conditioning is really a kick. It's like they're saying, "Let's trade places." No way!

You can't be a high-maintenance gal and ride hard like I do. The fun you have is the fun you make because you're going to hit rain, ride in sweltering heat, and essentially experience everything out there. It's a real connection with nature and your personal freedom. It's learning to appreciate simple things in life—the sun, a light breeze, fresh asphalt, and a 75-mph speed limit with no traffic.

Nancy Nemecek, California

1981 Harley-Davidson Low Rider Trike
Travel agency manager and motorcycle rights
   advocate officer for ABATE

M otorcycle rights have been my main focus for the past 20 years. I've been on the ABATE of California board of directors since 1988 and chairman of the board for eight or so years. I probably was the first female in this position in the U.S., but I am proud to say there are a lot more lady riders these days and there were very few when I started. There are many more women in Motorcycle Rights Organization (MRO) leadership positions.

I started riding because I'm very independent and wanted control over what I do and don't do. Waiting to be "taken" someplace was not my idea of fun. My husband started riding when he was in his teens. He taught me to ride a trike and built me my Harley trike. I have a 36-year-old stepson who thinks my riding is great. At age 59, I have no plans to stop. I love the wind in my face, the freedom, and mostly the camaraderie.

Riding my motorcycle put a lot of purpose in my life and it got me very involved in important political issues. Motorcycles taught me what it means to truly experience freedom! Don't judge anything unless you've tried it.

Darcy Betlach, Minnesota
Victory V92C, V92SC, V92TC
Marketing manager for Victory Motorcycles

Motorcycling is the release needed after the stress sets in from work. I work in the motorcycle industry and still find riding the most enjoyable stress release. It doesn't get better than speeding down a country road without a care in the world.

My first ride was on the back of a motorcycle with my dad. I was 18 months old, my helmet tied on with a black-and-white polka dot scarf. I rode around the neighborhood. Then at seven years old I got an Indian minibike. We still have it!

My most memorable riding experiences involve my family. I have four sisters and all but one rides. Each Sunday, we get together and ride to brunch or just ride. My mom rides on back with my dad. It's a great way to bond as a family. I generally take a niece or nephew on back with me, so we have quite a group.

For the last four years I have participated on the Kyle Petty Charity Ride (KPCR) Across America. *Wow!* In one word that describes the experience for me. We go 3,500 miles in six or seven days with 200 of the best people you could ever be fortunate enough to meet. To date, the KPCR has raised over three million dollars for children's hospitals across the country. Victory Motorcycles has been a corporate sponsor for the last four years and hopes to continue participating well into the future.

Jennifer Anderson, New Hampshire
1999 Yamaha V*Star 1999, "Baby"
Director of Laconia Motorcycle Week
   Association and masters in social
   work student

Between work, school, and more work, it sometimes seems like there is no time for just me. I spend time with my friends and loved ones but I am never fully happy with myself unless I can spend quality time with my thoughts. Being on my bike allows me that time and I cherish it. Riding cements my trust in myself and gives me a sense of accomplishment each and every time.

I remember the love my dad had for motorcycles, but it didn't really sink in for me until I worked with motorcyclists in Laconia, New Hampshire. I rode with him a little bit when I was younger but for me, it wasn't the riding that inspired me to love motorcycles, it was my dad's love for them. He always had at least one motorcycle around that he was fixing up to be his "dream bike." After a bad accident left him incapable of riding for a while, he would still tinker with a bike just to be attached to it in some way or other, and that's what I remember most.

Motorcycling has given me a new sense of trust in myself to accomplish something I believed to be difficult and it has also made me much more aware of others around me, mostly when driving. It has given me the courage to do something unfamiliar and scary.

There has definitely been a large increase in female ridership over the past few years at Laconia. I am still amazed each season when I see so many women on their own bikes. As for vendors, there is a noticeable increase in female riding apparel as well as apparel that celebrates the individuality and freedom of women.

Diane Howells, New York City
1998 Honda Superhawk VTR1000
Motorcycle Safety Foundation (MSF)
   instructor, Motorcycle Safety School
   president and founder; *Motorcycle Diaries*
documentary director

I had always loved motorcycles, but never considered riding myself. After growing tired of riding on the back, and with my father's backing, I took the MSF course. I managed to find a used Honda Rebel 250, but was horrified at the thought of riding in New York City. Every day for a month, I was frustrated at my own cowardice to leave Brooklyn and ride over the mammoth Brooklyn Bridge. I was so angry that I knew how to ride, and could drive a car in all situations, but was petrified about riding the motorcycle. But once I finally made it over that bridge, my self-esteemed soared! I found that once I conquered the motorcycle, I had the courage to tackle other areas of my life personally, creatively, spiritually, and financially.

With that positive momentum, I then went on to make a documentary about women motorcycle riders called *Motorcycle Diaries*. Next I started the largest motorcycle school in New York State, Motorcycle Safety School. I directly relate these accomplishments to conquering the Brooklyn Bridge. That experience empowered me to accept the challenges in life that you have to face alone. Mastering a motorcycle is a solo experience. You aren't dependent on anyone else, only yourself. Likewise, you are putting yourself at risk if you make a mistake. When you realize that you have that much power over your own destiny and your own life in a high risk situation and you're mastering it, that's very empowering.

Anne Deli, Florida
Co-Owner, Orlando Harley-Davidson
   Historic factory dealership

I grew up next to Mr. Harley on Kensington Boulevard in Shorewood, a suburb of Milwaukee, Wisconsin. When I was a very little girl, I walked out my front door to their house and announced that I was "Annie," which created an instant bond with motorcycles. It was Mr. Harley who took me on my first motorcycle ride in a sidecar and drove me up and down the boulevard. In a strange way, I grew up around both families, Harley and Davidson.

What I fell in love with most about Harley-Davidson is what the brand stood for: the individualism, freedom, and empowerment that is the ethos of the Harley brand. I worked at Harley-Davidson corporate for quite some time as a consultant and then became their vice president of global brand management and marketing. After that my husband, Steve, and I purchased a dealership. Dealers have a unique relationship with the customer. We see them, we speak with them daily and provide the services that help and enable them to become fully immersed in the lifestyle. A lot of what Harley-Davidson is all about is having fun—together!

In the backyard of our dealership, we recreated the 1903 shack in which the first Harley-Davidson motorcycle was built. We affectionately call this the "Love Shack" now because we hold Harley weddings there for people who want to be married on their motorcycles. Biker love is truly a universal bond. We even broke the record in the *Guinness Book of World Records* for wedding-vow renewals with the 325 couples on their Harleys at our dealership in March 2003!

Karen Thompson, Maryland
1996 Harley-Davidson Custom Softail,
 "ZBADGIRL"
Co-owner Sundown Scooters, Ltd
co-founder of Blessing of the Bikes
 in St. Mary's County

My inspiration for creating the Blessing of the Bikes stems from my faith, and I wanted to begin the riding season with a blessing. It also transpired out of our love for riding motorcycles and the bond felt between complete strangers. We started the blessing ten years ago, originally expecting

around fifty or sixty bikers to show up, but three hundred rode in!

Over the years the word and inspiration spread all over the East Coast and we outgrew a few locations until the eighth annual broke records and we had 8,000 bikes and 10,000 people join us! It's unbelievable to witness a sea of leather-clad bikers with their heads bowed in prayer, united together to bless their freedom, their bikes, and their fellow bikers. When we made a profit from the event we decided to give the proceeds to several different charities.

My husband, Mendell, and I started our shop as a small home business fourteen years ago and expanded into the full shop we are today. We have several award-winning bikes featured in a number of motorcycle magazines. I built and customized my current bike by myself. Your bike is an extension of your personality, your passion, and your life.

Our children are very used to our biker lifestyle. It's one of the many things they have always known about Mommy and Daddy. Their friends think it's way cool. My favorite quote is "Bikers Have More Fun Than People Do." I know this for a fact!

'Bikers Have More Fun Than People Do.'

Catherine "Katmandu" Palmer, Florida

1957 Harley-Davidson FL Panhead;
1976 Harley-Davidson Shovelhead;
1999 Harley-Davidson Fatboy
Motorcycle writer and photographer

I was born the same year as the first Duo Glide. One night in the mid 1970s, a wild man with long beautiful jet-black hair took me for a ride through the New England countryside at midnight and after that, my life was all about sex, drugs, rock 'n' roll, and Harley-Davidsons. I moved to Florida in 1978, and attended my first Daytona Bike Week.

I was 21 when I bought my first bike, a little cherry 650 Triumph Bonneville with a Cerrani front end. It cost me 350 dollars. I rode that pony all over south Florida and the old timers still call me Triumph Lady. I was a natural and I was on my way. I returned to New England to begin art school in 1982 and get reacquainted with my mother. I purchased a 1962 XLCH in parts and with the help of dear old friends, we put this little chopper basket case together.

In the mid-nineties, I took a chance and submitted my photography for publication. When my first photograph appeared in a national motorcycle magazine, I danced in the driveway and called all my friends. Since then I have taken more risks and submitted my writing along with the photos. I've made a name for myself as a great motorcycle photographer and writer.

Katmandu adores her ride, and writes about the lifestyle
Photo courtesy Katmandu

Beth Owens, Texas

Vice president, American IronHorse
  Motorcycle Company

*I*t never occurred to me as a little girl that
I'd be selling motorcycles and lots of
them. I've been so busy with my job that I
haven't had the time to master the power of
our bikes, so I ride on the back with different colleagues. I love the way motorcycles
make you feel. It is incredibly freeing and
removes the stresses that day-to-day life can
bring you. There's such a strong camaraderie in the motorcycle industry and
lifestyle. I don't think there is another pastime that has this kind of a spirit.

Part of my role, is to communicate information from our dealers and end users to
our chief designer and the rest of the staff,
so we can constantly improve and fine tune
the product line. I think there is tremendous
opportunity for women in this field. The
motorcycle industry is very receptive to
women. One of the reasons that I have
excelled here is because I am a relationship-
builder. Women are good relationship-
builders and multi-taskers. Generally
speaking, women have technically been the
good listeners and more detail and people
oriented and conscious builders in lots of
different ways.

Jennifer LeVan, Pennsylvania

2003 Harley-Davidson Ultra Classic Trike
Co-owner, Battlefield Harley-Davidson/Buell,
  Gettysburg; owner, Just Jennifer Art
  Gallery, Pennsylvania

*T*here are two things that I love, art and
motorcycles. Every motorcycle is so
beautiful. There are weekends at our dealership that I'll spend time wandering the
packed lot just looking at all the bikes. Our
customers love to customize their bikes, and
I love to see their new artistic concepts. The
Art of the Motorcycle Show at the Guggenheim Museum was great because it exposed
a whole different group of people to motorcycles as art, by way of art.

Owning a Harley-Davidson dealership
is really a labor of love. Can you imagine
being surrounded by really wonderful
people everyday *and* surrounded by motorcycles? Life doesn't get much better than
this!

Jill Zorn, Arizona

1996 Harley-Davidson Sportster, "Destiny"
Motorcycle event producer and founder,
  Jam Productions LLC

Bikers give more than any other group. If
someone did an actual demographic or
marketing study of charity events and
monies raised, my guess would be that
motorcyclists have raised more money in
total for all charities than any other type of
group, business, person, or organization. If
you gathered up all the information that

had to do with fundraising and generous people you'd realize, wow, bikers rule.

My kids learned what a real hug is by hanging around bikers. In this culture, the first thing you do when you meet someone is you hug them. At first, my boys felt funny hugging men because they weren't used to it. But now they see how people from all different walks from life get along and care for one another.

Kim Barlag, Ohio
Yamaha XT225; Kawasaki ZRX1100;
Harley-Davidson Road King
Editor, Thunder Press North

Motorcycling has opened up a lot of doors for me. I was fresh out of college and trying to find out who I was and who I wanted to be. Motorcycling shaped that for me because it became a hobby that introduced me to a lot of neat people. It also became a career, which has opened my eyes to the many different aspects of motorcycling. Before I only knew about Harley-Davidson and the Harley-Davidson community. The AMA opened my eyes to racing, sport bike, off-road riding, and every other aspect of motorcycling out there. I like to think of anyone riding on two wheels as part of one big family.

I think it's important to get more women in the AMA Motorcycle Hall of Fame. There's six women to 285 inductees into the Hall of Fame. I was instrumental in putting together the second and third Women in Motorcycling Conferences. It was really rewarding. I think women's involvement in

motorcycling has definitely improved the image of riders. We have contributed a lot to motorcycling. We need to encourage other women that riding is certainly an experience that they can accomplish. The AMA started the Bessie Stringfield Award to recognize women who have made significant accomplishments in the motorcycling world, and that was my idea. I'm really proud of that.

Brigitte Bourget, Arizona
Bourget's Bike Works

Most people are surprised to hear that I don't ride my own motorcycle. I very much enjoy riding as a passenger with my husband, Roger. He and I started our company ten years ago. He does the technical engineering and I do the aesthetic engineering as far as painting, rake and stretch and different things to make the bike more individualized and unique.

At Bourget Bikes we build fifteen motorcycles a week. Because we see them every day, we begin to take for granted how beautiful our bikes truly are, so when we see our bikes mixed in with other motorcycles at rallies and events we think, "Wow, we really do build a nice bike!" Our bikes definitely stand out in the crowd. And it's great when the customers personally thank you for your hard work; it makes you want to continue to do a better job for them.

Roger and I both make ourselves available to our customers. We're not corporate people who hide behind a bunch of executives. Bourget's is a family business. It's our name on the company, and we make sure that we not only do what's expected of us, but we go the extra mile for our customers and business, too.

Gail Worth Wilson, Missouri
2000 Harley-Davidson Road King;
1988 Harley-Davidson FXR
Drag racer and owner, Gail's Worth
  Harley-Davidson

I love to ride. I love to race. There is nothing like the feel of riding down a winding road and becoming one with your bike. The sun kissing your skin and the wind rushing by. Wow! What a way to relax.

I believe that a person can do whatever she wants in life. Sometimes it might be difficult, but if her heart wants it, she will do it.

My parents bought the Harley dealership so my dad would have something that he could pass down to his two boys. Kind of ironic, huh? At the time he didn't have a clue that I would step up to the plate and buy the dealership from him. My passion for Harley-Davidson is what drove me to buy the dealership.

I am very driven. I never stop reaching for the stars. As long as I am reaching upward, I have a beautiful view. A couple of years ago, I won my class in the All Harley Drag Races after beating out several men. Winning was great, but what made it so special was that after the race these young girls came up to me just so they could talk to me because they admired me. It was such a great feeling. One of them said, "My dad told me that I could just come right up to you and you'd talk to me . . . thanks!" My heart has never felt the same.

Laura Brengelman, Connecticut
Kawasaki ZRX1100, Kawasaki ZZR1200
Editor, *RoadBike* magazine

I belong to the Motor Maids, Inc., because of the wonderful lady riders at the heart of this class-act organization. I also belong to the International Brotherhood of Motorcycle Campers. Why? Because we love to camp, and there's nothing like sitting around a campfire at the end of a good day of riding, just hanging out with like-minded friends.

I first got involved in motorcycles when an incredibly attractive guy asked me out on a Friday night date and picked me up on his Yamaha Maxim. It was my first ride, and I fell in love with him and the ride. Almost 20 years later, I ride my own bike, as I have been doing for many years. My favorite rides are on two motorcycles, still with that same guy, who became my husband.

Motorcycling feeds my hunger for adventure, for touring the great outdoors. But the most important thing I've gotten from riding is an inner toughness. Riding a motorcycle is the best kind of fun, but it's not for wimps. To be a serious rider, one who travels long distances and does it well, you have to be determined, focused, believe that you've got what it takes, and just do it.

Pepper Massey-Swan, South Dakota

2000 Harley-Davidson Dyna Super Glide
Executive director, Sturgis Motorcycle
    Museum & Hall of Fame

When I was married to my ex-husband, a Goldwing rider, I told him that I'd like to have a motorcycle of my own one day. He said that it wasn't practical and not a very good idea for me. When I left him the first thing I did was purchase a motorcycle. You might say he inspired me to live a dream. I've been riding ever since. I met my new husband through my passion for motorcycles. He's the love of my life and my favorite riding partner. Our best times are when we can get out and ride together.

The ride that pops into my mind as being the most memorable was the time my husband and I went to the Sacramento Toy Run. We lived about 400 miles away. The weather was great when we left, but it didn't stay that way. All of a sudden, we began to see huge amounts of smoke as if a tractor-trailer had crashed and caught fire. The smoke was thick and white, filling the entire six-lane roadway.

We rode smack into it and instantly, it was 20 degrees colder. That smoke was actually fog. We continued on a mile or so until we could pull into a gas station, and threw on all of our woolies. The temperature continued to drop as we rode through the cold, wet fog. We eventually made it through the cold and had a wonderful time with friends at the Toy Run. I love the freedom and being one with nature on a motorcycle. You feel everything when you ride.

Kris Tigerlady, Illinois

1989 Honda NT650 GT Hawk;
1950s Vincent Firefly (a basket case)
Motorcycle Journalist

I've been riding for 26 years. I rode when there were women out there but I didn't know where they were so I ended up riding with men. When I first started riding, people would tell me, "You can't ride a motorcycle, you're a girl." People had been telling me that all my life, you can't do this or that because you're a girl, and I'd say screw that. When I got my bike, I had to hear, "Oh, that's your boyfriend's bike, huh?" And I think women riders still hear that.

What's great about biking is that a lot of people are completely connected. I mean, it's like "You ride a bike, you're a member of my family." We wave to each other like, "Hail to you, other special person." Getting my motorcycle was a major thing for me. Discovering the Vincent Owners Club and riding with them shaped my whole future.

Do women ride because they're empowered or is getting the motorcycle what has empowered them? I think it goes both ways.

Riding a bike is about pursuing your passion and not letting people tell you what you can't do, making your own decisions, knowing you can do whatever you put your mind to, and knowing that riding a bike will improve your morals rather than corrupt them. Indeed, the ones who have tried to stand in my way are the misguided. I have enjoyed more love and democratic living as a motorcyclist than others experiencing their "straight and narrow" lifestyles. I thank God that I found bikes, and that I found the people I ride with and have met through riding.

Motorcyclists are the most giving, loving, and honest people I know, and my best role models. And being able to give and love and be honest is real freedom. Who would think that a gleaming, snorting machine could do that for a person?

Brenda Fox
Photo by Randall Cordero

Sasha

Living & Riding Free

A woman who rides a motorcycle is in tune with the universe,
a candidate for high adventure . . . you ought to try it.

—Celestine Sibley, celebrated journalist and author

As women motorcyclists, we live and ride free. We are candidates gripping the handlebars of our destiny, singing at the top of our lungs, unable to contain our sheer bliss as we glide down the highway.

"Oh that you would bless me indeed and enlarge my territory . . ." (from the *prayer of Jabez*, 1 Chronicles 4:10).[29] I love this prayer, and it sums up so much of the living and riding free experience. When I saddle up on my motorcycle for any journey, I'm like a kid in a candy store, hungry for that next great experience. In order to have it, I've got to get out there and expand some territory because I want to reach beyond what I know; travel out of presupposed boundaries and catch some wind. I want to be blessed and receive a fascinating good time on my ride, expand my body, mind, soul, and heart, and enjoy my free will.

I want to be blessed to melt with the changing landscape, as the landscapes transform me. I want my two wheels to drive me to expansive territory physically, mentally, and spiritually that I surely would never have known otherwise. I want to be blessed to expand my sense of self and reach far beyond my usual busy, stressful routines. I want to be blessed so that I can experience the highest form of free will, connected with my higher purpose and greatest talents. I want my territory to expand so that I can utilize my greatest talents and enjoy my life free and uninhibited by confusing and dumb-ass boundaries and limitations.

I crave to experience all the treasures and the good times of a long motorcycle ride, because every ride transforms me and brings me to a new space and undiscovered territory. The ride opens up all six senses and once again I am whole. Prior to technology and a highly materialized world, we had the use of the sixth sense, the inner knowing, that revered dialed-in nature that acknowledges a higher self and thus leads us to ultimate freedom using our free will in a positive and encouraging manner. Intuition surely guides us. Motorcycle riding restores the sixth sense and connects us with Mother Nature and Father Sky, all things divine that equal living and riding free. I experience an inner road song that harmonizes with my essential divine nature to become a journeywoman symphony. All six senses are delivered into a supernaturally blessed sensitivity of heightened awareness and glowing insight.

Riders often equate the feeling of motorcycle riding as closest to flying. I agree. The power of the wind rushing through you, embracing your total being, is testimony to the inner need to soar and reach beyond and mingle with destiny; realize our inner

gifts and purpose. Simply Be. That's high on life, high from the ride and the wild makings of fond memories and far out fun. That giddy childlike laughter that wells up at the gun of the throttle flushes out all the darkness and gives way to clarity, the gentle nudge into an awareness never before known.

When territory expands and road blessings begin to occur, a new kind of road sign pops up on the voyage. A direct connection with the Creator through heightened senses gives subtle directions in life to the rider. We are revitalized and refreshed after the ride and we hope to carry our blessed territory expansive experiences into our everyday lives. Intuition becomes more keenly developed. Our oneness with nature, people, and the journey helps us to communicate our passion symbolically as we evolve and transform from the experiences of heeding the divine "road signs" in our lives during our motorcycle voyages.

Motorcycle riding is an ecstasy that expands our perception and understanding on so many levels and delivers us into a lifetime of camaraderie and good times while living and riding free.

Friends, God bless you and may the ride set you free!

Love and S'miles,

Oh sun shine down on me

And warm me from a cold past

Big sky of possibility

Help me retrieve my dreams

Everlasting

Wind whispering angels

Oh hear my highway prayers

The road is my home

Takes me back where I belong

Riding free is my song.

—from the song "The Road Is My Home,"
by Sasha

©2002

experience beautiful freedom®

Friends, may the ride set you free!

Appendix

So, you want to learn to ride or take an advance riding class?

Motorcycle Safety Foundation
1-800-446-9227 for a rider school near you.
www.msf-usa.org

Harley-Davidson
Rider's Edge®
www.ridersedge.com

See other schools listed within chapters below.

Additional Resources:
American Motorcycle Association
(800) AMA-JOIN
(614) 856-1900
www.ama-cycle.org

Motorcycle Industry Council and Discover Today's Motorcycling
www.motorcycles.org

For more in-depth motorcycle resources and web links, please visit
www.bikerlady.com

Web Resources

Chapter 1: She's Gotta Roarrr!
Author's website: www.sashamullins.com

Chapter 2: Watch Out! Curves Ahead!
Effie & Avis : www.wheelsinmyhead.com
Alice Brady and Viola Pelaquin: www.wallofdeathonline.com
Dot Robinson and Betty Robinson Fauls: www.motormaids.org
Louise Scherbyn: www.wimausa.org

Theresa Wallach: www.wima-gb.co.uk
Jean Davidson: www.jeandavidson.com
Susie Hollern: www.pinkrosepub.com
Jerry Hooker: www.motorcycle-memories.com

Chapter 3: The Road Is My Home
Michelle Dell: www.hogsandheifers.com
Erica B. Smith: www.wimausa.org and (WIST) www.magpie.com/digests.html
Shelly Hukkanen: www.foxysweb.com
Tiffany Weirbach: www.sportbikegirl.com
Jacquie Littlejohn: www.littlejohncontemporary.com

Chapter 4: Queen of the Road
Dixie Deb: www.dixiedeb.com
Cruel Girl: www.cruelgirl.gunsnet.net
Debbie "Breed" Amaya: www.waam.homestead.com/WAAMhomepage.html
Dawn Glencer: www.dealwithitcalendar.com
Luisa Gervasi: www.motocicliste.net

Chapter 5: Motorcycle Mammas & Women Who Wrench
Elisabeth Piper: www.motorcycles.org
Vicki Roberts: www.accidentscene.net
Jennifer Bromme: www.werkstattsf.com
Barbara O'Connell: www.indianmotorcycles.com
Lisa Martin: www.sandiegoharley.com
Lori Eby: www.paintyourharley.com
Leilehua Yuen: www.wrench-wench.com
Jennifer Lefferts: www.madmaps.com

Chapter 6: Wild Wind Sisters
The Motor Maids: www.motormaids.org
Women in the Wind: www.womeninthewind.org
Leather & Lace MC: www.leatherandlacemc.com
Devil Dolls MC: www.devildolls.com
Women on Wheels: www.womenonwheels.org
Speed Divas MC: www.speed-divas.com
Women's International Motorcycle Association: www.wimausa.org (USA)
Moving Violations MC: www.smokycity.com/MVMC
Ebony Queens MC: www.angelfire.com/mi3/queens
Sirens MC: www.sirensnyc.com
Women's Motorcycle Foundation, Inc: www.ponyexpressrides.org
Total Package MC: www.totalpackagemc.com
Dangerous Curves: www.dangerouscurveshawaii.com

Spokes-Women MC: www.spokes-women.org
Christian Motorcycle Association: www.cmausa.com
Soul Patrol Ministry: www.soulpatrol.org
Amazon MC: www.amazonsmc.org

Chapter 7: Racy Ladies

Freddie Spencer's School: www.spencermotorcycles.com
California Superbike School (Keith Code): www.superbikeschool.com
Reduc Sportbike Association: www.reduc.com
Sportbike Track Time: www.sportbiketracktime.com
American Federation of Motorcyclists: www.afmracing.org
Drag Bike: www.dragbike.com
Class Motorcycle School (Reg Pridmore): www.classrides.com
Star Motorcycle School (Jason Pridmore): www.starmotorcycle.com
Frank Hawley's Drag Racing School: www.frankhawley.com
Trials Training Center (Laura Bussing): www.trialstrainingcenter.com
Penguin Racing Schools: www.penguinracing.com
Sidecar Racing: www.sidecarracers.com
Women's Motocross League (Dominica "Miki" Keller): www.wml-mx.com
American Historic Racing Motorcycle Association: www.ahrma.org
Twisty Sisterz: www.twistysisterz.com
Angelle Savoie: www.angelleracing.com
Debbie Matthews: www.dmsports-wsmx.com
Vicky Jackson Bell: www.vjbracing.com
Lucie Stone: www.girlsonmotorbikes.co.uk
Zina Kelley: www.ducatigirl.com
Kris Becker: www.krisbecker.com
Vicki Gray: www.racegirl.nl
Katja Poensgen: www.katja-poensgen.de
Carina Sjutti: www.c70.com
Barbara Toribio: www.diamondbackmx.com
Marie Whittaker: www.sidecarracers.com
Debbie Knebel: www.godebgo.com
Kerry Watson: www.pithyproductions.com/kerrywatson
Jessica Zalusky: www.roadracinggirl.com
Stefy Bau: www.stefybau.com
Eliane Pscherer: www.team-octopuss.com
Jodie York: www.jodieyork.com

Chapter 8: Long Distance Lovers

Iron Butt Association: www.ironbutt.com
Ayres Adventures: www.ayresadventures.com
Motodiva: www.motodiva.com

Lotus Tours: www.lotustours.com
Towanda Women: www.towanda.org
Bikers Plant: www.bikersplant.net
Voni Glaves: www.mindspring.com/ ~ p_vglaves
Airyn Darling: www.bikergirl.net
Carol "Skert" Youorski: www.pinkribbonrides.com
Erin Ratay: www.ultimatejourney.com
Dee Gagnon: www.deegagnon.com
Nicky Austin: www.horizonsunlimited.com/tstories/austin
Susan Johnson: www.horizonsunlimited.com
Doris Maron: www.untamedspirit.net
Carla King: www.carlaking.com
Mariola Cichon: www.rideoftheheart.com

Chapter 9: The Bikerlady Artiste

Catherine Bell: www.catherinebellonline.com
Stephanie Finochio: www.stephaniefinochio.com
Lynelle Corbett and Hardley Angels: www.hardleyangels.com
Maria Willers: www.thevmmc.com
Cris Sommer-Simmons: http://home.att.net/ ~ patrickride
Sam Morgan: www.wallofdeathonline.com
Christina Shook: www.cshook.com
Rose "Bams" Cooper: www.3blackchicks.com
Gevin Fax: www.gevinfax.com
Melissa Harris: www.cycleportraits.com
Kathleen Brindley: www.newbikerart.com
Madusa: www.madusa.com
Debbie Evans: www.stuntrev.com
Erika Lopez: www.erikalopez.com

Chapter 10: Healing Winds

Brenda L. Bates: www.bikepsych.com
D.J. Jones: www.divaskinz.com
Xochi Hughes-Madera: www.cancergifts.com
Linda Back McKay: www.visi.com/ ~ lbmckay/index.htm

Chapter 11: The Motorcycle Lifestyle

Motorcycle Events Online: www.motorcycleevents.com
Daytona Bike Week: www.daytonachamber.com/bwhome.html
Laughlin River Run: www.laughlinriverrun.com
Myrtle Beach: www.myrtlebeachbikeweek.com
Laconia Bike Week: www.laconiamcweek.com
Americade: www.tourexpo.com

Hollister Independence Rally: www.hollisterrally.com
Sturgis Motorcycle Rally: www.sturgis.com
Street Vibrations: www.road-shows.com/street_vibrations.html
Biketoberfest: www.biketoberfest.org
Love Ride: www.loveride.org
Old Time Newsies: www.oldtimenewsies.org
The Ride for Kids: www.ride4kids.org
Children's Craniofacial Association: www.ccakids.com
Rolling Thunder: www.rollingthunder1.com
Harley Owners Group: www.hog.com
ABATE of California: www.abate.org
Darlene Betlach: www.victory-usa.com
Diane Howells: www.mssnyc.com
Anne Deli: www.orlandoharley.com
Karen Thompson: www.devoted.to/blessingofthebikes
Beth Owens: www.americanironhorse.com
Kim Barlag: www.ehlertpowersports.com
Jennifer LeVan: www.battlefieldharley-davidson.com
Brigitte Bourget: www.bourgets.com
Gail Worth: www.feelthepower.com
Pepper Massey-Swan: www.museum.sturgis-rally.com
Kris Tigerlady: www.kristigerlady.com

Notes

1. (p. 13) *The Rugged Road* by Theresa Wallach was also written in part by Barry M. Jones for Panther Publishing, Ltd., High Wycombe, UK, 2001. Available in U.S. through Whitehorse Press.

2. (p. 14) *Women of the West*, Volume 5, Tales of the Wild West series by Rick Steber. Prineville, OR: Bonanza Publishing, 1988.

3. (p. 14) Susan B. Anthony. "untrammeled womanhood" speech, 1896; in "Life and Work of Susan B. Anthony," ch. 46, by Ida Husted Harper, 1898. Indianapolis: Hollenbeck.

4. (p. 15) Marie E. Ward, *Bicycling for Ladies*. New York: Brentano's, 1896; and Reginal de Koven, *Bicycling for Women*, 1896; quoted from "Women on Wheels—Riding the Freedom Machine," article by Nancy Botkin, March 2000, Tube Times Issue #67, published by the San Francisco Bicycle Coalition. NancyBotkin, www.sfbike.org/OLD_site/www/news/html/2000/march/01march2000.html

5. (p. 15) *A Wheel Within a Wheel: How I Learned to Ride the Bicycle: With Some Reflections by the Way* by Frances E. Willard, Sunnyvale, CA: Fair Oaks Publishing, 1991. Reprinted edition, Applewood Books, 1997.

6. (p. 16) David Hendricks, "The Possibility of Mobility: The Rise and Fall of the Bicycle in Nineteenth-Century America," University of Virginia American Studies Programs, 2002.

7. (p. 23) *Hear Me Roar: Women, Motorcycles and the Rapture of the Road*, © 1996, 2000 by Ann Ferrar. New York: Crown, 1996. 2nd edition published by Whitehorse Press, NH, 2000.

8. (p. 27) *Motorcycling for Women—A Book for the Lady Driver, Sidecar Passenger and Pillion Rider* by Betty and Nancy Bebenham, London: Sir Isaac Pitman & Sons, Ltd., 1928. Intro. by Major H. R. Watling, Director of the British Cycle and Motor-cycle Manufacturer's Union. Reprinted in Susan Hollern's *Woman and Motorcycling, The Early Years*, Summer Hill, Locke, NY: Pink Rose Publications, 1999.

9. (p. 36) "The Rubaiyat of Omar Khayyam," in *Wine of the Mystic: A Spiritual Interpretation, from Edward Fitzgerald's Translation of the Rubaiyat* by Paramahansa Yogananda, Los Angeles, CA: Self-Realization Fellowship, 1994.

10. (p. 37) Statistics from the J.D. Power & Associates 2001 MCIS Study; the Motorcycle Safety Foundation Report, 2001; and the American Motorcycle Association (AMA) research on women motorcyclists, 2002.

11. (p. 39) *Gutsy Women: More Travel Tips and Wisdom for the Road* by Marybeth Bond, San Francisco, CA: Traveler's Tales, 2001.

12. (p. 40) *Deep Play* by Diane Ackerman, New York: Vintage Books, 1999.

13. (p. 40) *Polar Dream: The Heroic Saga of the First Solo Journey by a Woman and Her Dog to the Pole* by Helen Thayer, New York: Delta, 1995.

14. (p. 61) *Women's Bodies, Women's Wisdom* by Christiane Northrup, M.D. New York: Bantam Books, 1994, 1995, 1998.

15. (p. 74) *Motorcycle Safety Foundation's Guide to Motorcycling Excellence*, ©1995 by the Motorcycle Safety Foundation, North Conway, NH: Whitehorse Press.

16. (p. 95) *A Woman's Worth* by Marianne Williamson, New York: Ballantine Books, 1994.

17. (p. 98) Jhenah Telyndru, "Seeking Her Within"; www.sisterhoodofavalon.org/seeking.html

18. (p. 124) "Motorcycle Racing" Encyclopædia Britannica entry, from Encyclopædia Britannica Premium Service: www.britannica.com/eb/article?eu = 55336

19. (p. 140) *Riding Windhorses: A Journey into the Heart of Mongolian Shamanism* by Sarangerel, Rochester, VT: Destiny Books, 2000.

20. (p. 145) *DeeTours: One Woman, One Hundred Days, One Unforgettable Adventure* by Dee Gagnon, Brockton, MA: Pegasus Publishing, 2000.

21. (p. 155) *The Perfect Vehicle: What It Is About Motorcycles* by Melissa Holbrook Pierson, New York: W.W. Norton & Company, 1998.

22. (p. 157) "Patrick Wants To Ride" by Cris Sommer-Simmons, Haiku, HI: Steel Pony Press (P.O. Box 1088, Haiku, HI), 1994.

23. (p. 159) *3 Black Chicks Review Flicks: A Film and Video Guide with Flava!* by Rose Cooper, Cassandra Henry, Kamal Larsuel-Ulbricht, New York: Amistad Press, 2002.

24. (p. 162) *Bike Lust: Harleys, Women, and American Society* by Barbara Joans, Madison: University of Wisconsin Press, 2001.

25. (p. 163) *God on a Harley* by Joan Brady, New York: Pocket Books, 1996; *Heaven in High Gear* by Joan Brady, New York: Pocket Books, 1999.

26. (p. 170) *Back in the Saddle Again: Psychological Recovery After a Motorcycling Accident,* ©2002 by Brenda L. Bates, M.A., C.Ht. E-book: www.bikepsych.com

27. (p. 177) *Ride That Full Tilt Boogie,* ©2001 by Linda Back McKay, St. Cloud, MN: North Star Press of St. Cloud, 2001.

28. (p. 181) *Community Building: Values for a Sustainable Future* by Leonard A. Jason, Westport, CT: Praeger Publishers, 1997 (p. 72).

29. (p. 201) I learned of this passage from reading *The Prayer of Jabez: Breaking Through to the Blessed Life* by Bruce H. Wilkinson, Multnomah, OR: Multnomah Publishers, 2000.

Index